D0016530

# The ParentPreneur Edge

## What Parenting Teaches About Building a Successful Business

Julie Lenzer Kirk

John Wiley & Sons, Inc.

Published by John Wiley & Sons, Inc., Hoboken, New Jersey.
Published simultaneously in Canada.

Wiley Bicentennial Logo: Richard J. Pacifico

For general information on our other products and services or for technical support, please contact our Customer Care Department within the United States at (800) 762-2974, outside the United States at (317) 572-3993, or fax (317) 572-4002.

Wiley also publishes its books in a variety of electronic formats. Some content that appears in print may not be available in electronic formats. For more information about Wiley products, visit our Web site at www.wiley.com.

*Library of Congress Cataloging-in-Publication Data:*

Kirk, Julie Lenzer.
  The parentpreneur edge : what parenting teaches about building a successful business / Julie Lenzer Kirk.
    p. cm.
  ISBN: 978-0-470-11987-7 (cloth)
1. Entrepreneurship.  2. Parenting.  I. Title.  II. Title: What parenting teaches about building a successful business.
  HB615.K557 2007
  658.1′1–dc22                                      2006102240

Printed in the United States of America

10  9  8  7  6  5  4  3  2  1

To Keenan, Sydney, and Madison: Your continued love and support means the world to me. I could not have done this without you!

To my mom, Beth Lenzer, who is also my biggest cheerleader: You never stopped believing in me, even when I didn't believe in myself. Thank you for your unconditional love!

And finally to Daddy: It ain't Howard the Duck, but it's the best that I could do. I miss you every day and know you're smiling down on me.

# Contents

# Foreword

As a businesswoman who has had to juggle the demands of my family along with a work schedule of meetings, travel, stressful negotiations, and more, not only can I understand the message of Julie Lenzer Kirk's *The ParentPreneur Edge,* I have lived it!

It's not about who brings home the bigger paycheck or whether one spouse works part time or how much work is involved in being the primary stay-at-home parent caring for your children. It's all about the delicate balancing act that many, many parents face today. Whether you're working for yourself or for a large successful company, you are confronting challenging responsibilities that demand your time, energy, commitment and more every day. How you face these tasks determines not only how successful you are professionally but how happy and fulfilled you are in your home life.

Just as the book offers profiles of people who have successfully combined running their own business with parenting, I too believe that it is possible to combine professional success with parenting. In fact, as Julie explains, parenting can help you manage your workload. After all, isn't staying up all night with a sick child or running after a toddler while trying to figure out why your infant is crying sometimes more difficult than holding a meeting with adults who all speak the same language?!

In fact, the multitasking that is part of parenting actually helps entrepreneurs. Parents constantly have to make quick decisions, choosing one option over another while trying to satisfy children who almost always want instant gratification. It is the ability to assess a situation and make a clear-headed decision—or postpone making one—that is a crucial skill for both parents and entrepreneurs. Parenting requires you to focus on your children, helping to teach them the skills they need to mature—and the behavior that you hope will help them become mature and successful. This requires you to be an effective communicator and also conscious of your own behavior. After all, telling your children to "Do as I say, not as I do" isn't nearly as effective as being a role model whom they want to emulate, at least most of the time.

*The ParentPreneur Edge* is an excellent handbook for all entrepreneurs and business executives alike. If you're a parent, you'll readily identify with many of Julie's experiences. And, if you're not a parent, this is a refreshing guide to improving the skills that will help you in situations from the boardroom to the sales floor to the negotiating table.

Carolyn Kepcher, CEO of Carolyn & Co.
Former advisor to Donald Trump
on NBC's *Apprentice*

# Running a Business Is Like Raising a Child

"It's a girl!"—three words that changed my life forever. Six months later, another three words had a different yet similarly life-altering affect as well: Applied Creative Technologies, the company I founded when my first child was six months old. Outside of multiple births, adoption, or marriage to someone with kids, I know of no other way to have "children" so close in age.

Starting my own company was not something I had been dreaming of. In fact, I fought the notion for months before I finally took the plunge. Though I always knew I would have children, I did not see myself as an entrepreneur. Now over a decade later, I cannot imagine *not* being an entrepreneur. What changed?

## My Third Child

My leap into entrepreneurship was somewhat of an accident. I was, in fact, looking for flexibility. My previous job required me to travel three out of four weeks every month. Don't get me wrong—I loved what I did. Something changed, however, when my daughter was

1

born. When I first looked into her eyes, I knew I could not continue to travel at that pace. It was too much time away from home. At the same time I also felt strongly that I could not be a stay-at-home mom. Stepping out on my own seemed my best, albeit scariest, option at the time. I felt strongly, however, that I had nothing to lose. If it did not work out, I could always go back to my employer and work something out with my travel schedule. Besides, every other significant opportunity for change that I have encountered in my life had been frightening initially, but all of them turned out well.

The first year on my own, I was essentially aiming to replace my income by working from home. In reality, I made more that first year while working 30 hours per week than I had the previous year working 40-plus-hour weeks. Although I was going to work from home, we chose to keep our daughter in a family day care. She was in a caring, loving environment that we did not want to lose if things did not work out with my self-employment. Since she was only two doors down from my home office, I was also able to drop in and see her whenever I wanted.

My second year in business also saw the birth of my second child. I had continued a partnership with a company I had worked with in my previous corporate life and they were able to cover my contract for me while I took some time off to be with her. I went back at the end of my unpaid maternity leave and again saw an increase in my income from the previous year.

My third year in business was a turning point. That was when everything changed. My husband, Keenan, was frustrated and burned out with his engineering job. He started taking a computer programming class at night thinking he might be ready to change careers. We had toyed with the idea of his joining me in the business, but did not feel we were ready to make that commitment. At the same time, I was being offered more work than I alone could handle. I made an offer to a former colleague to join me on an hourly part-time basis.

Shortly thereafter, an argument with a colleague at work set Keenan off. The next day he resigned. Rather than finding another job, he decided to join me. We had some money saved up, a strong prospect for future work (though not a contract yet), and a fallback option to go out and get a "real" job should the business not work out.

Suddenly, I had three employees including myself. I needed to identify opportunities for additional work. Our timing could not have been better. One of my clients was searching for a vendor to develop a new production and warehousing system. The company was erecting two new manufacturing facilities and their current system (which I had designed 10 years earlier) was not equipped to handle the new business requirements. The timing could not have been better. I boldly approached the client and offered an alternative proposal: I could grow my company to develop and support the software it needed. I was able to convince the client that, given my in-depth knowledge of its operations, we were their best option for meeting their tight deadline. With that, Applied Creative Technologies (ACT) changed from a sole proprietorship to a corporation and my third child was born.

I have found that being an entrepreneur has been one of the greatest opportunities for personal growth I have ever experienced. In the 10 years through starting, expanding, and exiting my business, I learned more about myself than through any other period in my life. Like most working parents, I struggled at first with the notion of being away from my children. Many of my friends thought I was crazy. For me, that guilt did not last as I discovered the flexibility that prompted me to go out on my own in the first place. I believe strongly that I am personally a better mother because I am an entrepreneur. How did I fit owning a business in with being a parent?

As I grew my business alongside my children, I observed that there are actually more similarities between these two roles than differences. Many of the skills I developed as a mother and an entrepreneur were nurtured simultaneously. As my children grew, my business evolved, and the crossover of skills, joys, and challenges allowed me to pool my internal resources and tackle both tasks head on. Being an entrepreneur provided me with benefits I could not find anywhere else, and being a mother helped give it all meaning and keep it in perspective.

Parenthood and entrepreneurship are *both* the toughest job you'll ever love. Each offer unparalleled growth opportunities and require similar skills to make it through with your sanity intact. The details of every individual's approach to making it all work for them is unique. For me, I found that integrating my work and my home life provided me with the ability to achieve the life I wanted. That is not to say that I never shut off work when at home or did not focus intensely on projects at work. Rather, being flexible about how and when I worked and played afforded me the ability to do both. By not erecting unyielding boundaries between the two and living my life holistically, I found that embracing the parallels provided an edge in business.

## Embracing the Parallels

The word *ParentPreneur* is meant to describe entrepreneurs who are also parents. The number of people I have talked with, however, convinces me that many of the characteristics, and especially those that provide an edge, are not reserved for business ownership. Indeed, most working parents share the same experiences and develop comparable skills that can be drawn upon to provide an advantage in any business. The common bonds are the abilities and lessons they have learned in one facet of their lives that can be applied to the other. In talking with younger folks as well, they can learn from the similarities by drawing on their experiences with their own mom and dad or from caring for siblings. Unfortunately, not everyone recognizes the parallels nor embraces them to their advantage.

What parent has not had to clean up the mess from their child's uncontrolled bodily functions? Parenting can be hard and filled with ups and downs. The ability to remain passionate and persistent through the tough times is something all parents need to embrace. I have several friends whose babies experienced medical problems, and they could not come home from the hospital for weeks—sometimes months—after they were born. Those parents were at the hospital full time and would do whatever it took to get their babies home. That shows their love, passion, and persistence. These are also critical characteristics that add to business success.

As much as we love our children, there are days when we question whether we are really qualified to be parents. I left the hospital less than 24 hours after my first child was born. I could not remember the last time I had held a newborn. Keenan had never held a newborn, though he was a quick study. But they let us leave the hospital with our baby, and from there we were solely responsible for her well-being. The same was true for our business. We were essentially on our own.

Many entrepreneurs and leaders, even the successful ones, wonder if anyone will ever discover that they are not qualified to be running their companies. I absolutely had periods through my decade in business where I was in that camp. It was clear I did not have a degree in parenthood, either. There is no entrance exam for becoming an entrepreneur or a parent. Most of us start businesses without all the skills or tools needed to succeed, but we do it anyway. Some are successful, many are not. If you are not successful, you can take what you learned and try again. While you can (and do) make mistakes as a parent, there are no real do-overs. We are, however, able to do things differently with subsequent opportunities. Both business and parenthood end up requiring some amount of on-the-job training. You don't give up on parenthood because you don't know how to do something—you figure it out. Treat business the same.

In both parenting and the business environment, you'll be working to get results through people. For that reason, I have often pondered whether a degree in psychology would have helped me. I have heard many a business manager refer to instances where managing employees had been like dealing with children. Some are maturing teenagers, while others regress to a much earlier age. Every experience is different. But in the end, your job as a manager is to help people grow, and the rewards of seeing that development can make all the frustration worth it.

The ultimate similarity between parenting and entrepreneurship or any type of leadership is that you are building a legacy. As parents, we want to raise children who are happy, responsible, contributing citizens. We want them to make a positive impact on the world. They are our legacy.

As entrepreneurs, many of us are also creating companies that we hope will make a contribution to our customers, our employees, and our community. We want our business to make a positive impact on the world, or at least our corner of it. I have talked to many entrepreneurs over the years who maintain that their business fulfills their desire to be part of something bigger than themselves. They want to make an impact that is greater than their own financial gain. Even if financial independence is their goal, many cite philanthropy as one of the positive impacts that their success in business can enable. Providing people with gainful employment, at a minimum, is a significant contribution. There were 15.9 million people in the United States employed by businesses with fewer than 10 employees in 2003 (U.S. Census Press Release for Small *BusinessWeek* 2006, April 9–15), and those numbers have been rising. An estimated 25.5 million small businesses in America employ more than half of the country's private workforce, create three of every four new jobs, and generate a majority of American innovations (Small Business Administration, 2000). Small business is truly the fuel of the American economy, and what we have learned as parents can help us open our own service station to distribute that fuel.

## Business or Parenting?

Jack Woelber had been at his new company as a manager for only three weeks when he received a Saturday morning call from his boss, the owner of the company. Not knowing his boss that well yet, he couldn't imagine that the call was a good thing.

"Jack, we need to discuss one of your employees."

The worst thought went through his mind—something tragic had happened to one of his team members. Before he could respond, his boss clarified.

"I came into the office last night to retrieve my theater tickets that I had left in my desk and I caught Elliott* (* indicates the name has been changed) running out of my office with his pants around his ankles. He was there with Bridget*, one of the new secretaries."

Silence.

"You know, Jack, I just redecorated my office and they were on *my* couch. I was fit to be tied last night, but," he said chuckling, "I realized the reason I was so mad is that I had not yet been able to enjoy my new couch. They beat me to it."

This story could have just have easily come from the parent of a teenager as a business owner. This notion is continually reinforced when I hear entrepreneurs—both men and women—refer to their company as their baby. There are, of course, differences that can't be denied. I would never sell my children (unless the price was really good!) or shut them down because I was out of money or got tired of them. But after all, we give our business life, we nurture it, and then at some point, many of us let it go.

While Keenan was not involved in the conception of ACT, he adopted it when he joined me two years later. We both considered the company as our child even though it was kind of an accident.

Similarly, Jan King's entrepreneurial adventure was unplanned. She had been working as an editor at Merritt Publishing for seven years when the owner approached her to run the company. While his offer surprised her, it did not take her long to accept it. When the owner passed away a year later, Jan adopted what she calls his 40-year-old baby. She considered it a start-up, albeit an *old* one, because she literally had to reinvent the company from scratch. They had to figure out who they were, overhaul the product development process, and change a culture that was deeply rooted. Just like taking in someone else's older child, she had to define a new reality while preserving the things that worked. The changes came over time, as she could not disrupt everything at once, but she was eventually able to build her newly adopted baby into a company an outsider wanted to buy.

Donna Stevenson's experience was quite different. She didn't marry her business partner until years after they started their company together, which is why they claim their business, Early Morning Software, as their child out of wedlock. Today, some of her employees even jokingly call her "Mama."

Graham Weston refers to the starting point of his now over $200 million baby as the "magic moment of conception." He met three recent college graduates in the early 1990s when they set up his office building in downtown San Antonio to provide a shared but secure high-speed Internet line for all of his tenants. At the time, such connections were uncommon. He was providing a differentiated service to maximize his occupancy rate.

After reading one of the first editions of *Red Herring* magazine, a periodical aimed at the growing base of technology businesses, he was compelled to ask his future business partners if they had any ideas for a technology company. Coincidentally, they had already started a small company, which at the time had 12 clients but not enough in revenues to cover their expenses. With Graham's business development and financial savvy and the founders' technical and business skills, they had the right mix of businesspeople and geeks to make it work. Even though there were approximately 200 other vendors vying for room in their chosen market, many of whom were better funded and further along, the time still seemed right to conceive this business. With a cash infusion from Graham, he adopted their baby and Rackspace was born.

Hollywood even gets it. In one of the final scenes of the movie *RV,* Robin Williams is trying to convince a small, family-run soda company to merge with his large national beverage corporation in order to take their products national. In the midst of his presentation to them, he has a change of heart as he describes their company as their "baby." He talks about the pains of labor, seeing their baby learning to walk, growing up, and then the idea of letting it go. He proposed that they did not want their baby to be adopted and raised by his large (and now former) employer because of the severe differences in their parenting style. The nodding heads of the founders of that small company indicated that he was right on. Later, in the final scene of the movie, the owners come looking for Robin's character to hire him because he gets it. It *is* their baby. Seeing the connection paid off for him. They want him to help teach their baby to walk and take their products national.

Jindra Cekan sees the similarities between parenting and her business as a matter of complex logistics. As the founder and principal of Cekan Consulting, she coordinates humanitarian assistance efforts to get food aid and development to hungry people across third-world countries. She has to coordinate U.S. government food aid supplies and shipping, and juggle competing demands of the nonprofits and the local communities to get help to those in need. She likens this mobilization of food assistance to parenting. Her work efforts require constant juggling, diplomacy, and a community of involvement, much like her role as a single mother of two active sons. In addition to the daily grind required to ensure that her kids are well fed and get to school, she also has to coax them to share in chores, teach them good habits, and encourage them in best choices for after-school activities such as soccer, piano, and reading. Never mind what it takes to get her family and all their stuff to the beach for a week. Although these tasks differ in scope from her work, she cites them as requiring a similar personal effort. Additionally, once food is delivered, she has to help people set up the auditing systems to make sure the food reached the right people and provided a lasting impact on their ability to feed themselves better. With her sons, she is continually checking to make sure they are doing well in school, helping them make the best choices with their free time, and developing into caring, responsible kids.

As I raised my children and grew my business in parallel, the similarities became obvious and often humorous. It started when people would ask me if I was planning to have a third child, as if that was any of their business. I would quip that my business *was* my third child: It keeps me up at night, it takes all my money, and it sometimes sasses me back.

I realized the process that I went through when I was contemplating starting my company was similar to the steps I took in deliberating parenthood. I read *What to Expect When You're Expecting* when I was, well, expecting, but I could not find a *What to Expect When You're Starting a Business*. At least there was nothing on the bookshelves that seemed similar.

Naming my business and my baby involved similar difficulties. Control was not what I expected, either, as a mother or as a business owner. As I began to get my feet underneath me with both my new roles, I noticed some crossing over. At times when I was frustrated because I could not get my toddler to behave, I would think about some of the problems I had worked through and survived with my business. Reflecting on that gave me a much-needed boost of confidence to take a deep breath and know that I could solve this problem, too. Likewise in business, thinking about my children often brought challenges I was facing into perspective. My kids were healthy and happy—everything else was secondary. As I pivoted back and forth between these demanding roles, I began to see more and more of the commonalities and realized that I could leverage lessons learned in one to the other.

As I progressed through the growth of my business and my children, I noticed that the progression of stages was identical. That observation inspired the organization of this book. Each chapter represents both a stage of development in parenthood and in business.

| Parenting Stage | Business Stage |
| --- | --- |
| Getting Pregnant | Preparing for Entrepreneurship |
| Labor and Delivery | Launching |
| Baby to Toddler | The Early Days |
| Elementary School | Ramping Up: A Time to Learn |
| The Preteen Years | Growing Pains |
| The Teen Years | Emerging Independence |
| Letting Go | Exercising Your Exit |

In addition, there are many lessons that are not exclusive to entrepreneurship. Business managers and leaders go through similar challenges as well. There is wisdom in this book for you whether you are thinking about starting a business, trying to grow your business, or looking for management and leadership tips you can draw on from your parenting expertise. The lessons actually span several business phases: Starting, Growing, and Managing.

Because there are so many different ways that a business can be successful, I did not want to provide only my side of the story. By bringing in the stories of other entrepreneurs, both male and female, I wanted to demonstrate that there are infinite ways to make it work. Your way may be yet another one to add to the list. The key is that being a parent is not a detriment to your business success; it actually provides you with *an edge.*

## Embracing the Edge

As I began to research entrepreneurs to interview, I discovered that it was not easy to find those who had been successful in their business and had also raised children. Upon further digging, I discovered that entrepreneurs who are serious about their business, in general, do not like to advertise that they are also parents. It seems that there is a societal bias that says that you can't be serious about your business and be a good parent, or if you're a good parent, you must let things slide at work. I even had one entrepreneur indicate that she does not talk much about her family because she is worried that it will make her appear weak.

Realizing that your parenting skills can be an asset in business is half the battle. The other half is recognizing the benefits you provide for your child when you pursue your dreams and live a satisfied life, whether that means working a job you love or staying at home to raise kids. In reality, we are providing a service to our children by offering them a role model of someone who has a fulfilled life.

Children learn more by our actions than by our words. Carol Koch-Worrel teaches music to children. One particular child was having a difficult time with a specific note on the violin and was prepared to give up. Carol brought the child's mother over, who had never played the violin before in her life, and showed her how to hit the note they were working on. The child watched as his mom became frustrated but persevered. When she accomplished the goal, the child clapped and grinned. He proceeded to pick his violin back up and do the same. She modeled success and he emulated it.

Some entrepreneurs I have met, usually women, tend to use their children as an excuse for why they can't start a business or the reason their businesses are floundering. They claim that their kids have to come first and they just can't find time to do what they want to do. I cannot argue that our children should take priority, nor would any of the entrepreneurs I have talked to. Our children do come first, just not every single time. We are actually teaching them that life is about balancing priorities and give and take.

I contend that if you are serious about your business, you can find the time. Sometimes you just need to get creative, and often you have to get help. There is no guarantee that your business will thrive, as there are a number of other factors that contribute to a company's success. But if the business is more than just a hobby and you are passionate and persistent about solving a problem for your customers while keeping an eye on the bigger picture, you have within you what it takes to make a go if it. Parenting helps us to hone those skills.

Test the resolve of a mother whose baby is in the intensive care unit. Measure the persistence with which a father works to teach his child to play baseball or tie his shoe. Calculate the moxie of a parent who remains calm when seeking help for his or her hurt child, only to collapse hours or days later when the danger has passed. As parents, we gain useful skills that not only help us to be entrepreneurs, but actually give us an edge if we're willing to embrace them.

## The Personal Side

Donna worked with her father, who was an entrepreneur. In doing so, she saw that a family could be sustained through self-employment. Without that role model, her willingness to take the risk of entrepreneurship may not have not been there. She had seen firsthand that, at the end of the day, it is possible to be self-sufficient. In addition, Donna found that through being an entrepreneur, she uncovered wells of talent within herself that she had no idea were there. She believes strongly that the greatest gift of self-employment is that you find the best within yourself.

In the beginning, my measure of success was strictly financial. I did not realize at the time how much more there was to it. I compared what I made in revenues against my final year's salary at IBM. The first year out, I made more money on a part-time schedule than I had made the previous year working full time. The year that I first paid more in taxes than I had previously made was beyond what I had imagined. Although it hurt to write that check, it was a good pain. When our company first hit $1 million in revenue, I thought I had reached the top, but it just kept getting better.

I started to see the impact that the company had on others and on the community. We were able to provide good jobs for people. For some of the staff, we offered the only option for them to work and still be home with their children when they needed to be. We began to receive awards for our approach to work/life balance as we continued to give and to innovate. We were active in the American Cancer Society's Relay for Life to raise money for cancer and provided Christmas baskets to lower-income families. My business was so much more than just a job.

Each milestone achieved and life touched increased my belief that I could do *so* much more than I ever thought possible before. I found strengths I never knew I had and untapped capabilities that had yet to be exploited. I was an entrepreneur and I never knew it. The parable of "The Eagle and the Chicken" captures the challenge I overcame on my road to this discovery.

### The Eagle and the Chicken

A man once found an eagle's egg
and put it in the nest of a barnyard hen.
The eagle hatched and grew up
With the rest of the brood of chicks
but noticed he didn't look the same.
Nonetheless, he scratched the earth for worms and bugs
and played the chicken's games.
The eagle clucked and cackled,

he made a chicken's sound. He thrashed his wings,
but only flew some two feet off the ground.
That's high as chickens fly,
the eagle had been told.
The years passed by and one day
When the eagle was quite old
he saw something magnificent flying very high
and making great majestic circles up there in the sky.
He'd never seen the likes of it.
"What's that?" he asked in awe.
While he watched in wonder
at the grace and power he saw.

"Why, that's an eagle," someone said,
"He belongs up there, it's clear.
Just as we, since we are chickens,
belong earthbound down here."
The old eagle just accepted that,
most everybody does.
And he lived and died a chicken,
for that's what he thought he was.

*—Author Unknown*

If you've got the itch, maybe you are an eagle. How will you know unless you believe it is possible, and spread your wings and really try to fly? The worst thing that can happen is you learn just how high you can soar. If you fail to reach the heights you were aiming for, life goes on. At least you flew higher than you would have had you not tried and you learned more about yourself than you ever knew before.

The greatest danger for most of us is not
that our aim is too high and we miss it,
but that it is too low and we reach it.

*—Michelangelo*

CHAPTER

# Preparing for Entrepreneurship

My husband, Keenan, was ready to begin a family on our honeymoon. I wanted to wait. There were things I wanted to do that I assumed I could not do once I had kids. I wasn't ready to give up my freedom. I wanted to travel with my husband, join a soccer team, and learn to speak French. Besides, what did I know about being a mother, much less a good one? It had been at *least* 10 years since I had changed a diaper. While I saw scores of books available to enlighten any novice parent, they couldn't possibly cover everything, could they?

The more I contemplated parenthood, the more I began to wonder if there ever really is an ideal time to start a family. I started seeing young families and pregnant women everywhere I went—like noticing the model car you are thinking about buying where you had never seen it before. My filters had changed once I began to contemplate parenthood. I also started meeting more people who were pregnant or had kids and they seemed to be managing. None of them appeared to show any signs of slowing down. Women have been doing it since the dawn of time! If they can do it, I mused, why can't I? I made it through college while paying my own way by working three jobs, I rationalized—can it be harder than that?

A few months and several wine-guided conversations with girl-friends later, I realized that whatever I was waiting to do, children didn't have to stop me. I envisioned my husband and me raising our child and balancing my hectic travel schedule. I was determined not to let this baby derail my career—I would somehow figure it out. Feeling empowered, I decided it was time to get pregnant.

## Introduction

The timing is never right. It can take several attempts, but just having a go at it can be fun. Does this sound like entrepreneurship? How about parenthood? What about both? The similarities between having a child and creating a business—from deciding to take the plunge to thinking about the future and keeping it simple—are at hand from the very beginning. Who would have thought that having a financial plan and needing to redefine control would apply to both?

As I launched into both entrepreneurship and motherhood within six months of each other, I had no idea what an adventure it would turn out to be or how my life would change over the course of the next several years. What I also did not realize is how many parallels there are between these two major roles and how embracing these similarities could give me an edge in my business through the insights and lessons I would not have otherwise had.

## Deciding to Take the Plunge

While I planned my entry into parenthood, I actually stumbled into my business about six months after my daughter Sydney was born. At the time, I was working as a consultant and traveling three out of four weeks per month. Before she was born, I boldly (and naïvely) thought I could handle being on the road and away from home. Then she was born. One look into that beautiful face and I knew immediately that not being able to tuck her into bed most nights would not work for me in my new role as mom. It was a personal choice.

I also knew that I could not stay home full time. It wasn't that I didn't want to be with my child, but even in the three months at home after she was born I felt a part of me was beginning to atrophy—my brain. I became addicted to my Game Boy game, Zelda. It was the closest thing to critical thinking I had at the time. I would even sit and play the game while I was nursing. Being at home all the time was also becoming costly. Suddenly, the window treatments in the kitchen needed replacing, the wood floor looked worn, and couldn't we do something about our old couch? However, I knew I did not want to raise my child remotely from a hotel room. Unfortunately, I was not being paid enough to bring Sydney and a nanny on business trips with me. I realized I had to make a change.

My company's attempt to be accommodating was to put me on a local project, but their definition of "local" was an hour-and-a-half commute each way. Moreover, I was required to be at the client's site four days per week, three weeks out of the month. I felt strongly that this was not a viable option for our family. Since I worked for a large corporation, I could have taken another position elsewhere in the company that didn't require travel, but I loved what I did. I considered starting my own business but with the same fear and trepidation I had encountered a year earlier in deciding to start a family. What to do?

My dominant thought, admittedly, was to polish up my résumé and find another job. Looking back, I believe I was in denial. After all, my father was an entrepreneur, as was my grandfather. The signs were there growing up, I just didn't see them until my father helped me by recalling stories from my childhood.

When I was around 10 years old, I would hold carnivals in my backyard. I used to create big, colorful signs and post them throughout the neighborhood to advertise the event. Kids flocked to my house from across the neighborhood, being otherwise bored on a hot summer's day.

The carnival itself wasn't much, unless you were 10 years old and living in the 1970s when Atari's PONG was the next best entertainment option. I drew a penny toss in chalk on the driveway and sold little plastic bags of homemade popcorn with lemonade to wash it down. I even had a ride; for a nickel I would spin the kids around in Dad's old recliner. The funny thing was that kids actually paid me for that "thrill." As my father helped me recall, my entrepreneurial spirit was evident from the beginning. I could not deny it any longer.

With those thoughts and memories nagging in the back of my mind, interview after interview, I kept coming back to the idea of being my own boss. What was the worst thing that could happen? If things didn't work out, I mused, I could always get a "real" job. After some discreet fishing around, a long-term client of mine indicated—hypothetically, of course—that they would use me as a consultant if I were available independently. I can still remember that day—we were on an airplane, across the aisle from each other, and the look in his eye told me that he saw a real opportunity.

Before leaving, however, I wanted to make sure that my current employer knew that I would be working with this client. I did not want to burn any bridges or risk violating a noncompete agreement. Who knows if I might need to come back or even want to work out a partnership agreement with them in the future? I saw handling my exit with honesty and professionalism as the only option.

Once I cleared the pending arrangement with my then-current employer, I decided to take a life-altering dive into the unknown. I left the comfort and certainty of the secure job and ventured out on my own without, admittedly, much thought about where I was going with it. My situation was not unique. As I conferred with other entrepreneurs, however, I found that there are many different reasons that incite people to get started in entrepreneurship and equally many divergent ways to do it.

Paul Silber started his company by taking an approach that was on the other end of the spectrum from mine. While I wasn't sure where my entrepreneurship would lead, he knew exactly where he wanted to go with his company. Economic maximization. Build it to sell. As a scientist with a large cosmetic company, he saw a market need for toxicology research services that did not involve live animals. With a wife who stayed at home with his four-year-old daughter and newborn second daughter, he left his high-paying job in search of more challenge. That was when In Vitro Technologies was born.

Sheila Heinze also took a totally different approach from mine in starting her own business. When the company she had been working with was bought out, she had a difficult time reconciling the values of the new parent company with her own. Fearing that she may become bitter if she stayed, she decided to venture out on her own and create a business with an environment and culture that better reflected her own ideals. She knew in her heart that if she focused on keeping both her customers and her employees happy, her new firm would not only survive but thrive. And thrive it has. Ten years later, her baby SM Consulting has almost 500 employees and hundreds of happy customers.

Sheila's plunge into motherhood likewise took a dissimilar path from my own. She waited until she felt her company was stable enough to operate without her for several weeks before taking that step into motherhood. When her first baby, her company, was seven years old, she felt her management team was strong enough and her business was operating sufficiently smoothly that she could take the time off she needed to begin building her family. She then took several weeks off to travel to China to adopt her first of two children. The initiation of her family was deliberate; her plan and subsequent execution were fairly close in step. Not everyone so meticulously plans their growth, however. Some, like me, get into the business and are willing to follow it wherever it takes them. Sam's law practice followed that philosophy as well.

Sam Roberts*, an unusual combination of lawyer and certified public accountant, was tired of the lack of humanity he found in working for large accounting and law firms. He had a very strong notion of how he thought a law practice should operate and it was his interest in paying attention to the personal service side of law that nudged him to venture out on his own. Ultimately, he was looking for the control to do it his way. He wanted to price his services moderately and use technology to bring down his costs, a concept that was foreign to many law firms in the early 1990s. Although he had a wife at home who did not work and two sons under five years old, he took his 30 clients and boldly set out on his own entrepreneurial adventure that took him to a multimillion-dollar practice of 15 lawyers and 4,200 clients in 15 years.

For most, entrepreneurship demands such an adventurous nature. For many, it also takes a catalyst: an event or condition that makes their current employment situation unbearable. Mike Prizzi has been talking about starting his own business since I met him 11 years ago, but at this time remains gainfully employed. His challenge is that he is doing quite well with his current employer. He is a successful sales manager making enough money that his wife Laura was able to quit her job when their third child was born to stay home with the children. Mike has gotten "comfortable" with what he calls the golden handcuffs and fears he has more to lose by stepping out on his own. Not to say that he won't, at some point, venture into entrepreneurship as it is something he thinks about almost every day, but making the decision has been made more onerous by his current level of sufficiency. It will likely take some shake-up in his life or job to force the move. Hopefully, he will not have missed the timing in the market when he finally makes the jump.

The catalyst for Kathryn (Kathy) Freeland to start her own business came when she was passed over for a promotion. She had been with her former employer for five years. When she ended up having to train the person (a white male) who was given her job (she is African American), her disgust and anger drove her to prove that they were wrong in passing over her. She was determined to use her skills and talents to build her own company, one based on strong values and principles. Her experience is, unfortunately, not unique.

When a former boss told Marissa Levin, founder and chief executive officer (CEO) of Information Experts, that she would never be worth more than $44,000 per year, it was the last straw. The saying her mother used to tell her about never letting another person determine your worth came to her mind. She had already been considering venturing out as an independent consultant, and this was just the catalyst that she needed to make the move. Sitting in a restaurant one night, she and her husband mapped out a business plan on the paper tablecloth. Working on weekends and over her lunch hour, she was able to secure her first contract while still employed full time and immediately resigned to build her business. With over 20 employees and $5 million in revenues, she is now bringing home a lot more than that $44,000 annually.

Pete Linsert, former CEO of Martek Biosciences, was a venture capitalist before he became an entrepreneur. He had watched hundreds of business owners succeed and fail and decided he wanted to take a shot at it. When he was asked to develop a business plan for Martek, they asked him to come in as a temporary CEO to help the company raise money. He became excited about doing his own thing. Twenty years later, he retired from his "temp" position and started thinking about doing it all over again.

Linda Frost is one woman who has done it over and over and over again. Owning one business is not enough for her—she owns three: Brunswick Mortgage Company, Inc., which originates conventional loans on residential properties; Brunswick Builders, LLC, which specializes in semicustom homes in the $1 million-plus price range; and Brunswick Renovations, which buys townhomes below market, renovates them, and then sells them at or just slightly above market value, thus earning a profit. While all three businesses are distinct, there are some obvious synergies around residential construction and home building. She became disgusted working in the corporate world as she observed many managers turn greedy and look out for their own best interest without real regard for the customer. She claims she did not find one business she worked in where the customer was more important than money. She was tired of watching home builders take short cuts, use lesser-quality materials, cover up mistakes, and then charge inflated prices for their houses in order to turn a quick profit for themselves. Her vision was simply to build a decent product using quality materials and knowledgeable and experienced subcontractors, and provide superb customer service. She is now having fun (and making money) doing just that.

Unequivocally, the entrepreneurs I talk to all say that at some point, you just have to jump. Like parenthood, you can read all of the books available on owning a business and still not know how to handle everything you will encounter. While you shouldn't let that stop you, there are critical issues that must be addressed before plunging into entrepreneurship:

- Learn what you can. Read the books but do not overlook the value of talking to others who have gone before you, whether they were successful or not. Often, you can learn more from failure than from success. My father was an entrepreneur, and his input throughout my weeks of deliberation was critical to my eventual decision to dive in.

- Accept the worst-case scenario and then focus on a plan that ensures it never comes to fruition. I made sure I did not burn any bridges in leaving my former job and knew I could go back there—albeit with my tail between my legs—if I couldn't make a go of it on my own.

- Know how you are going to make money and how long it is going to take to be able to pay yourself. See the section on business planning for more discussion on this topic.

- Save enough money to cover your personal expenses or have a back-up income or revenue stream (consulting contracts on the side, spouse with a good job, or an inheritance from Grandma). Getting used to ramen noodles doesn't hurt, either. Unless you have a committed customer with a contract or steady customer base from the start, which most do not, it will take longer for you to make money than you think. Get used to *not* eating out and to living below your means. Do whatever you need to do to support yourself (that is legal) until your business can.

- Take out credit cards, buy a car if you need one, and make sure you can live in your house for a few more years. Once you leave your job and plunge into self-employment, it becomes increasingly difficult to obtain personal credit without a steady income.

- When a new business has no credit, the financial assurance falls on the owners. Make sure your personal credit report is solid because you may need it to secure early financing for your business.

- And last but not least, consider what it is that you want to get out of your business and put together a plan to get there.

## Thinking About the Future

As parents, we don't create business plans for our children—or do we? So maybe we don't sit down and write a 30-page plan with financial projections of their future income, but we do spend time dreaming about their future.

Once the reality of a pregnancy sets in, it is hard not to start imagining what your child will be like. Keenan and I both hoped our children would have his math ability and my love of reading and writing. If they got my math and his writing, we joked, they would be waiting tables for the rest of their lives. Thankfully, they got a little of both.

We parents begin at an early age envisioning the vast opportunities we will make available to our children and what type of parent we will be. We are, in essence, defining our model of success for them and envisioning our hopes and dreams for them:

"I want her to go to a good college."
"My son will play football."
"We will put him in a top-notch preschool program—I don't want him to struggle as I did."
"I want her to love reading as much as I do."

### Worlds Colliding

I spent the first six months of my pregnancy sick. Contrary to common sense, eating actually made me feel better. Since I was still traveling for work, I walked around toting so much food that a colleague commented that she expected a light to come on whenever I opened my briefcase.

We also had to make some big decisions: What type of day care will we need, or will we give up an income so one parent can stay at home? How are the public schools in our neighborhood? In our case, they were not up to our standards, which is why we considered moving. We had to decide if we should move into a new house for the school district or consider private school. We also had to start looking into ways to save for the ever-increasing costs of our child's college education. Trade-offs had to be made as we were creating a life plan for our kids.

In a similar way, you should not start a business without thinking about the future and creating a plan for executing your business concept to reach your goal. How else will you know what trade-offs to make? There are many specific questions that must be asked, most of which need to be answered before spending much time or money moving forward. The ultimate question to be answered, however, is "Can this business idea make money, and will it align with the other priorities in my life?" Note that this question has two distinct parts, both of which need to be addressed. One is personal, the other is business. Clearly, you need to have a good grip on what your life priorities are before you even begin. Refer to Chapter 9 for a broader discussion on how other entrepreneurs have addressed this.

Although people are generally good about researching opportunities for which they need to spend money, many forget that their time *is* money. For any new business I have considered, I have conducted a high-level feasibility analysis to answer the ultimate question. In order to get to the answer to that question, several contributing factors need to be explored:

- What is my product or service?
- Who will pay me for it, and what will they pay?
- What kind of profit can I make?
- Why will they buy mine over the competition?
- How much time and money will it take to get this business going?
- Where is the needed money going to come from?
- What is my definition of success? What do I want out of the business?
- Am I willing to put in the time and money it takes to make this business successful?

Ultimately, a thoroughly researched feasibility analysis will provide indications about whether a venture is worth your most precious asset—your own time and energy. Sometimes, the answer will be "no" and it can be hard to let go after you've already put so much time into it. It is integral at this point to separate emotion and the strong desire to start a company from the facts. If the idea is really something you're passionate about, think about modifying the concept to provide what the market really needs or finding other ways to charge customers in order to make enough money. Whatever shift needs to be done, persistence is a vital element of successful entrepreneurship. Resist the temptation to quit just because the first idea doesn't pan out. Research has shown, in fact, that it takes most entrepreneurs three tries before they hit the "big one"—the business idea that really works. If you're lucky enough to get one out of the way via a feasibility analysis, you're already on your way!

---

### Feasibility Analysis vs. Business Plan

The difference between a feasibility analysis and a business plan is the question being answered. A feasibility analysis should answer "Should I?" while the business plan shows not only why I should but how I will. While the contents should be tailored to the audience and what they will want to know, a business plan describes the design of the company to execute the vision.

---

Once you have a feasibility analysis that indicates you should move forward, you have to design a business to execute the concept. That is where a business plan comes in. Too many businesses start off without a business plan and the owners are then surprised when they don't achieve the level of success they had hoped for. Whether it is actually written in one formal document or scattered among various documents or kept in the entrepreneur's head, the business plan and the process used to develop it are a pivotal contributor to the success of a business.

It isn't hard to find training or good books to help write a business plan (see Resources at the end of this chapter). The formality with which you should undertake this task depends on your motivation: why you're doing it and for whom.

Common reasons to write a business plan are to obtain outside funding or attract business partners and key employees. Even if these milestones are not in your vision of your business, you still need a business plan to work through how the business will operate to reach your end game. If you haven't thought about what you want out of the business or how and when you will get out, then that is the first step to completing the business plan. Know where you're going so you can chart the path to get there.

For example, if your plan is to develop a company that you can hand down to your children, you will make one set of decisions. Under that scenario, you might be more conservative about bringing in outside investors. If your plan is to develop a company where your employees can buy you out, you will put different incentives and compensation systems into place than if you were hoping to merge with a competitor. Disparate decisions will need to be made along the way depending on where you want to end up.

A common misconception about a business plan is that once you write it, you are done. Just like our plans for our kids morph as they develop and grow, our business plans must change, too. My dreams of my daughter's picking up on my pursuit of Broadway were thwarted when I discovered that she was as tone deaf as I was. Many successful entrepreneurs I speak with who maintain their business plan for funding or other reasons say that they can't keep track of the number of revisions they have made to it. It is revised that often.

Furthermore, our priorities change as we traverse the seasons of our lives. What worked for us when our kids were young may not be what we want when they're heading off to college. I kept my traveling down to no more than one week per month when the kids were young. As they have grown I have been willing to increase my travel schedule, especially when there is the option to take them with me.

A business plan should be a living, evolving document that is constantly revised as these outside forces mold and shape our business and change our industry. All businesses need to have a

Plan B and be willing to shift when market conditions, opportunities, or life changes warrant it.

I have to confess that I did not have a business plan when I left the comforts of my job at IBM. What I did have, which many other new businesses do not, was a customer—a big one. And the customer had committed to providing me with a level of contract work that, at a minimum, could equal the salary I was making before I quit.

The first time I had to start thinking about the future was when the work available began to reach my personal capacity. At that point, I had to decide whether to turn down the additional work or identify more resources to help me. This is a good problem to have, but a challenge nonetheless.

Taking on more work and growing my business was a tough decision. I could keep it small and manageable or I could let it grow and see where it could take me. I had just gotten used to the "small and manageable," but now that I had taken that first step out on my own, I was hooked. Declining new work did not seem like a viable option to me. I had to find help.

It so happened at the time that Keenan was getting burned out at his job and was looking to change careers. His background is in engineering, but he had just completed a computer programming class at nights and was interested in helping me in my business. His skills and interests complemented mine with no overlap, which made it clear that there was a gap he could fill.

While relying on one endeavor for our financial security and future seemed risky—all our eggs would be in one basket—my customer was able to foresee (though not promise) the work continuing to increase. In order to take advantage of that, I had to be able to find suitable resources to perform the tasks. After some intense discussions, we resolved to give it our best shot, and *my* business became *our* business. Besides, we reasoned, one of us could always go out and get a "real" job. What we didn't realize at the time was that our journey through starting and growing a business would be the most *real* job we had ever had. I have personally been transformed. Although before I hadn't seen myself as an entrepreneur, I now know it would be arduous for me to return to work for someone else. I would make a terrible employee, anyway.

## Keeping It Simple

A couple of months after our first child was born, we hosted a couples' baby shower for a pregnant friend. As part of the entertainment, we played a game. A tray full of baby gadgets was laid out in front of the mother- and father-to-be and they were to guess what each one was and what it was used for. The man had to go first. The first item was a large bulb syringe, which was identified quickly. What stumped the future parents was what the device had to do with a newborn. When the utility was revealed—it is used to suck the snot out of a baby's clogged nose—hoots of laughter erupted. It only got better from there.

When my sister-in-law found out she was pregnant, she immediately went out and registered for every baby gadget she found. She had to have the top-of-the-line stroller and only the *best* accessories. My jaw dropped when I saw the prices and added up what the ideal accompaniments for a new baby could cost.

The number of tools and devices invented in the past 20 years that a new parent can't live without is amazing. It is astonishing to think our parents raised us without all these necessities. When did raising a baby get so complicated?

Starting a business can dangerously follow a similar trend away from simplicity. When you finally make the decision to take the plunge into entrepreneurship, the first thing most people do is outfit their office. Whether it is in or out of the home, setting up a place to work makes the decision feel real. For women, this may even seem like nesting. Let's face it—there is something about shopping for office supplies. When I was a kid, I used to go into my father's office and rummage through the supply cabinet; it was like browsing a candy store. The new pencils, pads of paper, and extra highlighters somehow made me feel instantly organized. It must be genetic because my children always flocked to the supply cabinet when they came into our office.

Now, with club stores like Costco or Sam's, you can purchase enough office supplies in one package to take you through to your retirement. You must be careful, at this point, not to go overboard. For example, do you really need a pack of 100 Post-it notes or 50 Sharpies just for yourself?

When it comes to office furniture, there are many options for keeping expenses down. I can still remember the excitement of going to Office Depot to outfit my basement office. I selected a medium-priced U-shaped desk with a hutch. I knew that there would be some assembly required, but I did not realize it would take my father-in-law and me all day to put it together. As a consolation, I still use that desk today. When we eventually moved into our first office, we again worked to keep our expenses low by purchasing previously used furniture from a rental company. Even though it had been rented out, we were able to select pieces that looked like new. Rackspace CEO Graham Weston took the same approach. Their first offices were furnished with scratched and dented clearance desks and chairs bought at auction (Patricia Gray, "What's Your Magic Number?" *Fortune Small Business,* November 2006).

Creative companies have even been inventive in obtaining equipment for a scientific lab. When Pete Linsert and his small team were building out the facility for their company, Martek Biosciences, they were disgusted at the high price of counters and cabinets for labs. They actually went to Home Depot and bought kitchen cabinets and Formica countertops for use in their lab in lieu of the expensive specialty products. He shared that even though acid has been spilled on a counter every five years or so, the cost to replace it is still significantly less than if they had opted for the high-end equipment in the beginning. Just don't ask what they used a mop bucket for.

Creativity can help bring down the price of marketing collateral, too. Many new business owners add unnecessarily to their overhead early by rushing out to get high-end business cards printed. When I first took the plunge, I found some preprinted papers in a catalog and printed my own business cards on my printer. The paper technologies were not where they are today, and with obvious perforated edges, the cards weren't that great looking. To me, however, they were a sign that I was serious, which seemed important at the time. It wasn't until I encountered someone else who had the same design that I decided to go to the next level.

My second set of cards came from a local postal store. They had catalogs for business cards from which I could choose varying styles and quality levels. I ordered the ones with raised lettering because I thought those would look more professional. Unfortunately, what I designed on my PC brought the level of professionalism way down. Looking back, it was a waste of money at that point in my business. I gave away about 50 of the 500 I had ordered and would have been fine going with the lower-end cards. They made great luggage tags, though.

Today, the papers and templates available for printing business cards and even logos have come a long way. There are also web sites available where you can order business cards on a variety of paper stock and from your own design or a predesigned template. Web-based services are also available to design a custom logo for your business. Where you are in your business should govern the type and level of business card you have.

- Start-up: Seamless-edge business cards printed on your color printer.
- Growing with employees besides yourself: Web-based printing or a local printer such as Kinko's. These are also good if you are starting to raise money and need to upgrade your image without looking like you are wasting (investors') money.
- Profitable with a professional logo: Professional printing shops that can match your logo's color choices exactly. This is key to maintaining consistency and perpetuating your company's brand image.

When Keenan left his job and joined me in the business we were still working out of our home and keeping our business overhead low. While the prestige of having an office outside the home was tempting, we recognized the undue financial burden it would put on us at this point in our business's growth. This is an important consideration, especially when starting out. It is prudent to build up cash reserves to fund expansion and growth. By keeping overhead low, the money will be there when you need it. For us, our seven months of working from home after we hired our first employees provided us the ability to build the cash reserve we needed to outfit an office when we finally moved into one. Rather than go into debt—something we did only briefly when we had our first growth spurt—we were able to self-finance our growth through conservative cash management and continuing to keep our overhead low.

Having the office at home was convenient as well. More than once a support call came in during the wee hours of the night. With our office down the hall, we were able to stumble to our office and address the issue without having to put on shoes or get dressed. We *were* the image of the professional on the conference call wearing fuzzy bunny slippers. We even dressed in bathrobes and big slippers that year for Halloween, touting our costumes as "self-employed home office."

Thankfully, our home office was big enough to accommodate both of us, though I had to learn to adjust the volume of my voice when talking on the phone so as not to chase Keenan out of the room. We both also enjoyed the morning commute. We found we could dig into work before the kids woke up, take a break to have breakfast with them, and get back into it when the nanny arrived.

One disadvantage appeared when I tried to multitask by coloring my hair while doing e-mail. I got so engrossed with my e-mail that I left the color on too long. That afternoon when I stepped out into the sunlight, my hair looked metallic purple—not exactly the color I wanted.

We did have to adjust to having our young kids around while we worked. We hired a nanny to come into the house and care for them while we worked, but it took some time for them to understand that Mommy and Daddy were working and were not available to play. Whenever we would leave our office and walk into the kitchen or another part of the house, they didn't have to see us to know we were out—they had that on radar. We eventually bought a small refrigerator to put in our office to minimize the number of times we had to venture out. At least that helped eliminate *that* temptation.

As the children got older, they were able to understand our situation better. They were allowed to come into the office when the door was open, and most of the time we would stop to talk with them. Frequently, they would come in and color quietly in the corner while we worked. Just to be near us was somehow comforting to them. If the door was shut, however, it meant we were on the phone or otherwise did not want to be disturbed. It took some time but they eventually came to respect our office hours because they saw the benefits at times when we were able to be more open and available.

As the workload continued to increase, we needed to expand our resources. I made the decision to hire people rather than use subcontractors for a number of reasons. First, quality was a major consideration for me, and I felt that paying someone as an employee would provide greater leverage and control over that aspect of the software development. Second, based on my long-time relationship with my customers, service was a critical element of my success in working with them. I needed congruity in the people who were dealing with my clients and in the delivery of our services (see the "Creating Consistency" section in Chapter 6). That approach paid off. Consistently, our customers cited our interactions with them and our approach to customer service as one of the reasons they continued to grow their business with us.

The story of our decision to move the office out of our home is not unique. Essentially, the work crossed the line into our personal lives one too many times. It was New Year's Day and I was entertaining Keenan's family. At the same time, we had a new software release that had to be delivered to the client within the following week. This particular software required a special printer and associated computer setup, both of which just happened to be in our home office. The person who was working on the project for us was encountering unforeseen problems and needed to have access to that computer and printer in order to solve them. We didn't anticipate the issue would take long to work through, so we let him come over to use the equipment in our home office. That was a mistake. He ran into problems he could not personally address, and I was the only one who could guide him to a solution. I got pulled into working while I should have been entertaining. The next day we decided it was time to move the office out of our home. We needed more separation.

Many entrepreneurs are quick to rush into expensive, Class A office space because they want to feel successful. The term *Class A* refers to an office building that is priced the highest because it is new, in a convenient location, and professionally managed. Depending on your business, that can be a waste of money. Admittedly, some professions need to project a certain level of accomplishment and financial success through their office environment. That said, Martek Biosciences *still* operates out of their strip mall office building even though they have received almost $500 million in capital investments. They claim that being within walking distance to restaurants and services is more important than the prestige of a high rise. Investors seem to like that about them.

Our clients rarely, if ever, came to our place of business, so image was not an issue for us. Consequently, when our business finally left the home, we continued to work to keep our expenses down and overhead low. This is also called keeping our "burn rate" low—the rate at which our fixed costs burn through cash. The office we moved into was only 800 square feet and as we quickly grew to eight people, we had to get creative with the use of our available space.

The office had a lobby, a large open room, and two small offices. I shared one of the offices with our project manager, though he often worked from home. We had people sharing L-shaped desks and working on computer printer tables. Not the environment I would recommend, but everyone was working hard and we were growing.

In the middle of the office was a small kitchenette and a single bathroom. Anything that was being cooked in the microwave or transpiring in the bathroom was known throughout the whole office, and it was not always pleasant. When we reached 12 people in that space, we knew it was time to move, even though our lease had another year on it. We assumed we would lose our deposit since that was what our contract indicated, but it was a risk we needed to take. Thankfully, we were able to find another company to take over our lease, and our landlord released us from it and returned our deposit. We were pleasantly surprised that they were able and willing to essentially renegotiate our contract. It made going into the next one a little easier and less ominous. In fact, we broke that lease, too, because of rapid growth and did not lose our deposit. Contracts can be amended and negotiated. What a promising discovery.

## Having a Financial Plan

As we started looking into our baby's future, we began to realize that feeding another mouth—albeit a *small* mouth in the beginning—was going to require a shift in our spending habits. As we discovered overpriced baby furniture, clothes they grow out of after one wearing, and gadgets that we just must have, the realities of the financial obligations that come with having a child began to sink in. Then there was the soaring price of a college education to consider. Children are not cheap. We had to make a plan.

Running out of cash is one of the largest reasons small businesses fail—either it took longer for their product to take off than anticipated or the customers said they loved their product or service but not enough to actually *buy* it. Sometimes, companies can have ample customers and plenty of work and still run out of cash because they pay their vendors too quickly or their customers don't pay them fast enough. Large customers, including the government, can take longer to pay than the agreed-upon terms, and if you don't have the cash reserves you need, you could find yourself thinking about using credit cards to make payroll, which I *do not* recommend.

We made it a policy in our business to build up and keep at least three months of operating expenses in cash as a buffer against such issues. We also obtained a line of credit to cover us during periods of growth when it took some time for our revenues to catch up with our added expenses. If you're just starting up, at least three to six months or more of your personal living expenses should be set aside for the same reason.

Even after hiring our first few employees and moving into an office outside of the home, we still didn't have a formal financial or business plan. We also didn't really have a business; we had a contract with a single, albeit substantial, customer. Although I didn't realize it at the time, there is a big difference.

We finally recognized our need for a business and financial plan when questions began surfacing regarding where to spend our profits. The good news was that we actually *had* profits, in part because we had kept our overhead low. We were contemplating how to branch outside of our large, single customer and acquire other clients. We wanted to turn our contract into a *real* business. To accomplish that, we would need to begin investing money into the company in the form of infrastructure and much-needed sales and marketing. The business plan would make sure that we were going in a viable direction and that we were spending money on the right things to get us where we wanted to go. The financial plan ensured that we would have the money we needed when we needed it.

Up to that point, our flagship customer was consuming every new resource we hired. While the growth within that one account was helping our revenues grow, it wasn't adding to our future security. Security? I hadn't even realized prior to that time that security was even something I was concerned about. Sure, it had been in the back of my mind since Keenan joined me in the business, but I had never put a formal plan into place to make sure I achieved that goal. I discovered the hard way that running a business without a plan is like traveling without a map—you're not likely to get where you want to go. Likewise, if you have no designated place to go, any place will do—including bankruptcy. Thankfully, we didn't have to learn that lesson the hard way. Our large customer funded our product development and we continued to bring in revenue from services as we began to look at, and actually succeed in, growing our customer base. Ironically, our success wasn't where we had thought it would be. The markets began to change from the time we developed our business plan to the time we started to execute on it. That's when it pays to be flexible.

In starting up a company, we're constantly warned about losing focus. It has been proven that trying to be everything to everybody is *not* the path to success. Focus is good, but not with blinders on. Markets shift unexpectedly, customers' needs change, and competitors continue to innovate or move into our territory, interrupting our original plan. It is imperative to adopt a model of *focused flexibility*. Think of focused flexibility as equivalent to peripheral vision. You continue to focus straight ahead, but you don't ignore anomalies that you catch out of the corner of your eyes. If you were skiing down a hill and spied another skier coming toward you, you would adjust your heading so you would not collide. So, too, with your business you should watch for signs that your current path forward needs correction or, perhaps, a whole new direction.

We worked hard to negotiate the ownership and licensing rights for the software we developed for one of our clients. As part of the negotiation process, we had to create a plan for marketing and selling the product to new customers. The market at that time seemed open, with 58 percent of the market share belonging to the "other" category and no real market leaders in sight.

By the time we finished negotiating the contract and took time to look again at our opportunities in the market one year later, the landscape had changed drastically. Two companies had emerged as strong players in the industry and had begun buying up their smaller competitors. The race was afoot and we were still tying our shoes.

The impact this consolidation was having on the price of the software in our industry was to drive it down. Our software was becoming a commodity, and in a commodity market, winners emerge based on price and volume. We did not have the volume and did not want to compete on price. The only alternative other than finding a new market was to develop a specialty. In order to survive, we had to alter our plans and practice focused flexibility. We needed to hone in on our competitive differentiation and find a niche that was still underserved and become the market leader there.

I hired a consultant to interview our customers and prospective customers to find out why they bought from us and what *they* believed our competitive advantage was. The consultant also asked customers who had opted to go with another solution why they didn't buy from us. That information was just as useful as the other, but, unfortunately, we had not gone after a lot of business at that time so there wasn't a large field from which to get input. The results of that study were nonetheless invaluable.

Based on the results, we adopted two changes to our strategy. First, we redefined our offering so as to highlight the true benefit the customer told us they were getting from our software. Interestingly, it was not what we had thought. We also found out from our customers that they considered our experience in their industry to be a significant competitive advantage. Although there was no contractual reason to do so, we had previously stayed away from other companies in this industry for fear it would jeopardize our relationship with our principal client. Upon further research we discovered that this market was easily accessible and virtually untapped. As a result, our second modification was to focus on the industry we were already in. What we learned later is that by not wanting to offend our main client, we had been cutting ourselves off from our path of least resistance and highest probability of success. We had let emotion cloud our business judgment, which is rarely a good thing but, unfortunately, happens often.

We developed a plan to carve out a niche in this industry. We opted to remain somewhat under the radar so as not to invite the market leaders into it as competitors. At some point our plan was to emerge with enough traction to attract a large company's attention so they would purchase our company. In essence, that is exactly what we did; while we didn't get bought out by a competitor, we were able to sell our software to a business partner that was in the same niche and looking to expand their offerings within that market.

After the sale and some much-needed time away, Keenan and I began to look into several other business opportunities. Throughout our research we found several times that we needed to shift our business concept due to information we uncovered about competition, industry trends, or consumer buying habits. We practiced focused flexibility. We finally decided against going with a particular business opportunity when we discovered that the typical industry profit margins were well below what we were used to and the work associated with getting the product to market was not congruent with our personal objectives. Had we not taken the time to conduct a feasibility analysis (little of which actually made it off the whiteboard onto paper), it is likely we would have wasted a great deal of time and money and been sorely disappointed with the results. Some companies, however, get the message directly from their customers after they're already operating that they need to change directions.

When Graham Weston, CEO of Rackspace Managed Systems, first bought into his business, his partners sold him on a completely different business model than they ended up with. Since Graham's background had previously been in real estate, he envisioned the business as a leasing company. They were leasing computer servers to their customers. Then the first angry customer reached him. The client was having trouble with his server that Rackspace hosted and was looking for some assistance. The founders were not initially looking to start a customer services company. The original business plan drove them to recommend the customer go out and hire an information technology (IT) person rather than provide the needed support. Over time, it became clear what their customers wanted. They were not interested in just renting hardware. They wanted services to go along with it to make sure their computers remained online. Graham saw the opportunity to turn computer servers into a service, and the whole business took on a new life. He likens the difference between their two business models as the difference between taking a taxi and renting a car. The taxi provides a service, while renting a car leaves the driving to you. They both get you where you want to go but with different methods and pricing. Rackspace decided they were a taxi.

Contrary to what I thought in the beginning, markets, customers, competition, and my changing goals and priorities had a great deal of reign over the changes needed in my business. I learned quickly that the control I sought when I started my business wasn't the same kind of control I experienced. I had to redefine what control really meant.

## Redefining Control

Some of us begin to learn early in our parenting career that we are not truly in control. When I got pregnant in our second month of trying, I thought, "This isn't so hard!" When I had a miscarriage 12 weeks later, I should have seen the signs about who was in control. Thankfully, I got pregnant for keeps the following month and we were on our way.

My next lesson in painful patience and complete lack of control started around week 34. I was swollen and achy and so large that I had to wake up out of a sound sleep just to turn over in bed. It was such a humid July that every time I took off my sandals, the indentations in my feet made it look as if I still had sandals on. As my due date approached, I tried every trick I had ever read or heard about to bring on labor, from the seemingly sane to the outright bizarre. While walking to hasten labor seemed to make logical sense when you consider the downward pull of gravity, I couldn't imagine what eating spicy food did to prod the baby along down the birth canal. Logic aside, I found myself opting for spicier food rather than mild on the outside chance that there might actually be some truth to the urban legends. The bottom line, I realized, was that the baby comes when it's darn well ready unless you look to outside furtherance from your obstetrician.

The idea of starting my business so I could have more control seems naïve in hindsight. While as a business owner I do have more control over some things, the thought that I have total control over my schedule is laughable. My customers, the marketplace, my employees—everyone controls my business more than I do.

Early in my business, control seemed easier to find. Looking back, it was in direct proportion to my revenues. In the beginning, I had a customer request a proposal that required me to work over the weekend. Because it was an account I really wanted to obtain, how could I refuse? When that had happened in my previous life before kids, it was no problem. I would stay at work in the war room (the room we destroyed through the course of proposal writing), eat pizza, finish the proposal in marathon-like all-night sessions and catch up with my husband when it was all delivered. The difference in approach once I had kids was that I took the kids to the zoo by day and worked on the proposal after the little ones went to bed at night. Sometimes, I was able to get some work in while they were temporarily entertained by television. Although I invoked the electronic babysitter sparingly, it did come in handy when I was desperate. I owe a great deal to Disney, PBS, and Nickelodeon. The only downside is that to this day the "I Love You" song from *Barney & Friends* can still send chills up my spine. As the kids have gotten older, not much has changed. The Internet, iPods, and instant messaging have filled in where Barney left off, though their use is still equally regulated in our house, much to the kids' chagrin.

As those proposals turned to contracts and my revenues grew, control became elusive. I had customers depending on me as the control was slipping away.

We had created custom software for a large manufacturing company and our deadlines and installations revolved around our customer's production schedules. Since they operate on a 24 hours per day, 7 days per week schedule, *they* let *me* know when they had down time in their operations so I could install or upgrade their computers and software. My schedule was their schedule, and most often it involved what would otherwise be a holiday. I would also get support calls at two in the morning, which, thankfully, in the beginning required me to only walk down the hall to my computer to diagnose.

When I started hiring employees, I envisioned taking a big step back toward control over my schedule. Once these bright young people were trained, they could be available to travel to the customer sites and answer the early morning support calls. While this was a great idea, I began to see that it would take some time to get to that point and that my employees, too, exerted some amount of control over me and my schedule.

Having people to take over the 24-hour support we provided our clients relieved one of the biggest challenges to my time. Rather than staffing our office on a rotating 24-hour schedule, we chose to adopt an outgoing pager system. When the call was not answered within a certain period of time, I was paged as a backup. I wasn't tagged often, but when I was, it was usually ill-timed. Thankfully, failure to answer the call was most often due to dead batteries in the pager or simply not hearing the beep, both of which were easily remedied with improved procedures and training.

It also took some time for the customer to get to know these new people and trust them as they had trusted me. Eventually, because I had hired excellent people, others gained the customers' trust and I stopped getting support calls directly. It took me longer than I expected to become the most expendable person in my company from an operational perspective, but the flexibility did come back, albeit in a different form than what it was before employees.

Donna cites the lack of governance from others on how and when she does her work as what has given her the control she sought through self-employment. She has been able to build her company around her personal life, but that does not mean she is always available when her children want her. She believes strongly, however, that she is more accessible to her children now than if she were working for someone else.

While the control available as an entrepreneur is different than what I had expected, I found that I did have control over the role my business took in my life and the way I achieved what I needed to. I could schedule time to be with my children and complete certain tasks at night or in the early morning. I was able to grow my company at a rate I was comfortable with and in a way that complemented my goals as a mother: to be available for my children when they truly needed me while teaching them independence at the same time.

## From Diaper Bag to Briefcase

- There is really never an ideal time to start a business or a family, and you will never have all the answers before you do. There are, however, several critical factors that must be considered before diving into a new business:
  - Do your homework, including talking to others who have done what you want to do.
  - Look at the worst-case scenario and then work to improve upon it. For example, for me, the worst case was that I would have to get a "real" job. I made sure I did not burn bridges in case I needed to go back to my former employer on my knees.
  - Save up your money or make sure you have a back-up income stream.
  - Conduct any personal transactions where your credit will be reviewed and make sure it is in good standing. You'll likely need it later for your business.

*(continued)*

- Know clearly how and when you will make money in the venture before taking the plunge.
- Developing a business plan to design how your business will be successful is a critical first step and an ongoing concern for profitable, growing companies. However, don't let the exercise of planning put blinders on your eyes. It is prudent to keep your eye on the market in case you need to shift to avoid a big tree in your path.
- Keeping overhead low for as long as possible is critical to remaining flexible and keeping the cash from flowing out the door too quickly. Work out of your home for as long as possible—your clients don't even have to know! And do you really need those fancy business cards and mahogany desk?
- When you do lease your first office, don't overdo it. If customers are not coming to visit you, it is prudent not to waste your money on expensive office space. Many other lower-priced office options are available that can be equally as effective and meet your needs. If Martek, which is poised to reach $1 billion in revenues, still maintains their original offices in a strip mall, why can't you?
- Contracts can be renegotiated. Do not hesitate to explore your options with leases and other contracts when you need to make moves based on company growth.
- Cash is king. Know how you will make it, where and when you will spend it, and, more importantly, where you *won't* spend it.
- The control experienced in parenthood and entrepreneurship is not what you would expect. While customers and employees have more control over you than you might anticipate, the flexibility that comes from setting your own work hours and arranging your priorities make it all worthwhile.

## Resources for Writing a Business Plan

### Books

Rhonda Abrams, *The Successful Business Plan* (Grants Pass, Ore.: Oasis Press, 1993).

Lee E. Hargrave, *Plan for Profitability: How to Write a Strategic Business Plan* (Four Seasons Publishers, 1999).

Jan B. King, *Business Plans to Game Plans: A Practical System for Turning Strategies into Action* (Hoboken, N.J.: John Wiley & Sons, 2004).

## Web Sites

www.sba.gov

www.logoworks.com

www.psprint.com

## Other Resources for Starting a Business

Jane Applegate, *201 Great Ideas for Your Small Business* (New York: Bloomberg Press, 1998).

Michael Gerber, *The E-Myth Revisited: Why Most Small Businesses Don't Work and What to Do about It* (New York: HarperCollins, 1995).

Thomas Ittelson, *Financial Statements: A Step-by-Step Guide to Understanding and Creating Financial Reports* (Franklin Lakes, N.J.: Career Press, 1998).

Robert Kiyosaki, *Before You Quit Your Job: 10 Real-Life Lessons Every Entrepreneur Should Know about Building a Multimillion-Dollar Business* (New York: Warner Business Books, 2005).

Norman Moore and Grover Gardner, *Forecasting Budgets: 25 Keys to Successful Planning* (New York: Lebhar-Friedman Books, 1999).

### Linda Frost's Top Five Tips

1. Create a product to meet a need that you believe will people will pay to have met.
2. Formulate a plan on how you will sell to that need.
3. Organize your plan and put it into action.
4. Keep good records and provide excellent customer service by following through on what you say you will do.
5. Thank your customers for their business and send a small thank you gift (e.g., a gift card to a restaurant, flowers).

CHAPTER 3

# Launching

My second child was born 19 months after my first but didn't come in second for pain. She tried to come too early, sending me into premature labor at 36 weeks and, of course, in the middle of the night. Unfortunately, I had to cancel a training class that had been scheduled for the next day. I was supposed to teach various computer applications to the sales reps of a new, major client. Interestingly enough, if I had taught that class and it had gone well, my company might have taken off in a completely different direction. It wasn't to be.

After several hours, the labor pains stopped progressing and my doctor sent me home to sleep. Not wanting to take any chances, she preferred that I go another couple weeks before the baby was born so that the lungs were more fully developed. That was a great idea, except that I was walking around dilated to four centimeters. I used to joke with my friends that my daughter could stick her hand out and wave to them if she so desired. It was a good thing she had decided it wasn't quite time to come out because I was not anywhere near being ready. I still had to get my older daughter, who was all of nineteen months old, to move out of the crib and into her big girl bed. I had hoped to have it already done, but time had gotten away from me. This "false alarm" woke me up and gave me the extra time I needed to be prepared. It also taught me how much real control I would have over this child—very little.

My doctor was able to schedule me into the hospital to induce labor by breaking my water two weeks later and still two weeks before her original due date. The doctor was concerned that if I just let it go naturally, she would have to teach my husband how to deliver the baby himself.

When the scheduled day arrived, we went into the hospital early in the morning. I remember hearing the Beatles' song "Birthday" on the radio and feeling so much more in control and ready than the first time weeks before. I should have known better. After the doctor broke my water, she recommended that I take a walk through the hallways to let gravity do what it does best. On my walk, I stopped by the room across the hall to visit with my neighbor who had been scheduled for induction that same morning. She was two weeks overdue and because they were dispensing medication that quickens the effectiveness of labor, she had already been given an epidural to ease the pain and was bed-bound. As I was standing there chatting with her, my labor pains had started and were beginning to quickly get uncomfortable. Within a few minutes, we were summoned back to our room by our nurse so she could check my progress.

Once I got back across the hall, the contractions seemed to kick in where they had left off two weeks earlier. Like the wave of sickness that overcomes you from food poisoning, the labor rose quickly to a furious, burning pain in a matter of minutes. The pain became increasingly unbearable and had me yelling at my nurse for drugs. I finally got the epidural I had been oh-so-calmly asking for just in time for the two pushes it took to deliver daughter number two. Although I can remember a great number of details about that delivery since I had no drugs to alter my perception and journal entries written soon after the experience to refer to, I can no longer *feel* the pain. The pure exhilaration of looking into my baby's face made all that melt away. The lesson that I took away from the experience was that if I ever considered giving birth to a third child, I would likely have even less time in labor and need more time up front to find an anesthesiologist *fast*. But would I have another child? Not now with so many years between. Besides, I had my business as my other baby, and it required as much energy, passion, and planning as the real thing.

## Introduction

The effort required in childbirth is in many ways not unlike the labor pains associated with starting up a company. Building a company is hard work, but somehow we forget that and do it over and over again. Perhaps after the first one it gets easier, or maybe it is because we are passionate about what we do that we are able to withstand the hard times and sleepless nights. Naming both a business and a child is a difficult task as well, but once you've bonded with baby and business, you find yourself unable to envision anything else.

## Forgetting the Pain

Like childbirth, the only way I remember the early days of starting up my business with any accuracy is because I kept a journal through it. Before going back through the chronicles of my early days as an entrepreneur, I would recall from memory coming home early from the office to play with my baby. After she went to bed for the evening, I would launch into my productive period. I would sit snuggled and comfortable in my bed with my laptop from 9:00 P.M. until 1:00 in the morning programming and never seem to get tired. I had inexhaustible energy and could do anything and everything. I felt as if the world were at my feet and I was *empowered* because I loved what I was doing.

When I go back and read through my journal, reality smacks me on the head like they used to smack newborns' butts. The only world at my feet was in the piles of dirty laundry that needed to be done within viewing distance of my work space, or the heater under my desk because our basement was so cold and damp.

In the beginning, I was terribly depressed working out of my house. I missed the personal interaction of an office environment and felt the pull of the household chores that were all too visible in front of me. It took me almost six months of working from home to realize that I didn't have to wait until lunchtime to go out and run errands with everyone else. I could go at any time! And if I took a little more than an hour, who was going to chastise me?

Then there was the uncertainty. I had one assignment, but what would be next? How could I get more contracts lined up when I was so busy doing the work I already had? I couldn't really enjoy any breaks and treat them as a vacation because I needed to go out and find my next job. Had I made a mistake by giving up my seemingly easier, nice-paying position with the company I thought I would retire from? Would they rehire me if I ran back and told them I had made a mistake? Were my friends right—was I really *crazy*??!

The good news is that I settled into a rhythm quickly and those initial fears and anxieties began to fade. I had it down. Unfortunately, the beat of the drum started to speed up as my company got more successful and the workload increased.

As the company started to grow, a new set of challenges emerged. I could no longer do all the work by myself—I had to hire people. With employees came a health care plan, workers' compensation, and liability insurance. We had to hire not just people but the *right* people, find an office, outfit it, and obtain a line of credit with that nasty rider that claims my house if we default. Adding to the stress was the uncertainty of not knowing, in the early days, if we were even going to make payroll. And yet somehow, looking back, that is not what I first recall. Mostly, I remember that I was having fun doing what I enjoyed. And the payoff—the camaraderie of the family of people I worked with and the customers we serviced—made all that start-up pain seem so much lighter, somehow not as bad. The joy of being my own boss and following my passion overshadowed it all.

Working on starting up a couple of new business concepts and leaving the babies to others brought some of the "pain" rushing back. When I sat down to do the weekly accounting, my heart began to pound stronger as my breathing quickened. It didn't take long to remember why bookkeeping was one of the first functions I outsourced. I am obviously not cut out to balance pennies. I know why it is important and do it because I have to, but it just isn't my thing.

As I move forward, I use the schooling I obtained through hard knocks to help others start up new businesses and am personally taking the lessons forward with me into my next venture. There are many other things I will do differently the next time around, but pain be damned, I am doing it again!

Before you write me off as insane, there are others who have been diagnosed with SED (serial entrepreneur's disease). Jay Butera, a self-proclaimed start-up addict, was so convinced that he was done with entrepreneurship that he drove 100 miles to throw his cell phone into the Atlantic Ocean after selling his first company, Cedar Fresh Home Products, to a group of investors. Although he twisted his shoulder when he declared his freedom by hurling his phone, he was able to relax at the beach with his family and find peace. Unfortunately, it did not last long.

One morning while his wife and kids were at the beach, Jay stole away and went to an Internet café. In a matter of a few hours he started a company around one of the products he had held out of the previous company's sale. In his mind, he could create a small business—enough to keep him engaged—but keep it contained. If only. Like other entrepreneurs with SED, he was drawn into the challenges of building a business and soon began adding products to his line. He had not so much forgotten the pain; rather, the thrills and joys of building a business overshadowed the hardships and pain. He was right back into it, cursing it and loving it at the same time (Jay Butera, "Addicted to Startups," *Fortune Small Business*, October 2006).

Terry Chase Hazell took less than two months off between her "babies," and there was actually no "off" time in there. After she left her first business baby, Chesapeake-PERL, she was constantly evaluating and considering her next opportunity. When she finally settled on her next venture, SD Nanosciences, some of the familiar pains began to resurface. First, although Terry had gone for almost two years without a salary building her first start-up company, she had forgotten what it was like to go without money. It did not take long for her to recall that not drawing a salary and forgoing benefits is difficult. Also, the first few months when you are the only full-time person in an early-stage company can be lonely. She had become so accustomed to the bustle of a growing company that the solitude of start-up hit hard. Additionally, there is no real company location—no castle for the flag, as Terry puts it. She had forgotten how grounded it made her to walk into a building with her company name on it. As difficult as these pains are, however, she is well on her way to bringing home business baby number two.

## Keeping Names in Perspective

What is in a name? Quite a bit! Ask a boy named Richard Cranium how important it is to consider nicknames. Many couples spend hours analyzing possible names for their child: Should we use a family name? Do we want something classical? Should we select a name from the Bible? Or something no one else has and *doesn't* remind Mom or Dad of someone they once dated. Naming a child can have a lasting impact on their life and their future to boot. For example, will there ever be a President Paris? Not likely. The good news is that names can change. For example, would Bruce Willis have become a multimillion-dollar action star with his birth name, Walter Willison? Would John Wayne have become the ultimate man's man with his given name, Marion Morrison? Tom Cruise as Tom Mapother (the IV!)?

Sometimes, names grow to fit the person. In college, I decided to stick with my given name of *Julia* instead of *Julie*, the name that everyone had been calling me since I can remember. One day I just stopped correcting the teachers when they called roll based on the registration records. All the new friends that I made called me Julia and I didn't correct them. It began to grow on me, or I grew into the name. After college I reverted back to *Julie*. In talking to an old friend from college who knew me as Julia, she commented how much I looked like a Julia and not a Julie. Those who knew me as Julie said just the opposite. Perhaps it is all in how it is presented and what you get used to. Does anyone remember what Accenture used to be called?

As difficult as it is to name a child, naming a business or product is just as exasperating, with similar far-reaching implications. First, the name should mean something that is relevant to the business and its customers. A restaurant named Good Eats might work, but a drugstore named Tombstone? Some marketing folks will tell you a company's name must not leave any conjecture to what the business is about. The challenge is that many companies are not sure what they are about when they start up. Even if they are sure in the beginning, it often changes over the course of getting to know your customers and the true value you bring to them. I labored long and hard over our name: Applied Creative Technologies. We were a technology company that applied creativity to solve our customers' problems. I thought it fit well. It didn't hurt that starting with an "A" put it at the top of alphabetized lists.

The name must also be unique in a particular field. While having three Megans in your daughter's class is fine, there can be only one Microsoft. We did find another Applied Creative Technologies in Texas but they manufactured computer hardware. It was close, but we applied for a trademark just in case as protection.

You must consider any acronyms as well as nicknames. Would you hire a services firm with the name Services United in Knowledge, or SUK? ACT as an acronym worked well for us.

It is so challenging to find a meaningful, unique name for a business that companies have started making up words. Verizon. Manugistics. Cingular. Intelligistics. Biotechnology companies have become especially bad at making up names. They take parts of scientific words and force them together into a new word. Sci-GenTech Corporation. BioMed SciZyme. To scientists, these seem to mean something. To the rest of us, they come across as sterile.

Naming a business has spawned new services in an already thriving multimillion-dollar marketing industry. Companies and consultants charge thousands of dollars to name companies. Add more money if the company plans on taking advantage of the explosive global marketplace, because the name must be internationally unique and it cannot be offensive in a foreign language. Folklore has it that when Chevrolet went to sell their "Nova" automobile in Mexico, they realized they had to change the name when someone pointed out that the word *nova* in Spanish means "no go." Who wants to buy an automobile that doesn't go? It is possible to alter perceptions through exemplary execution but at what cost? If all else fails, business or product names can be changed, too.

My good friend Mary Cantando was doing well as a small business consultant. She had been a successful business owner herself and was sharing what she had learned in her 20 years in business with others to help them grow and prosper. Her company, Cantando and Associates, was assisting a number of different types of entrepreneurs to grow their companies, but Mary felt like something was missing or was not quite right. She couldn't wait to get to some of her projects, while she faced others with dread. One day she sat down and divided her clients into two columns: those she loved to work with and those she merely tolerated. Looking at the list, she experienced an "aha" moment. The companies she derived the most out of working with—the ones in the "this is fun" column—were all owned by women.

Researching the market of women business owners, Mary found a severely underserved but growing niche market. She noticed the domain WomanBusinessOwner.com was available and realized that no one else was focused on this market. Cutting off 70 percent of her revenues to focus only on women was far more monumental than changing the company name, but once she decided to go that way, her business was reborn. She did what many new business owners fear and changed her company's focus and name to Woman Business Owner. With that tough decision and simple name change, her business began to soar. Would Mary have been as successful in addressing her new niche market if she hadn't changed her company name and subsequent focus? It is possible, but by branding herself and her company around her target market, she's been enjoying growth beyond her wildest dreams and has become the go-to expert for helping women-owned businesses grow. She did not realize when she set out as Cantando and Associates that there was a different market in which she would find her passion and purpose. Taking the risk in focusing her efforts as well as changing her company name paid off in success beyond what she had previously imagined.

Amy Nichols also found that she had to change her business name when her strategy shifted. When she had created her "dog spa" several years earlier, she researched the name "Happy Tails Dog Spa" and found nothing like it in the Washington, D.C., metro area. She enjoyed immediate success and was able to open another facility a couple of years later. The time and energy involved in opening these stores was immense—it took a great deal of work. As is often the case with entrepreneurs who open a business based on their passion, this was not what she had envisioned for her life. She actually wanted to grow faster than her own reach could take her. Smartly, she decided to franchise her concept to accelerate its growth.

Within the first year she had sold six franchises in the same geographic area but, again, was not satisfied with the pace. She realized that she needed to take her concept national in order to experience the growth she envisioned. In researching national expansion, it became clear that the name of her spas had to change. In other parts of the country there were many different pet services and outlets that used the "Happy Tails" name. Happy Tails Grooming. Happy Tails retail store. While none of these establishments were spas, the risk of confusion was too great. That was when Dogtopia was born.

## Passion Is Required

When we finally brought our baby home, we used to sit and stare at her for what seemed like hours. The bond that both my husband and I felt with her is indescribable, and unless you are a parent, it is hard to understand. The night we brought her home from the hospital, we put her in the bassinette at the foot of our bed and even moved our pillows down so we could be near her. Although we didn't sleep much, we were in awe.

As the sleepless nights went on, it became physically difficult to continue. Keenan went back to work, which meant I had to wake for all of the nighttime feeding shifts. Although I was able to occasionally go to bed early as he took the last feeding of the night, the weeks of interrupted sleep had my mind in a dense fog. There were times when I felt like I was losing it. The growing love I felt for my baby was the only thing that kept me going. I am convinced that the ever-increasing bond of affection is nature's way of protecting both parent and child. Without it, caring for a newborn would undoubtedly lead to insanity.

A scene from one of my favorite comedies, *Monty Python and the Holy Grail*, depicts in a disgusting but funny way the passionate insanity and persistence that a successful entrepreneur feels. A knight is guarding a bridge, and anyone who wants to cross the bridge must defeat him. As another knight approaches to cross the bridge, he is met with the challenge, and quickly draws his sword and chops the defending knight's hand off. The handless knight, in reply, quips, "It's just a flesh wound!" They continue to fight. One by one, the defending knight's limbs are severed (don't worry, this is actually funny!) while he continues to spout retorts such as "That's all right, I've got another one!" when his leg is removed. Finally, at the end of the scene, the defeated knight has no arms and no legs, and sitting there on the ground concedes, "All right, we'll call it a draw." Now *that* is passion and persistence: always looking at the glass half full—or the other limb still attached—and not refusing to back down. It has also been called insanity by many who do not understand it. I believe they are not totally wrong. After all, one step away from crazy is passionate.

Amy Nichols refused to give in. She doggedly approached seven banks before she found one that would loan her the money to open her business. It took finding someone who believed her story, saw her passion, and owned a dog himself—she wanted to open a doggy day spa—for her to finally receive the money. While many businesses have difficulty obtaining early funding from banks, which is why businesses are not deemed "bankable" until they are established and generating profits, Amy's passion for her vision finally led her to the right person and she got the check.

Someone once described a measure of entrepreneurial passion as "the fired-up factor." When you talk about your business non-stop with a smile on your face and appear to others as fired up about it, that is a strong sign that you have the passion. Positive energy exudes whenever you discuss your baby. Mary Moslander, founder and CEO of LiveHealthier.com, has that level of intensity. She describes working in her start-up company as "crazy, hard, exciting—I love it!" Her web site provides online social networking for people interested in improving their health. She is passionate about applying technology to make a difference in people's lives, which is what she is doing. Seeing her members get online with each other and forming communities around losing weight or getting in shape pumps her up. As crazy as it has been to manage cash flow and build something from absolutely nothing, her passion for what they are doing keeps her energized.

Mary Cantando claims her passion for her client niche has made the biggest difference in her business. She gets up every morning fired up about meeting with her clients, or delivering a keynote to women entrepreneurs, or writing an article for a women's magazine. She *loves* her target audience and knows she's making an impact in their businesses and their lives. To her, that makes all the difference in the world.

Randy and Chris Anderson were driven to entrepreneurship by their love of coffee and music. They worked with partner Kurt Esche and his wife to open The Music Café, a music-themed coffee shop in the small town of Damascus, Maryland. Randy had been a musician and played music all his life. He also had an obsession for good coffee. Chris reports that Randy's relationship with coffee was so strong that he had to stop at Starbuck's on the way to the hospital when she was in labor with their first son. "I'll just run in, you sit there and time your next contraction." Opening his own café had been a dream for 10 years until he finally made the decision and took what he calls a leap of faith. Having been open for only a few months, they are already making plans for their second store.

Paul Silber found that he was driven by succeeding at a challenge. Entrepreneurship was a challenge to him, and his main focus was on being successful. In order to do that, he had to learn what it was that his customers wanted and then provide that. While that sounds too simple to be true, it is. His business, for example, started out as purely services based. One day, one of his clients asked if they could provide product, so they found a way to do just that. At the time he sold his company, the revenue mix had shifted to 80 percent product and only 20 percent services. Listening to the customer and focusing on his passion for success brought exactly that.

In my business, my passion was driven mainly by two things: (1) seeing our customers delight in receiving a tangible benefit and (2) proving you could have a successful business and a life at the same time. Because I felt the burning passion to make these things work, I did whatever it took to make my business sustainable. The passion fueled a boldness—a fire—I had not experienced before. People saw the fire in my eyes, and if they understood what I was saying, I could have sold them on whatever it was I needed from them. Part of the key is to know exactly what it is you want from them.

My first appointment to ask for money was with the president of a local bank to ask for a line of credit to cover our anticipated growth. We did not have a business plan (shame on us!), but we did have a letter of intent from a major customer. Not knowing any better, I wrote up a one-page description of our company and what our contract (which was in negotiation) was hopefully going to look like. Our attorney had set up the meeting, which was the only reason we were meeting with the top guy and not delegated to some lower-level associate (which illustrates the value of having the right advisers). Against all odds, we were given a generous line of credit. When I asked later what convinced him to take a risk on our start-up company, the president mentioned my enthusiasm and passion for what we were doing. He felt compelled, based on my presentation, to believe that we could do what we said we were going to do. The passion sold it.

## Worlds Colliding

Terry Chase Hazell learned how to hide labor contractions during a pitch for investment money. A few days before she delivered her son, she was giving a venture pitch and had some pretty strong contractions. She couldn't talk momentarily, and everyone in the room was staring at her—probably thinking she was going to climb up on the podium and start heavy breathing and pushing—so she just held her nose and pretended she had a terrible sneeze coming. The contraction passed and she went on with the presentation. While the elapsed time was only about 10 seconds, it felt to her as if half the time was wasted with her standing there holding her nose. She ended up having the baby a couple of days later and closed on the investment before his umbilical cord came off.

That fire continued to grow because it was continually stoked in two ways: First, it spread through my employees as they caught the fire of providing a service that was valued by our customers. They also valued being regarded and treated as total human beings and not just employees. A perfect example of this was our part-time employees. We had several who worked reduced hours so that they could be home for their children after school. I was consistently impressed to witness these staff members accomplishing as much in their reduced-hour work week as others achieve working full time. They not only believed in what we were doing for our customers but were also driven by their appreciation for what we were able to do for their family life by providing a flexible work environment. Feeling valued not only as an employee but as a person motivated everyone at the company to strive to provide the best service in the industry. Keeping our customers happy meant keeping us in business, which in turn meant maintaining their ability to be flexible. They got that connection and worked hard to make it work.

The fire also grew through our customers. They loved us because we truly cared about their business as our own and they kept working with us because of the value we provided to their business. In fact, the first several years of our business growth were due solely to referrals from our customers. We actually called one of our customers our "VP of Marketing" because he would go to trade shows with me and make stand-up presentations on the great projects we did for their company. What an incredible feeling. Happy employees along with good execution truly yielded happy customers.

One afternoon, a customer called the office to report that their manufacturing facility was down due to a problem with their system—*our* system. At first, one or two people were working the issue but as time wore on and a clear solution was elusive, everyone in the company started to get involved. While this might sound like a waste of time, we all had shared sense of responsibility and no one was going home until the problem was solved and the customer's plant was operational. Even though we weren't all engaged in the actual solution process, we were there for moral support and to order the pizza. Personally, I knew I wouldn't be able to sleep knowing this had not been resolved. Well into the night, our team finally found and corrected the problem. Even though the problem turned out *not* to be our fault, we all felt a sense relief and celebration. Once the caffeine wore off, I was able to go home and sleep soundly. I might have even gone to sleep with a grin on my face. We were all on fire.

I confess: When I worked for someone else, I did, on occasion, feel like not going to work. If I did not actually call in sick, I went into work without any makeup on so that I would not look well. That way, when I went home sick at lunch time, no one would question. Since I've found passion in my work as an entrepreneur and in helping other entrepreneurs, I keep going no matter how bad I feel. Fever? As long as it isn't over 101 degrees. Sniffles? Take a lot of tissue. I have even gone to events wearing *extra* makeup just so I *don't* look sick. That is what passion does for you.

If you had asked Margaret Pressler a week earlier if she had time to work a new project into her schedule, the answer would have been unequivocally "no." But when a major national retailer called, Margaret knew what she had to do. Whatever they wanted. Not only did the retailer want to order her BurpCatcher burp cloths for its stores, the buyer also wanted a photo of a mom and a baby using one of her products to put in their catalog. Where she could not previously imagine having time to fit a photo shoot in, her passion for her business took over. Margaret lined up the baby of a friend and a photographer to get the work done to meet her customer's tight deadline.

Some of Terry Chase Hazell's happiest times as an entrepreneur starting up her first baby, Chesapeake-PERL, were when she was passionately focused on the task at hand. She can remember running through the Sears parking lot with her chief scientist and a microwave on a shopping cart. They were in big trouble on a project and needed the microwave to replace a special heater they had broken in their lab. They were laughing the whole time they were pushing the cart. They ended up working 18 hours straight to save that project using, as she calls it, that dumb microwave. She recalls that as one of her best days at the company. Passion and creativity pulled together to accomplish the task.

When you are passionate about what you do, no one has to wake you up in the morning to get you going or convince you to shift your schedule to work in a photo shoot for a customer. On the contrary, you can't wait to get to it. There is not an entrepreneur around, however, who hasn't thought about throwing in the towel at one point or another. Because there are so many ups and downs along the road, it takes passion to keep moving forward. It also helps to come to see your business as your baby, something you can't just abandon when the going gets tough. That is when the bonding occurs.

## Becoming Bonded

I tried to describe the bond between a parent and child to my younger brother when his wife was expecting, but he just couldn't get it. After his baby was born, the light went on. The delay in his understanding makes sense, though. His only reference until that pivotal point of parenthood was his experience as the child. As a child, the bond is completely different. I can remember being convinced as a teenager that my mother worried too much about where I was or what I was doing and who I was with. Then I became a mother.

When our younger daughter was 18 months old, she was running through the living room and fell and bumped her head on the wooden leg of the ottoman. My husband ran to pick her up, and I'll never in my life forget what happened next. She stopped breathing. She just went limp in his arms. I can still feel the fire rise in my gut when I think about it. Thankfully, she started breathing again within a couple of seconds, but that was the longest couple of seconds I have ever endured. The doctor speculated that she had cried so hard she had stopped breathing momentarily. That one moment was enough for me—I didn't want to go through *that* again.

It wasn't a month later, however, when she was sitting on a stool at our breakfast bar and accidentally fell off. I can still see it in slow motion in my mind—her little body tumbling down as a fire once again rose up in my belly. As she fell, her wrist hit the stool next to her. We weren't sure at that point if it was broken because she didn't really cry, though she was noticeably favoring that hand. We thought perhaps it was bruised. It wasn't until days later when she fell down running and was inconsolable for an hour that we realized this could be more serious. She refused to use that hand at all. The emergency room doctor confirmed our suspicions that it was broken. Now after two trips within months to the hospital with the same baby, we were expecting Child Services to come to our house for a little *interview*. Thankfully, that didn't happen and the arm recovered fully. We even kept the cast and laugh when we compare it to her arm as she has grown.

That same bond that comes across as a fire in the belly we feel with regard to our children is what drives many entrepreneurs to do incredible things. This can also be called *commitment*. When we've embraced our business baby, we are as committed as the pig that gave the bacon for our breakfast.

Margaret first bonded with her start-up company, Williamboy Products, when she saw the logo that her graphic designer had developed for her. It embodied everything she wanted her company to be: fresh, cute, whimsical, modern, and bright. Once she saw it, she knew she could make this idea work. Although she had the product name and the first production samples from her manufacturing partner in China, this was the first concrete evidence of her brand, and it provided her with a visual connection to her business. She could actually envision her BurpCatchers on the shelves at Target with that logo. Seeing it convinced her that this baby, her business, could be successful. She even carried her logo around in her purse like you would a baby picture.

Randy bonded with his business even before it was born. While designing, planning, and getting organized, he could actually feel the café come to life. Compare it to the euphoria you get from looking at that first sonogram. Something was there. It was alive and waiting for someone to love, nurture, and guide it into becoming a well-groomed and -oiled machine.

In business, that bond can also be a negative force when it comes across as defensiveness. Although the intense feeling of defensiveness motivated me to get things right the first time and to quickly fix anything that went wrong, it also resulted in initial outbursts that weren't so favorable for retaining customers. It took me some time and maturity to realize that it wasn't all about *me* and that a customer's perception can be reality.

In the beginning of my business's growth, I took every bump in the road personally. Any little software problem a customer brought to our attention felt like a personal attack. Any capability that wasn't exactly what they wanted or how they wanted it was a personal failure for me. Immaturely and arrogantly, I would posit that any problem they found had to be theirs. They weren't doing what they were supposed to be doing or they were using the system in a way that was never intended. If I had continued to do that, I would have ended up with no clients and personally needing to be locked up with padded walls. It took a caring customer and trusted adviser to help me learn not to let my bond with my business cloud my judgment.

The difference in my approach became clear years later when my oldest and largest client took me on a long lunch to tell me that they were going to be replacing our software (notice I didn't say "my" software) with their company's *standard* software in all five of their facilities. I still had that fire in my belly, that "how dare you call my baby ugly" feeling, but I masked it and took a deep breath. I then opted, instead, to handle the news as a professional.

I endured the five-hour meeting with grace and then went back to my hotel room and screamed into the phone to my husband. The actual transition took several years to even get started and they continued to be our customer through that time. Had I overreacted during the meeting and let my emotions show, it is possible that the relationship could have been damaged or completely severed, resulting in millions of dollars in lost revenue. As it was, it cost me only gray hairs and hours of lost sleep, though that wasn't the only sleep that I ever lost.

## Sleep Is a Luxury

From the time they are born, children have an uncanny way of robbing their parents of a good night's sleep when they most need it. They have no regard for the sanctity of their parent's sleep. Their stomachs are so tiny, most have to eat every two hours, day and night. Since Keenan had gone back to work, I was the lone designated night feeder. I don't know whether it was postpartum hormones or the delirium caused by the lack of continuous sleep, but by the time my daughter was two weeks old, I would reply to her cries for food with a loud "MOOOO!" I felt like a cow. I don't know why I even bothered to put a shirt on. By the time she finished nursing one side, fell asleep, woke up, and fed on the other side, I sometimes had only 30 minutes to myself before the next feeding. At that point, I decided to forgo everything that I had read about the purist view of not wanting to create "confusion" and started pumping so my husband could share in the joy. For him, it actually *was* joy. He at least could feed her without exposing himself. And neither of my children got confused over the multiple sources of sustenance—they chowed down on both.

When my children were old enough, I taught them the connection between waking mommy up in the middle of the night and mommy being grumpy the next morning. It took a couple of rough mornings for it to sink in and it still doesn't *always* work. Even today, my daughter seems to know instinctively when I need to get up for an early morning flight. With my alarm set to go off at 4:30 A.M., she comes into our room at 3:30 complaining of a bad dream. Although she goes right back to bed and is immediately asleep again, I am awake and, knowing I have to wake up in an hour, can't go back to sleep.

Show me an entrepreneur who doesn't have bouts of sleepless nights and I will show you a stockpile of sleep medication. Whether it is a proposal that needs to go out, a nagging personnel issue, or just general concerns about whether you will be able to keep your business afloat—businesses rob owners and managers of sleep all the time. History has it that Thomas Edison slept only three to four hours per night, though it was reported that he also took midday naps (a benefit of a home office!).

Most of my late nights were on-site at a customer's manufacturing facility. My best and worst sleepless moment came early in the company's history when we were installing critical new capabilities at a customer's plant. We were working with an enhanced technology to enable them to print bar code labels at the end of their packaging lines so that they could then move the containers into the warehouse and track them via laser scanners. As such, this was a key point in the process and if it didn't work, could create a bottleneck in their production process. Simply put, their entire manufacturing process could stop if our function didn't work, so it had to work. Because the technology was new, we had some setup kinks that we worked through until the wee hours of the morning.

Once we got the system stabilized, we decided to continue covering the plant operations in shifts. I had to conduct user training the next morning so I was the first one to go back to the hotel and sleep. I left the plant around three in the morning and after the short drive to the hotel, flopped squarely into the middle of my bed and fell asleep, clothes and all. It had been a long day and night. About 10 minutes later, someone was pounding on my door, calling my name. I thought I must be dreaming, but the pounding continued. There was a problem at the plant and they were in danger of having to shut down their production line. After splashing water on my face and brushing my teeth, I was back up and out to the plant a mere 40 minutes after I had left. We worked through the night to resolve the issue and then to help the production personnel catch up since the system issue had put them so far behind. Thankfully, they didn't have to stop production, but I had to max out on caffeine in order to conduct my training the next morning. At least I was able to go back to the hotel and shower. Everyone was thankful for that.

Several years later I encountered another significant marathon work session. We were key players in a major system upgrade for a manufacturing facility in the Netherlands. We had developed the software to move manufacturing orders from the corporate scheduling system down to the plant floor to be carried out. Without the manufacturing orders, no products could be made. Our lead project manager had been on site for over a week with very little sleep, and there were still problems. He was hitting a wall and the customer requested that before they could let him leave, we needed to commit to sending a replacement. Tomorrow. It happened to be a busy time of year and we had no other qualified folks available that could take his place at the last minute. Except me. I had become the most operationally expendable person in my company (this, by the way, is a good thing, which you will see in the "Getting Out of the Details" section in Chapter 6). I had to go.

Less than 24 hours later, I was on a plane bound for the Netherlands. That particular time of year we had a tail wind flying from the East Coast to Europe, which made the trip fairly quick. The bad part about that was that there was very little time to sleep. In addition, I needed to get up to speed with the technical implementation while en route so I snuck in maybe an hour of broken and interrupted sleep. When I arrived in Amsterdam at 7:30 the next morning, I had no choice but to wake up. I had to get into the car and drive for two hours to get to the plant. Thank goodness I was able to catch a quick shower at the airport or I might not have made it. When I arrived at the facility we went right to task and worked straight through until midnight. By then, my eyelids felt like they were made of lead and I swear I was seeing double. When I got into my hotel room, I could have fallen into a bed of thorns and not noticed a difference. I was out. In the end, we were able to find and fix the issues and the customer was grateful for the quick response and customer service. It was worth it all, even though I slept so soundly on the plane ride home I know I was drooling. My story, however, is in no way unique.

It was 9:00 on a Friday evening when Terry called me. She was on her way back from the beach a day before her husband and kids because she had just found out her company was in the running for a portion of a multi-million-dollar contract and the final proposal was due in three days. She had stretched it out as long as she could—working nights after her kids went to bed, tiring them out at the beach so they would take a longer nap. She claimed she had slept only a couple of hours all week and was preparing for a weekend marathon performing the final edits on what turned out to be an over-100-page proposal. If her company won the contract, it would be the largest in their history, and as the founding CEO, it would enable Terry to pick and choose her next project. Personally, she felt as if she had no choice—the opportunity was too great. She would rather trade a temporary loss of sleep for the opportunity and continue to spend as much time as she could with her kids. That's just what we do as entrepreneurs.

Sleepless nights can be good or bad, depending on the individual. Paul claims that his sleepless nights have been very educational for him. Anytime he found himself waking up in the middle of the night, he knew that there was something that he needed to change: He had to either fire someone, hire people, or change the company direction. For example, it was repeated sleepless nights about five years into his company that indicated to him that it was time for him to build a strong management team so he could get out of running the day-to-day activities of the company. He needed to have time to focus on the bigger picture. He knew for sure that if his sleep was being interrupted night after night, something needed fixing.

I would often awaken in the middle of the night with an idea or product concept that I had to write down before I would even have a shot at going back to sleep. I actually keep old business cards next to my bed and write my thoughts or ideas down on the back of them so I can get back to sleep. They are my "night notes" and have yielded some of my best and most creative ideas.

## Maintaining Perspective

When I packed my bags for the hospital, one of my *What to Expect* books reminded me to put in a pair of socks to keep my feet warm. I made sure I packed a silly pair of socks, ones that had cartoon animals on them with bright colors. I wanted something that would make me smile if I happened to glance down and see them. It was my way to remember to keep things in perspective and to maintain my sense of humor. It is important for many of us in business to do the same thing.

When I was a co-op student, we used to play practical jokes on each other all the time. I suspect this is how the first computer hackers got started. One morning when I went into the lab and logged onto my mainframe terminal, a screen popped up that listed all of the files I had stored on my disk and indicated that they were being deleted. I panicked. At the end, after an appropriately timed pause, another message appeared that read "Are you scared? (pause) Some people will believe anything!" My heart was in my throat but I quickly started laughing and began planning my revenge.

Before the proliferation of e-mail chain letters and overabundant jokes became the epidemic it is now, I actually read some of the funnier notes that crossed my inbox. One particular e-mail caught my attention, as it suggested some silly things you could do to make people wonder about your sanity. I used a couple of them merely as stress relievers. For example, one day while sitting in my office I paged myself over the company intercom. Subtle. Not everyone got it, but I sure got a kick out of it. I almost couldn't do it because I was laughing so hard. I cracked myself up, and the laughing, even alone, helped me keep things in perspective.

To keep his sense of humor, Paul subscribes to online humor sites, such as *The Onion* (www.TheOnion.com). With daily farcical news feeds, he finds at least one or two chuckles help get his day started right when he has time to peruse. He also helps his employees keep things in perspective when they get out of whack. He has been known to remind them of the really important things in life, like health and family, at times of high stress. If he encounters one of his staff members blowing a specific situation out of proportion, he takes them to look out the window. He points to the nearest building and reminds them that there are lots of people "over there" having their own crisis, too. Things could always be worse.

Sitting back while watching and listening to the reactions of the patrons in his café helps Randy keep things in perspective. He witnesses his customers relaxing as their stress melts away and he is reminded why he has worked so hard to make his dream come true. His wife Chris points out the incredible joy she gets from seeing the positive impact their place has already made on their small community. One woman, who happened to be going through a divorce, confided in Chris that being able to bring her teenage daughter to the café has allowed them to open the lines of communication at a critical time. They have created a different kind of meeting place in a town that so desperately needed something *different.*

Sam Roberts thought that his giant saltwater fish tank would help him keep perspective, until one day his triggerfish ripped the head off of another fish. Sam was on the phone with a client when it happened and cut the phone call short. The fish was removed to "solitary confinement" and later given away, but the tank did not have the same sense of peace after that. He had to stick to his passion for baseball as his escape, his outlet to relax. Coaching both his sons' baseball teams and ardently following his Yankees helped him keep things in perspective.

Pete also found a great deal of perspective in his children. He too coached both soccer and basketball for his daughters and found that getting involved with activities that are totally different from work helped take his mind off business. It also reminded him of why he worked so hard—to provide good things for his family. As an added bonus, having time with the girls helped him to stay in touch with a younger generation. This proved helpful when managing his company, which was full of young postdoctoral "kids." It gave him a connection to them where he could at *least* understand their lingo.

His 55-minute commute every morning and evening helped him as well. He used the time driving into the office to contemplate the day's activities and the ride home to review what had transpired. He found the quiet time, which he feels too many business managers lack, gave him perspective that he would not have otherwise found. Even when he was in the office, he has been known to clear his desk and stare out his office window in deep reflection, watching a groundhog play.

One way that we kept things in perspective in our company was by assigning fun titles to people. We had a "Database Goddess," "Object Overlord," and our quality assurance manager was called "Release Police." My unofficial title was "Master Persuader." While these banners were mostly used inside the company, we did share them with customers we had developed a more personal relationship with and it always brought a chuckle.

Margaret notes that following her passion in starting up her company has actually added to her overall perspective about life. She has never felt more fully alive. She feels as though she is grabbing at everything she should be reaching for, overwhelmed but exhilarated at the same time. Because she is so crazed between home, her kids, her business, and her job as a reporter at the *Washington Post* (the moonlighting approach), she strives everyday to look for something that puts it all into perspective. For example, she has made a point to really notice the changing leaves of autumn and claims that she has never seen reds so red and oranges so orange. She is also keenly aware that her youngest child is growing up quickly, so she savors every minute she gets with him. In driving through the country one afternoon with her three children, she was so taken with the colors of the leaves that they stopped the car and got out to collect them. She then sent them to her sister in California—something she never would have thought of doing before. Furthermore, she claims she is more aware of her own capabilities and how much more she can accomplish than she previously thought. You cannot put a price on that type of perspective.

Keeping things in perspective has proven important for me personally as well. I bought a Mickey Mouse watch that made me smile whenever I glanced at the time. Many people keep inspirational quotes or cartoons posted above their desk. I also see parents posting pictures their kids drew for them, sometimes even framed. This reminds them daily part of one of the reasons they likely work—for their kids. The overwhelming need to connect these two parts of our lives further substantiates the benefits of a more integrative approach to managing work and home life. This is discussed more fully in Chapter 9.

## From Diaper Bag to Briefcase

- Forget the pain, remember the lessons and the joy. Go ahead and do it again but take the lessons learned on previous attempts with you.
- Think hard about what your company name says about your business and what images it evokes. Be prepared, however, to find a new identity if your strategy changes. The right name can propel your business where the wrong one can bring on cardiac arrest.
- Passion that drives that burning-in-the-gut for your company is required to stick with it in difficult times. Make sure your passion is in the right place—providing what your customers want, need, and are willing to pay for.
- Bonding with our children and our business is an incredible feeling. It can help us to do amazing things when used positively. When the bond is in the wrong place and not managed, it can come across as defensiveness and threaten to sabotage your relationships with your customers and employees.
- If you are too attached to your sleep, don't become an entrepreneur or have children. And *certainly* don't do both at the same time. The good news is the sleepless nights don't last forever, but they do come back every once in a while to remind you.
- Find ways to keep everything in perspective. Make sure you laugh at least once a day, and if you're not having fun at what you're doing, consider doing something else. Also, watch using a triggerfish for relaxation. They can be *mean*.

## Additional Resources

### Books

Jim Collins and Jerry Porras, *Built to Last: Successful Habits of Visionary Companies* (New York: HarperCollins, 1994).

Al Ries and Laura Ries, *22 Immutable Laws of Branding* (New York: HarperCollins, 1998).

Mark Sanborn, The Fred Factor: *How Passion in Your Work and Life Can Turn the Ordinary into the Extraordinary* (New York: Doubleday, 2004).

Any Dilbert or Dave Barry book

## Web Sites

www.JokeOfTheDay.com

www.TheOnion.com

www.uspto.gov (to make sure no one else has a trademark on your company name before you use it)

### Pete Linsert's Top Four Tips

1. The quality of an idea has to be sound. Research your market to ensure a demonstrable need is being met.
2. The quality of people, both employees and investors, is also critical.
3. Keep overhead down.
4. Pace yourself. Running a business is a roller coaster. Don't let yourself go all the way to the top or all the way down to the bottom.

CHAPTER

# The Early Years

Jennifer's son was three months old and she had not yet been out at night without him. Her husband's company Christmas party was to be the first time. She was excited about getting out, but also exhausted. Rallying, she wanted to pump some milk before she left so her mother could feed the baby while she was out. As she sat with the pump in place and beginning to do its duty, she felt creeping warmth across her lap. Looking down, she realized that she had forgotten to put a bottle on the other end of the pump. The outfit she had bought to go out in (because nothing else fit her!) was soaked through. Tears welled up quickly in her eyes, and then she just started to laugh.

When my older daughter was about two months old, I was faced with a similar situation. It was 2:00 A.M. and I was changing her diaper before her early morning feeding. The weeks of interrupted sleep must have been catching up with me because I was moving extremely slowly on this particular evening. I learned the hard way that I needed to be faster. When I lifted up her bottom to clean it, a brown runny substance came squirting out across the lamp on the changing table and splattered three feet away on the wall, leaving a trail to mark its course. I sat there for 10 seconds, completely stunned, and then started laughing uncontrollably. Was I just drunk on caffeine? My raucous belly laughs were enough to jolt my sleeping husband from his deep sleep. When he stumbled into the room and saw the tears of laughter in my eyes and trail on the wall, he joined in my amusement. My poor daughter—oblivious to what had transpired—just lay there and stared at us. Thinking back, the only other reaction I could have had at the time would have been to sit down and cry.

## Introduction

Once we parents bring our baby home, we settle in for the crazy ride of caring for a newborn. The lack of sleep continues, but we begin to recognize that no book could have prepared us for the roller-coaster ride of being a new parent. We also learn what it is truly like to get on-the-job training and to always be ready for the unexpected. It is during these times that we must stand tall through the "Terrible Twos," learn to say "no," and realize that we have to hold it all together, at least while others are watching. In business, as well as parenting, the early years are a roller-coaster ride with moments where we can choose to laugh or cry and maybe do both at the most inappropriate moments.

## Choosing Laughter over Tears

In business we are presented with opportunities, as in parenting, where we can choose to either laugh or cry in reaction to the same situation. I had just returned to my office after spending two weeks with my father and learning that he was dying of cancer. I tried to jump back into work as a diversion, but my heart was heavy.

That morning, Margaret*, a manager who had been at my company for only a few months, walked into my office and wanted to talk with me. She had not been happy for some time and proceeded to unleash on me the reasons she was unhappy—what a horrible manager and even worse person I was, and how she would do things differently and *so much* better than me. Ironically, I had received numerous complaints about her from her staff. It was clear from their comments that although she might be a good manager in a different environment, she did not fit into our company culture. This discussion made my decision easier, but she quit before I could fire her. Even though I knew the outcome was ultimately beneficial, it was a difficult encounter that left me feeling depressed and drained.

I called in one of my other managers, Carl*, who would take over Margaret's duties until we replaced her so he could review her outstanding projects before she left. After the discussions with Carl, she was to leave.

Before Margaret left, Carl poked his head in my office and said that she had given me something and wanted it back. Befuddled, I couldn't figure out what it was. Carl walked over to my desk and took the beautiful bamboo arrangement that Margaret had given me for Christmas a couple months before. "She wants it back." My chin must have hit the desk. Not since I was five and my brother took back the wheat penny that he gave me have I had someone take back a gift. At that moment, on the verge of tears, I started laughing uncontrollably. Clearly, the bamboo had meant more to her than it had to me. At least, unlike Jennifer's laughter through tears, it didn't cost me a dry cleaning bill.

My employees saw the humor in it, too. The next "Boss's Day," they pitched in and bought me my own bamboo arrangement. It became our own little joke from that time forward.

## Worlds Colliding

Nancy* was on her way to an important meeting with a potential client, but frantically picking up around her house. It was the day the cleaning service came, and she just wanted to make sure everything was picked up (why do we do this!?). Not thinking, she picked up one of her daughter's barrettes and without anywhere else to stash it, put it in her hair.

Her presentation was well received, and at the end of the meeting, one of the men she had been presenting to commented on how much he liked her barrette. She blushed, said thanks, and continued on. She won the business in part because she handled the potentially embarrassing situation with grace.

I relate the ups and downs of entrepreneurship and parenting to Space Mountain. It is dark so you can't always see dips or sharp turns coming, and while it can have moments of terror, it is also one hell of a ride. Maintaining a sense of humor has been an essential tool to help me get through the valleys to the next peak. Whenever I start to lose perspective, I listen to the words of one of my favorite musicians, Jimmy Buffet: "If we couldn't laugh, we would all go insane." I choose laughter over insanity any day.

## Learning "On the Job"

When we came home from the hospital with our first child, we were exhilarated and exhausted all at the same time. All the books we had read, while they helped, could not prepare us as parents for the adventure that lay ahead of us.

When we took our daughter into the pediatrician for her three-day checkup, we found out just how much there was to learn that wasn't in the books. Our daughter had lost two pounds since she was born. While losing some weight after birth is not uncommon, her percentage of weight loss exceeded the acceptable norm. The doctor concluded that she was not getting enough to eat. Since I was nursing and therefore solely responsible for feeding her, I took that on as a personal failure. What was I doing wrong?

Based on the doctor's advice, we began supplementing with formula immediately after she was done nursing. What a difference this approach made in her demeanor! She suddenly calmed down, slept longer, and wasn't as fussy when she was awake—incredible what actually feeding your child can do. My milk did eventually come in and I was able to continue nursing for a few months longer, but we decided to continue with a bottle as well because Keenan enjoyed being involved in that part of her care. The lesson learned was not based on something we read in books—we had to learn it "on the job."

Inevitably, novice entrepreneurs get more firsthand experience with "on the job" training than they likely expected. With no one but your customers to interview you for the position, who is to say whether or not you are qualified? ACT was not only my first business, it was my first formal management job. In truth, the majority of entrepreneurs start a business without ever having done so before. As many business owners with an advanced degree will attest, there is a lot to entrepreneurship that isn't taught in school and is best learned experientially whether through your own experiences or those of others.

There is information readily available on the Web and in print to help entrepreneurs with a variety of "big picture" issues such as developing a business plan, incorporating, and hiring employees. When I was looking for assistance on more detailed implementation issues such as selecting a phone plan or finding an accountant, I was largely on my own. I had to learn that on the job.

One of my most frustrating early experiences came from setting up my home office phone line. This was before competition from cell phones drove land-line phone companies to be creative with their calling programs. I did not, at the time, have any choice in my local phone carrier.

I made the mistake of being up front with the phone company and telling them I wanted a business line in my home. How was I supposed to know that it would cost more? When I found out that I had to pay for every outbound call, I was incensed. I tried to shift my story and tell them it was a "residential" line, but it was too late. The operator had flagged me. It brought back memories of paying for baby food. Look at the per-ounce cost of baby food and decide for yourself whether or not the prices of children's products are inflated.

The lesson that I learned was that businesses, like parents, often pay more than individuals for the same product or service. Airline tickets are a great example. When we would talk to a customer about coming out to their site to conduct a system review or requirements analysis, it was rare that we would be willing to put them off for 21 days to save on the airfare. We wanted the business and had to pay top dollar for the airline tickets. While we became better at using technology to reduce our airline expenditures, sometimes we just needed to be face to face. We found that many of our customers had a hard time spending hundreds of thousands of dollars with people they had never met in person. As I traveled, I continued to marvel at the person sitting next to me on a plane, knowing they likely spent hundreds of dollars less for the same seat. Perks from frequent flyer programs don't make up for that, at least not all the way. When you are traveling a lot, the last thing you want to do on a vacation is to fly somewhere. And while the free drink coupons are nice, I always felt that the person in the cheap seat should be buying me the drink!

Another area where I felt at a total loss in my new business was in pricing our services. My first customer knew me from IBM, so I had a hard time asking for the same hourly rate that they were previously paying for my time. It was not that the quality of work had changed, but the overhead rate had significantly decreased and they knew that. I also had no one to back me up if I was unavailable, meaning there was no "bench," which brought down the price they would be willing to pay. I had not yet built a broad reputation or published anything significant so I did not feel that I could call myself an "expert."

In researching hourly rates that other so-called consultants charged, I found a mixed bag with very little credible information that I could use as a true benchmark. I thought about asking my client but I did not want to look like I didn't know. Finally, I asked one of my colleagues who worked for a business partner if he knew what they charged the customer. He did not know, but he was nice enough to find out for me. I simply based my price slightly above theirs, rationalizing that I was located in a more expensive area than they were and consequently had higher overhead. It seemed to work because the customer did not flinch—should I have gone higher? I had no idea; I was learning as I went along. What I did know from my years at IBM is that it does not pay to lowball a customer because they attach a value to products and services based on price.

This is similar to some associations that I have counseled: Members expect a certain value based on the price they pay. Organizations that are trying to attract a higher caliber of members, for example, an entrepreneurial association that wants to lure owners of bigger companies, may actually need to *raise* their dues to get the attention of this segment. An association with fees under $100 is not likely to be perceived as providing the business benefits expected by larger companies. Unless the affiliation is philanthropic in nature, these member organizations are not likely to attract the attention of their desired targets.

Carol Koch-Worrel set the prices for her music program based on what she thought the market would bear. When she researched the market and the prices of other programs in her area, she concluded that they were not charging enough. She decided to price her program 12 percent higher than her closest, established competitor and see what happened. It did not take long for her programs to fill up and establish a waiting list. Apparently, it was not all about price. What she discovered is that the parents placed a value on the program based on how much it cost. They perceived Carol's program as having more value than others in the area. This gave her additional profits to put back into her business and eventually outsource some of the tasks so she was not doing everything, or wearing all the hats.

## Wearing Many Hats

When our daughter was born, Keenan and I had to do everything for her. She was helpless and relied solely on us, her parents, for survival. When she was hungry, we fed her. When she was wet, we changed her. When she cried, we picked her up. It became almost an automatic reaction. Essentially, we were Pavlov's dogs, except we were too tired to salivate.

Our business started in much the same way, with us, the owners, doing everything for it. Euphemistically, this is called "wearing many hats." We took care of the books, purchased the office supplies, talked to the customers, performed the work, and took out the trash. This was expected in the beginning without the funds to hire others to perform those tasks. We even developed our organization chart to show all the functional boxes we would at some point fill, but our two names were the only ones in them.

Many times, we had to perform tasks that we did not like or want to do. The one area that Keenan was skilled at but grew to detest was information technology (IT). As an engineer, setting up computers, configuring networks, and installing phone systems were simple jobs for him. These tasks also drove him crazy, not so much in the initial implementation but in the support and trouble-shooting that often followed. Given that internal IT support was not a revenue-generating position, we had to wait until we reached a certain level of profitability to comfortably afford the additional overhead. Many small companies I meet with today are able to successfully outsource their IT function. Our needs were different and more complex than most because we were selling sophisticated IT solutions to our customers that also needed to be supported. Years ago when we were in need, it was hard to find someone to perform those services on a contract basis at the level we needed them. Thankfully, we were eventually able to hire a highly compe-tent IT manager, who became a contributing factor to our success. A "Kirk" crossed off from another box in the organization chart.

Mike Tumbarello was in a worse position. He was starting his mortgage company and, without a background in computers, found setting up his systems to be exasperating. More than once he caught himself picking up the phone to call the IT help desk, only to remember that he *was* the help desk—truly, a hat he had not an-ticipated nor cared to wear, but tasks he slugged through as best he could. I would like to say that he learned everything he needed to know and now teaches others how to set up their systems, but he's still as un–techno-savvy as he ever was. At least now he has an IT staff to answer the help desk calls.

Because of the variety of menial tasks that must be done, bring-ing new people into the business in the beginning can be tricky. We found that if candidates had not worked in a small business before, they may say they know what it takes to be part of a small but grow-ing company, but they don't always. There is a risk that they will not be willing to do the more lowly tasks that have to be done such as wiping out the microwave or changing the roll of paper towels when it is empty. While this might sound trivial, being willing to do "whatever it takes" was critical for fitting in with our company's culture. We required that anyone we brought into the company have that can-do attitude. They could not act as if they were above others or they would not last long.

One day, fed up with the continually empty roll of toilet paper, I called my employees into the bathroom to demonstrate how to change it. I was trying to make a point that no one is above seemingly menial tasks. Those who felt that level of task was below them may not have been swayed by my demonstration, but at least they understood what I expected of them—to do whatever it takes to keep the company moving forward, even if it is a dirty job.

## Teaching Your Baby to Feed Herself

I found one of the dirtiest jobs in parenthood—and no, I am not talking about diapers—was teaching my baby to feed herself. Like most babies, Sydney started with the obligatory Cheerios. There is something about that small, round "O" that is the perfect size and shape for little ones to pick up in the tiny fingers. I remember that being a big milestone. From the Cheerios she graduated to zwieback toast. For those who have not endured this rite of passage in parenthood, zwieback is essentially like a kid's version of the Stella D'oro toasts that are sold in the cookie aisle or a biscotti, but not as dense. I don't know if it just felt good on her emerging teeth or she really enjoyed the taste, but she went to town on them. The problem with these treats, besides their marginal nutritional value, is that they make a mess—a huge one. The minute my daughter put the stick in her mouth, it turned to mush. Although that is a great thing for helping kids to swallow and digest the food without choking, it also makes it easy to smear. I could understand, perhaps, how she got the mushy toast all over her face, but how it got on the wall escaped me. Of course, that is part of the charm of watching your baby learning to eat solo and made for some great photo opportunities. Not quite as good as when she started eating sweet potatoes, but it was up there.

A business learns to feed itself when you can successfully begin to leverage customers to get more business. This can be in the way of additional work within a current account or through a referral.

I am amazed at how many people fail to formally ask for a referral. It is one of the easiest and least expensive ways to grow a business. In fact, we were able to grow our business to over $1 million in revenue based solely on referrals. To make sure we did not forget to ask the question often, we added it to our annual and quarterly customer satisfaction surveys. "Would you recommend our products and services to colleagues or contacts within your industry?" It is that simple. But do not forget to actually *ask* for the names and contact information if they do say yes.

There are also creative ways to leverage your satisfied customers in order to attract new opportunities. One of the most fruitful methods for us has been to present our successful projects at industry conferences. Because we tout them as "lessons learned," we always attract a strong showing. Even better—get your customer to speak with you or instead of you. Hearing the gory details from their perspective makes the experience so much more credible. I would recommend, however, that you make sure their version of the story is not too gory. One of my customers actually managed to offend anyone from Europe in his talk. He was the type of person who could get away with something like that, so there was no long-term damage. I can't say that we obtained any international clients from that particular presentation, though.

Another creative method for garnering referrals is to nominate your customers for awards. When one of them wins, host a reception in their honor and ask them to invite their industry colleagues. Better yet, host the party at an industry conference so you can invite prospective clients as well. Meeting your references in a social setting takes the pressure off everyone to say what they think they are supposed to say and gives your client's story even more weight. There is no better salesperson for your products or services than a satisfied customer. For that reason, a friend of mine who is in real estate offers to throw a housewarming party for her clients when they move into a new house in lieu of a gift. She is providing a service to her customer that may cost more than a gift, but it is also providing a way for her to meet her client's friends and build her customer base. The friends get to hear good stories about the buying process from the new homeowner in a nonthreatening sales situation. It is a win-win for everyone.

In addition to building your referral system for new clients, do not overlook opportunities to expand your reach within your current accounts as well. The chances are better and the cost is lower to make a sale to an existing client than to sell a product or service to a brand new customer. Leveraging your existing relationships can pay off in big money.

## Never Wake a Sleeping Baby

Asher Epstein, managing director for the Dingman Center for Entrepreneurship at the University of Maryland, has been classified as a serial entrepreneur. A *serial entrepreneur* is someone who has forgotten how much work went into building a company and he does it more than once. His family "start-up" came later when his daughter was born. That was when he realized that, although he did not know anything about being a father, his experience working in early-stage companies had prepared him for his most important job as a father. He discovered that many of the skills he had gained as an entrepreneur could be applied to raising his daughter.

Within the first several weeks after she was born, Asher discovered in talking with friends that they would wake their babies, even if they were sleeping soundly, in order to feed them. He did not agree with this approach. From his years of entrepreneurial experience he had learned: "If it ain't broke, don't fix it." To him, this meant that if his six-week-old daughter was sleeping peacefully, she should remain asleep until she was hungry enough to wake up.

He also knew better than to let his friends give him pause about his parenting approach. He did not second-guess his decision. If his doctor had advised him he was doing something that may harm her, he would have changed his behavior and learned from it. He knew, however, from his experience as an entrepreneur that to continually mistrust his own decisions was a destructive and slippery path.

Early in our start-ups, if we are smart, we are soliciting the advice of a variety of people, including, perhaps, a formal advisory board. With this type of board or any outside adviser, you will present them with the "CliffsNotes" version of background and information about your situation or pending decision. If you ever used CliffsNotes as a high school student, you likely realized that key details can be missing. You get an overview of the plot and themes but not necessarily the same feel you get from reading the full novel. Consequently, an outside adviser will rarely have the same information about any particular situation as you do. Only you, the entrepreneur, have all the information about your goals, plans, customers, markets, and historical events. As a result, you should not fall into the temptation to follow *all* of the advice you get. Your advisers will have different experiences, backgrounds, and objectives behind the suggestions they provide you. Sometimes you can even receive conflicting recommendations from different sources. Get all the information you can and then make your own decision, going against advice if the situation warrants it.

Terry Chase Hazell had a good relationship with one of her advisers and respected his opinion on most issues, except one. He did not think she had what it took to be a chief executive officer (CEO). Continually, he would advise her to find someone else to run the company. He did not feel, because she was a novice, that she had the skills required to grow the company to its full potential. Had she listened to him, she would have never gotten the company off the ground. Over the years as she drove the company to achieve funding and development milestones, he began to quiet his private protests regarding her abilities. Several years later when she was leaving the company, she told him that she was going to be the CEO of another start-up. His response shocked her: "Good—that is what you are." She almost cried. Her belief in herself and ability to make it work made him see her as she had seen herself: most definitely as a CEO.

Donna Stevenson would have gone into real estate development had she not joined her husband, Cecil, in his IT start-up. She essentially adopted his baby before they were even married. She felt real estate provided a solid grounding and had been talking about it for years. So when Cecil passed by an old building in downtown Baltimore that had a "For Sale" sign in the window, he did not think twice about walking in to make an inquiry. The older couple who owned the building had been running a business out of it that had been in their family for three generations. They were ready to retire. When they learned that another young couple was looking to locate their business in that building, they saw a mirror of themselves and wanted to find a way to make it happen for them.

When Donna and Cecil consulted with their main adviser, he recommended against buying the building. He believed that it would detract from the day-to-day running of their business. While he made good sense, both Donna and Cecil knew in their gut that they needed to go forward with this real estate deal. While it was hard work to convert the space into usable offices, they felt it was worth it. The building has been an asset that has given them a comfort zone—like paying off the mortgage on your house. They never once regretted their decision and could not imagine ever renting an office from someone else again. Had they listened to their outside adviser instead of their gut, they would have missed out. Businesses that put too much weight in their outside consultants can quickly lose direction.

One start-up group I had been working with had done an excellent job of identifying a strong cadre of outside advisers. Rather than meet with all of their mentors at one time, they opted to discuss issues and solicit input on a one-to-one basis. This approach had a major flaw: As people were providing them with different recommendations, they were left alone to filter through the suggestions and come up with a decision or solution. They became stuck as they swayed in the direction of the last person they had spoken with. They were so far engrossed in a specific decision or problem that they could not see what was happening. I recommended that they start holding advisory board meetings to bring all of their outside counsel together to discuss the issues and hear one another's thoughts and ideas. That way, individuals could respond to the insight of others or clarify their approach or intentions. Although it is possible that they could still receive disparate counsel they needed to sift through, at least they could collect more information on the pros and cons of each argument so as to come to their own resolution. Ultimately, they would need to make their own the decision.

Making decisions was not something Linda Frost generally struggled with. She was considering investing in a restaurant business and purchasing the building as well. She did not know anything about restaurants, but she knew a lot about business. Her partner on the deal had a background in the restaurant industry; however, it was not very strong. She saw this as an extremely risky venture. Her driving desire was to employ her teenagers as helpers, which would provide them with extra money as well as a way of keeping them close to her. It looked better as an asset in her portfolio of investments than it did on paper, and for the first time in her life, she felt she was making an emotional decision rather than a logical one. Everyone she consulted with advised her against this venture. In the end, her logic won out over the emotion and she did not go through with the deal. She has had no regrets. In fact, she was quite relieved because soon after her decision, she realized that she was handling almost more than she could at that time and this project would have pushed her over the edge. She was able to separate emotion from logic and went with her gut.

It is important as well that once you make a decision, you do not second-guess it. Follow-though is key. No wishy-washy moving ahead—make a decision and stand by it. Sure, you can change course if you discover new information or the situation changes, but all-out execution is critical. If you find you've made a mistake, learn from it and move on.

As we shifted our strategy away from selling our software as a commercial, off-the-shelf warehouse management system and into selling it as a piece of an integrated system, we knew we had to go all-out. We redesigned our web site and hired a marketing consultant to help us develop our messaging and collateral. We could not just *sort of* go there. We had to go all the way. At one point we became frustrated with our progress in locating a number of qualified customers and hired an outside firm to help us with prospecting. In short, we spent a significant amount of money in pursuing this new direction. Unfortunately, we found that while customers loved what we were offering and said they saw the need, they always had some other project that was more pressing. They did not need what we offered badly enough. We learned that agreement on the value of your product or service is not enough—they have to be willing to buy it as well.

## Spit (up) Happens

It happened so quickly that my husband had no choice but to react. It was clear our daughter was about to throw up on our new carpet and, without thinking, he just shoved his hands in front of her mouth to catch it. Immediately after that, he looked at me with a most disgusted look on his face. What had he just done? Doubtless most parents have similar stories. You can walk around with a rag to catch it or invest in a carpet cleaner (and most likely need both), but if there's one thing we've learned with babies—spit up happens.

It was messy burps hitting the floor that actually motivated Margaret Pressler to start her company, WilliamBoy Products, Inc. She got tired of continually wiping up the floor after her son, William, burped. In her frustration, she created the patent-pending BurpCatcher, a burp cloth with a pocket at the end to catch whatever came out. Never again would a parent have to be caught by surprise, at least not by what comes out of a baby's *mouth*.

Margaret maintains that her newly found company is like a baby who had received great Apgar scores in the delivery room (everyone thought it was a good idea), but now that the baby is home (she's on her own), it needs to eat every two hours (it is sucking money) and does nothing but poop and cry (it requires a lot of unglamorous work). She knows at some point in the future her "baby" will sleep through the night, but for now, no one is sleeping. In fact, she describes herself as walking around with a constant pressure on her chest from the anxiety caused by trying to hold together her fledgling new business, her three kids under nine, and her job as a reporter at the *Washington Post*. Her challenge has been that her business has taken off much faster than she expected.

When she recently attended a baby products show in Las Vegas, she had fairly moderate expectations. Throughout the show she noticed that while she had a flock of interested buyers constantly at her booth, some exhibits around her were quiet. She was not expecting the response that she experienced from potential customers nor the volume of orders she received as a result. These were all good problems to have, but they were problems nonetheless. After recovering from the exhausting trip, she rallied. She was able to meet the sudden spike in demand and was also much better prepared for the next show. She was ready to catch that burp before it hit the floor.

Mary Cantando had built what she thought was a thriving business, but she had only one key account: IBM. Then one day in 1992, she picked up the phone to hear that her key project, one that generated more than half of her revenue and employed 32 members of her staff, was being cut as of 5 P.M. that day.

She hung up the phone and sat there paralyzed. When she was finally able to get up, she went to the ladies' room and got physically sick. What would she tell her staff? She would have to lay people off. These 32 people weren't just employees, they were her *family.* As she called them individually into her office, she mentally vowed that she would never again let so much of her revenue rest with a single client. She kept her vow. Over the next few years, she closed multimillion-dollar deals with Glaxo, AT&T, SAS, H-P, the Environmental Protection Agency, Nokia, John Deere, and Cisco, just to name a few. She had wiped the spit up off the ground and, like Margaret, found a way to keep it from hitting the floor again.

Similarly in my business, we have been caught by several events that we were not expecting. We had been negotiating a contract with a large client for two months. It was pivotal to our company's strategy, as it would give us ownership of the software we were developing for them, which meant rights to sell it to other companies. We were putting the finishing touches on the contract when the news broke—our client's company had been sold. The company that bought them was a multibillion-dollar conglomerate and immediately put a hold on all in-process legal contracts until their lawyers could review and bless them.

I was actually working from home the morning the news broke and remember going on a long walk to contemplate our dilemma. What would this do to our contract negotiations? Were we stalled indefinitely? Would we lose the rights we had worked so hard to negotiate?

Although our contract was delayed by another few weeks, we were able to get the terms that we had fought so hard for: ownership of our intellectual property and the ability to license it to other companies. We were also able to negotiate a multiyear, multimillion-dollar support contract, which we discovered a year later was a critical maneuver when another unexpected event occurred.

Our relationship with this customer had been based around one particular person, Ernie. Ernie was the individual who had the most influence in convincing me to start my own company and believed in me personally more than any other person outside of my family ever has. He and I shared a deep trust that was developed over years of debating technical issues, often loudly, and realizing that we both had each other's interests at heart. Ours was a relationship built on mutual respect, and it extended to a personal level.

On one particular occasion, I had spent a week conducting training at the customer's manufacturing facility in Europe when Ernie flew out to the same facility to attend meetings. We were able to carve out time before I left to discuss several new system functions they wanted priced and argue over how they should be implemented. This was not unusual for us, as we constantly challenged each other and always ended up with a solution that was better than where we started. We resolved our differences as I was leaving to catch my flight home, and all seemed good.

When I landed at the airport, I called to check in with the office and received the news. Ernie had passed away from a heart attack shortly after I had left him in Europe. I stood speechless in the baggage terminal before crying inconsolably. He was 48 years old.

Not only had I lost a mentor and friend, but we had also lost our main contact within a major client. My personal loss was excruciating enough to endure, and without the contract we had fought so hard to get signed, that loss could have extended into my business as well. My personal connection was gone—it was all about business now. It was truly an unforeseeable event. Had we not had solid legal documents in place, it could have cost us everything.

The lesson I took away from this series of experiences was that although we had a strong relationship with our customer that was built on trust, it was a necessary but not sufficient foundation upon which to build our business. A customer contact does not have to actually pass away to be lost—people also get promoted, lose authority, or take a new job. It was imperative that we have all of our commitments in writing. Had we not backed up our handshake agreements with formal contracts, our business could have taken an irrecoverable nosedive.

I also learned that, while a customer can have a certain amount of control over many aspects of my business, I have control over how I react to unexpected events. A customer sent us a notice, abruptly canceling our contract without cause. Emotionally, I was angry. I wanted to get the lawyers involved and fight it. The other alternative, which felt really wimpy to me, was just to move on. When we looked at it from a practical standpoint and eschewed the emotions, we determined that the amount of money that we would have paid a lawyer to fight the case could be significantly more than we would have made through the remaining term of the contract. While some may see walking away as the gutless way out, we saw it strictly as a prudent financial decision. Donna's experience with "spit up" was very similar.

Early in their business, EMS experienced attempted sabotage. Someone from within a large customer was trying to disparage their firm—and succeeding. When they first met this program manager (PM) after the contract had been awarded, he seemed to be an ethical team player. Shortly thereafter, they began to observe that his actions did not match their first impression. He was able to get their contracts that they had five staff members working on for over five months transferred to another vendor. While some of those five employees could be redeployed to other projects, a couple had to be let go. The customer then also attempted to pay a mere 20 cents on the dollar for the work that had already been performed. Donna was furious. This person's false accusations and bad-mouthing of their work cost them over $250,000. At the time, they did not feel like there was any illicit activity that they could prove nor did they have the money to fight the issue with a lawsuit.

It was not until the lawsuits from other parties began to fly that they discovered the truth behind what had happened. This PM had EMS's contracts—and those of other vendors—transferred to the company his wife worked for. Eventually, he and his wife both quit their jobs and started their own company with the pilfered contracts.

As hurt and angry as Donna was over this loss, she could have absorbed it without a financial loss for the year were it not for the other circumstances occurring in their industry. The previous two years they had seen profitable double-digit growth, but this year was already different. This was 2001 and the telecommunications industry, where many of their clients were, was tanking. In addition, the 9/11 terrorist attacks put almost all projects on hold for a period of a couple months. It was the first and only year in which they posted a loss, and they vowed to never let that happen again.

Smartly, they had already learned the advantages of diversifying the industries they were in. They had previously acquired several Department of Defense contracts using their 8(a) certification (as a minority/disadvantaged business). Those contracts, along with others, began to skyrocket after the dust from 9/11 settled, but the bumps in the road were not without longer-lasting impact. Their core team of employees agreed to reduce their work schedule from five days to four days per week with the associated cut in pay in order to weather the storm. They all had to go back to their ramen noodles, but this time they did not even get to add meat. While those were the dark days, Donna knows it *always* could have been worse.

The other lesson that Donna took away from that experience was that she needed to expand not only her reach within a particular account but also to grow her own personal network. When a similar situation materialized several years later, she was able to minimize the damage by appealing to high-level connections to make calls on her company's behalf.

## Persuading Creatively

When Mary Cantando's first son, Keith, was about two years old, she put him in his car seat and went over to her in-laws' house to pick up a package. They lived out in the country, and she had to pull up in the driveway next to the back door of their house. She turned off the car and glanced into the backseat to see the baby asleep in his car seat. Rather than wake him, she ran into the house to get the package. She returned quickly to realize that she had locked her keys in the car. Fortunately, it was not a hot day, so her son was not in any danger. Mary was stumped. She tapped on the car window, thinking if she could get him to wake up, he could pull up the lock. Every time she tapped, he opened his eyes, looked at her, and immediately went back to sleep. She tried this about three or four times, with no luck.

She went back into the house and sheepishly told her mother-in-law what she had done. Her mother-in-law was an old hand, having raised five sons. She glanced around the kitchen, picked up a banana, and walked with Mary out to the car. She gently tapped on the window, and Keith's eyes opened. She held up the banana, and said, "Do you want a banana, honey?" He immediately woke up and nodded his head. She was able to get him to pull up the lock to get his banana. Essentially, she unlocked a car with a banana.

I did not have to use food to coerce two 10-year-old girls willingly and happily to help me tear down the nasty old wallpaper in my bathroom. Getting them to do it was simple: I told them that peeling away the wallpaper was like peeling away dead skin from sunburn. As disgusting as that might sound, peeling skin is a thoroughly addicting pastime for some people. Once you get started, it can be hard to stop. And so it was with the wallpaper. They ripped all the wallpaper off the walls in 10 minutes flat. By making an unfamiliar and seemingly boring chore seem like something else they could relate to and actually enjoy, I was able to get enthusiastic, free labor. I did not have to resort to force or mandate—I was able to keep it positive and fun.

I thought that using positive reinforcement to persuade my children to exhibit a particular behavior would be easier, but it has taken a lot longer than I expected. When they were toddlers, they had a hard time understanding the connection between a behavior and a reward unless the reward was immediate. That made it a challenge. As they got older, however, the connection became more obvious and easier to communicate.

Over summers, our kids are required to earn television time by reading. For every minute they read, they earn two minutes of TV. During the school year, they earn time on the computer by completing certain chores. We also try to provide special treats and privileges when they do something out of the ordinary, like emptying the dishwasher without being asked.

In the work environment, we attempted to provide the same positive reinforcement with employees to encourage desired behavior. At our quarterly meetings, we would often recognize staff members who had exhibited exemplary performance by hitting a tough deadline or had received special praise from a client. We discovered, however, that not everyone likes to be recognized in a public setting. Some people would prefer sincere, private appreciation and a genuine handshake. Everyone is different, and we needed to take that into account not only in recognition but in many other aspects of the business as well.

Graham Weston, CEO of Rackspace Managed Hosting, has employed different and generous methods for rewarding his employees. As a services company, he knows the only way the company will continue to grow and thrive is by keeping the staff engaged. Top performers in his company are given the keys to his BMW M3 convertible for a week. He also lets employees use his guesthouse on the water for extra special recognition. Their creative approach to rewarding employees has helped them expand their company to over 1,150 happy and loyal employees and growing. Of course, if they keep up the pace, he is going to have to buy another car.

While rewarding employees is a good way to encourage productive work habits and behaviors and foster loyalty, getting opinionated staff members to buy into ideas and decisions requires creativity as well. I wanted to encourage independent thinking in my company, but I often had visions that not everyone shared. As Donna asserts, you know you are an entrepreneur when you have visions—when you see things that no one else does. Incidentally, that is why people often call us crazy. These pictures are sometimes so clear to Donna that she has no doubt she has to follow through with them. Likewise, I had to bring my team around to see my vision on several occasions and get them to buy in on their own accord.

I've been fortunate to work with some extremely intelligent people with strong personalities, which forced me to learn early the value of "casting ideas" in order to get my vision across. Casting an idea is a persuasive technique that involves helping people to see a concept as their own. It is also called creating ownership or buy-in.

I've had many occasions to cast ideas, but the most memorable was early in my career while I was still working at IBM. I was trying to convince programmers to adopt my design ideas. On my boss's advice, I opted for working them through my thought process to get them to buy into the idea. In walking my colleagues through my logic, one of the most arrogant developers had a light-bulb moment. He acted as if he had suddenly come up with the design I had been trying to convince them of. In the interest of moving the team forward, I let him think he came up with the idea, and we nailed the assignment. Because I had previously consulted with my boss, she knew where the idea originated. As a business owner, I do not care if anyone knows it was my idea or not. The focus for me has been on getting things done. I continually used that technique to help prod employees along my mental path when needed. Manipulation? Maybe. Creative persuasion sounds better.

Marissa Levin takes a different approach in her company. She feels that if you hire the right people with the same basic values, you don't have to persuade them to do anything, they just do it. This works well if you are deliberate in defining your culture, expectations, and vision from the beginning so that employees know what to expect when they are hired. Unfortunately, markets change and companies grow, which makes it critical that these elements be continually revised and revisited. Bringing your company and employees along as the business morphs and grows requires paying attention to change and creating intentional communication to make sure that the behaviors and ideas being encouraged are appropriate and relevant.

## Waiting for Delayed Gratification

My older daughter loved her pacifier. She called it "pa." When she couldn't find one, she would walk around the house as if in mourning, whining, "pa . . . pa . . . pa. . . ." Rarely would she have just one pacifier; she would carry one around in each hand in addition to the one she was sucking on. We knew that it was not good for her teeth and consequently tried everything we could think of to get her to stop.

As she approached her third birthday, we pulled out the psychological bag of tricks. We told her that three-year-olds do not use pacifiers. Pa had to go in the trash. We started this about three months before her birthday, hoping it would sink in.

Two weeks before her actual birthday, Keenan and I were sitting in the kitchen talking when she walked in, opened the trash can, and threw all three of the pacifiers she was holding into the trash can. She then looked at us and said, "Am I three now?" That was the first indication we had that she was actually listening to us. Talk about delayed gratification.

Often, however, it takes even longer than three months to receive feedback that tells you that you are doing a good job as a parent. It can take years and sometimes even a lifetime. One mother relayed to me that the best indication that her message was getting through to her children did not come until her children were, themselves, parents. It was then that she heard them repeating the things that she had told them to their kids. They were parroting their parent. Apparently, her kids were listening, but it took a long time for her to realize that. That was one of the things that frustrated me the most about being a mom when my children were young. I had no idea if I was doing a good job or not. I figured if they were safe, loved, and fed, then I was on the right track. Hugs were the only indication my daughter thought I was doing a good job. That kept me going. Entrepreneurs, too, need to be internally driven and patient in order to wait for outside gratification. They need to be in it for the long haul.

If you entered into or are considering entrepreneurship for instant glory and praise, find another profession. Only the self-driven need apply. When you do a good job as the CEO and you don't have a board of directors, there is often no one there to tell you so. No immediate feedback. Even if you do have a board of directors, you could be getting slugs instead of hugs. While there are awards given to entrepreneurs by outside organizations, there is a lot of hard work and many years that go into a company to get to the point you would be eligible for such recognition. There has to be an accomplishment or idea worth recognizing. Most successful entrepreneurs realize that they eventually need to seek out validation and appreciation.

Donna made it a point to seek out recognition but still had to wait until the business was three years old for the accolades to begin. She knew that PR was cheaper than advertising and so applied for various awards. EMS's first award came when the company was recognized by Signet Bank as a "Rising Star." The honors continued to flow: Baltimore's Fastest Growing Business, the State of Maryland's TechnoRising Star Award. While awards do not get you a paycheck, they do help you build your brand in your customers' eyes and provide external validation. To many entrepreneurs, it also provides long-sought-after validation that they are doing a good job.

Awards aside, many entrepreneurs wait months or years before they receive a salary from their foundling business. Unless you start your venture with an already signed contract or a lot of financial backing, you will need to spend money before you make it. At a minimum, you will need a business phone line, computers, business cards, supplies, and so on. It is true: It takes money to make money.

If you are developing a product, you can consider services such as training or consulting to contribute revenue to the business while you are developing your product for the market. Better yet, find a customer that needs what you are developing and have them fund the development. Client-funded product development is a win-win situation that does not require you to give up any equity in your endeavor. Many companies appreciate the ability to influence the features of a product to meet their specific needs and may be willing to pay for its development. If the development cost is too big for any one client, consider organizing a consortium of clients who have input into the product capabilities and design and all contribute financially to get it to market. In the best case, it will cost you only royalties or favorable pricing. Don't overlook the opportunities for product training, upgrades, and maintenance as sources for follow-on and continuing revenue as well.

Another route some adopt to mitigate their risk of taking the entrepreneurial leap is to moonlight—work on their business around their full-time job. There are also people working on their business "side of the desk," which means that they are working on their own business while they are supposed to be working their full-time job. I do not recommend this. Moonlighting, however, requires an inordinate amount of time and energy and can be a tough way to get started. However, it is often, financially, the only option. Many entrepreneurs who have started this way hit a point where they are getting too busy to juggle the job and the business effectively but are not making enough money to fully replace their salary and quit their job. Marissa incorporated her company and found her first client before she quit her job. Margaret is still juggling part-time work for the *Washington Post* while she builds her business. There are no easy answers to the timing issue. If you find that you are not making any progress on removing the excuses that are keeping you from starting your business, the time or the idea may just not be right for you. Please refer to the "Deciding to Take the Plunge" section in Chapter 2 for additional considerations.

Some entrepreneurs have reduced their full-time job to part time or a compressed workweek to provide more time to develop their real interest. A word of caution: Review the employment documents you signed when you started work prior to pursuing any projects outside of your place of employment. What you are developing on your own time could still be owned by your employer.

Paul had contemplated starting his own business for a year before he left his high-paying job. During that time, he continued to live beneath his means, making frugal decisions and saving as much money as he possibly could. When he left the comforts of corporate life, he had to wait over two years to receive a paycheck again—a tough call when he was the sole provider for his family with young kids. Rather than buying a house when they moved, they opted to rent instead to preserve money that might be needed for the business. Even after the company was turning a profit and he was able to draw a salary, he brought in key people whom he paid more money than he was making. What he had that they did not was equity in the company. His reward, though not guaranteed, was to be delayed until such a time as there was a "harvest"—a cash event in the way of a buyout or an initial public offering. His patience paid off, though it took several years to get there (see Chapter 8).

Kathy Freeland, founder of RGII Technologies, Inc., went for four years without a salary. She started her company out of her house with $3,000 and used credit to get herself and her company through the tough times. She claims that she even had to cash in her 401(k) from her previous job to make payroll. She is quick to point out, however, that her method is not suited for everyone. She advises most people, in fact, not to do what she has done or to do so with great caution. With a financial background, she was able to balance their approach so that they were never too far gone to recover. Like Paul, her patience and focus yielded a solid return on her investment when she sold her company 13 years later.

Both gaining praise and getting paid in an entrepreneurial venture can take time. Many entrepreneurs that I have spoken with are quick to point out the various other benefits they have derived from entrepreneurship. Some cite the extreme satisfaction that comes with building their business, while others greatly appreciate the flexibility being their own boss has provided them.

Terry was getting dressed to go to a meeting one day when her two-year-old son asked her where she was going. He recognized she had on her work clothes and promptly asked her not to go to work that day. On many other days, she has had to apologize and leave to attend a critical meeting. On this particular day, the meetings she had scheduled could be canceled, and that is what she did. She knew at that moment that she could not go back to work for someone else.

Donna relays her self-discovery as one of her greatest benefits of starting her own company. She cites finding strengths and capabilities she never knew she had. She feels strongly that she has stretched herself more than she ever thought possible and now realizes there is much more she can do.

The joy of being your own boss and, like parenting, the rewards from personal growth are enjoyed regardless of where you or your business ends up. You have to be prepared to reap these rewards from inside of you, as the truest sense of gratification and pride are internal. In looking back, the sense of accomplishment and thrill of meeting daily demands head on made me stronger and more able to take on newer and larger challenges than I ever thought possible. I am *empowered.* Okay, so a positive cash-out didn't hurt, either.

## Surviving the Terrible Twos

Something happens to a child somewhere between ages 18 months and three years. The "baby" starts to melt away and a toddler emerges. At this age, children think they are much older than they really are and believe they are much more capable. They want to do things their body might not be ready to handle.

While it is common to hear parents talk about the mayhem that emerges when a child turns two years old as the "Terrible Twos," I actually experienced the "Terrible Threes" with my daughters. It was not uncommon during this period to witness my child on the ground screaming—at home or in public—because she did not get what she wanted. "No" seemed to be the only thing in their—and my—vocabulary over that year.

It was a period when they were still babies but at the same time wanted to approach tasks themselves or in their own way. My younger daughter's favorite saying during that time was "my do it" (which I am sure meant "Please, Mom, let me do it myself"). She wanted so badly to be like her big sister, who was five at the time. She was experiencing the first of many growing pains.

In my company, we experienced similar pains approximately two to three years into our growth. As we were bringing on new people, we had to have the cash to cover their salaries until our customer paid us for their services. Since our customers generally paid us 30 days after we billed them, and we billed them monthly for services performed over the previous month, we only had to "float" employee salaries for 60 days in the worst case. Having just moved into a new office that required a great deal more furniture, we unfortunately did not have that extra cash lying around, which is where that bank line of credit came in handy. We also relied on credit cards, which we found out was not always a good idea.

Peter was new with ACT but had been around long enough to have his own company credit card. He and I were on a traveling road show to introduce him as the new support manager to our customers. Imagine the horror I felt when his credit card was rejected as we were checking in to get our rental car! I was hoping that perhaps there had been a problem in activating his card so I promptly offered my corporate card as an alternative. Same result. Completely abashed, I had to use my own personal credit card so that we could be on our way and not miss our meeting.

When I got back to the office, I discovered the source of the problem. We had a corporate account in which all of the cards shared a pooled credit limit. When we added more cards to the account, we forgot to request an increase to our limit. To make matters worse, Keenan, as IT manager, had recently purchased a great deal of equipment for the new office, which he charged on his company credit card. It didn't take long after that embarrassment for us to make some changes. First, we made it part of our procedure to allocate a certain amount of our credit to each employee card issued and monitor the overall credit limit. Second, we secured a separate credit card without a limit for Keenan so his capital spending would not freeze out our on-the-road consultants. Thankfully, Peter did not run for the hills as a result of that first experience, but the story continued to circulate throughout the company for years.

Another story that continued to promulgate was Faye Ann's first week on the job. I had worked with Faye Ann at my previous company and knew based on her work ethic and capabilities that I would hire her if I could. When we were at the point of needing her services, it took only a couple of phone calls to convince her to come on board. She and I had not seen each other since I left my job three years earlier and didn't meet in person until she had already been working for me for a couple days.

Her first day on the job was spent traveling to a customer's site. She actually met one of her new co-workers for the first time in the back seat of taxi at 5:00 A.M. They were riding together to the airport in order to catch an early flight. I was already in Ohio and was going to meet up with them a couple of days later. When

I finally joined the group, Faye Ann let out a little scream as I entered the conference room. I had dropped over 40 pounds since the last time she had seen me. I was not hiding it from her, it just had not come up in conversation and I did not think to mention it. The change in my appearance surprised her. This exchange occurred in our customer's conference room with them looking on. The customer was puzzled that we had not seen each other in such a long time until I explained the nature of our previous relationship. I also pointed out that the speed with which entrepreneurial companies have to operate sometimes means finding the right people sight unseen!

Another particularly sharp growing pain came when we moved out of an office with cubicles into real, walled offices. At first, everyone was thrilled with having privacy, even those who were required to share an office. What we didn't realize was how much benefit there had been to being out in the open—communication with a colleague was easy if not unavoidable. When we were in cramped quarters, it was effortless to share thoughts, ask questions, and know what everyone else was working on. Once we dispersed from 2,000 square feet into 4,000 square feet with only a few added people, everyone seemed so far away. You had to get up and *walk* to talk to someone about a function you were working together on. Meeting at the coffee pot started to have more meaning. True, there was more focused quiet time but we had not made any provisions to compensate for the informal communication that had been taking place previously. As a consequence, many people felt isolated and no longer a part of a group. They did not know who was in the office, who was out on travel, or who was working from home. They felt clueless.

Once we realized communications was an issue and needed to be more intentional, we formed an internal communications committee to make recommendations on how to do it better.

One of the first problems the committee set out to solve was the flow of information between folks in and out of the office. We did not have an office manager at the time, and with more than one entrance, there was no way of knowing who was around. As a result of an employee's suggestion, we created an intranet—an internal network application that not only provided news and information, but also included an "employee locator" system. Using this application, people inside the company could see who was in the office, and if someone was out, whether they were working from home or when they would return. It took some time to get everyone to keep it updated, but once people began to see the value of the information, the system was rarely out of date.

Once we had mitigated the expanded office space communications issues, the communications committee remained intact to address additional issues that emerged from our rapid growth. Consistent use of meeting agendas, improved communications processes, and a customer support newsletter all resulted from this group and the suggestions it acquired from other employees. We found that when we put our heads together, we were better equipped to identify the problems and arrive at creative solutions. That belief in the power of teams remained as one of our company's core values.

## Embracing "No" as Good

Right around the "Terrible Threes" time with my toddlers, I felt like I never said anything but "no" in different forms:

"Stop that."
"Don't touch that."
"Don't put that in your mouth."
"Don't tackle your sister."
"No candy before dinner."

I began to dislike saying "no" because it felt so negative. I longed so much for opportunities to say "yes" that I would actually invent ways to be positive by suggesting an alternative:

"You cannot have candy but you can have a piece of fruit."
    (Does that statement really work for anyone?)
"Why don't you play with this instead."
"Let's go outside and you can tackle me instead of your sister."

Contrary to the way it feels, when we say no to our children, it is actually a good thing. They are testing their limits, and it isn't until they go beyond their limit that they reach a "no." Perhaps we tire of being told "no," as many of us seem to lose that ability to push the limits as we grow into adults. Pushing the limits in business, however, is a must in order to be successful.

The day I told my chief operating officer that we were not hearing "no" enough from our customers, he looked at me like I was crazy. Surely, boasting a 100 percent proposal win rate was a good thing, right? Wrong! The odds are that you will win some and you will lose some, but what I realized is that if you're winning them all, you're not going after enough. In truth, we weren't losing business because we weren't pursuing enough new contracts. In contrast, we were actually missing out on opportunities both with new customers and within existing client accounts.

When we started going after additional business and writing more proposals, we started hearing more "no" responses. Although we never actually celebrated a "no" from a client, we did evolve to where we were not afraid of failure and embraced it as an opportunity to learn more about what the customer wanted that we were not providing. After every loss, we held a debriefing meeting to discuss the customer's feedback and how we could change our proposals or services for the next opportunity.

What I have noticed that many companies do not realize is that if you are not saying "no" to any clients, you do not really have a strategy. We have also had to say "no" to a potential client. We decided early on that we did not want to become a "body shop"—an organization that merely contracts out our people for specific tasks over a period of time with no cohesiveness or consistency in application. If we adopted a business model of contracting out individuals on a project basis, we would need to focus on building generic technical skill. We would not be selling to our broader, higher-level, and more valued capabilities of analysis and design. We felt that this approach, while it may work fine for many companies, would diminish our true value and not enable us to grow our internal intellectual property. Our plan was to leverage our projects to build internal assets that could be reused. By following this model of reusing certain intellectual capital, we had found that we could increase our profit margins on similar projects significantly. Revisiting our strategy led us to the conclusion that we did not want the type of business that was being offered to us.

We also decided that at that time we were not interested in working on government contracts. What I knew from my previous employment was that working for the public sector is an entirely different world, with disparate processes, requirements, and even sales approaches. We believed that in order to fully leverage our past performance in the private sector we needed to stay in the private sector unless we hired separate and appropriate resources to get us into the government market.

One particular opportunity surfaced to partner on a large government contract. While we would have been only a small piece of the several-million-dollar, multiyear, contract, our portion of the project would have stretched our capabilities and resources far beyond our current abilities. It would have also taken us into an area that we were not focused on as a core competency and would change our strategic direction completely. After several hours of intense conversation, we opted not to participate in the proposal effort. While there were some people who felt the opportunities in this uncharted area could take us in a whole new direction and growth, it was a direction we were not, at the time, willing to undertake. It did not fit into our current strategy and we were not interested in altering it to fit in this particular project.

Another place where "no" became important was in our approach to work/life balance. Read on before you too hastily predict what I mean by that.

When I founded my company six months after my first child was born, flexibility was a key motivator. I set out to prove that you could build a successful company and still have a life. I wanted that not just for me, but for all my employees as well. I longed to create the kind of environment that matched my values—my belief that people are more than just employees, they are total human beings with needs and responsibilities outside of work that have to be acknowledged and dealt with.

In the beginning, we approached this philosophy of work/life balance as "balance at all costs." I tried to accommodate every request for flexibility that was brought to me and realized quickly that we could not operate our business that way. What we needed were guidelines for what we could accommodate and what we could not do. We had to be able to say no.

For example, not all positions within the company were suited for telecommuting or part-time work. When my office manager requested that she work from home one or two days per week, I could not grant her wish. One of the duties of that position was to answer all incoming phone calls as the company operator to keep others from having to interrupt their work to answer the phone. Her consistent absence in that position even one or two days a week would be felt, and others would have to step in to fill that role. That was not acceptable.

People who were new to a position were also required to be in the office. Because we believed in encouraging people to stretch into new areas, we provided many opportunities to move people around within the company and essentially start a new job. When a particular employee transitioned into a role that was new to her, even though she had been at the company for a year, I told her she would have to wait 90 days before I would consider her request to work from home. I felt strongly that because she was new to that particular job, being in the office to ask questions and receive guidance was critical to her future success in her new role.

Nat had the opportunity to pursue a master's degree with all expenses paid, but he would have to attend classes on Wednesdays. When he first brought this to his manager, his request was denied without consideration. I had to step in. After further counseling, we looked more closely at his request and determined that we could work it out. It wasn't always easy as his colleagues learned to adjust to his altered work schedule, but with management reinforcement and good planning, the shift in his schedule was rarely felt.

After going from one extreme to the other, we adopted the policy to consider all requests for flexible work arrangements and created a process around it so as to remain fair and consistent.

## From Diaper Bag to Briefcase

- Choose laughter over tears whenever possible, even if it means laughing through tears, which can be an extremely satisfying emotion. I rank it second to laughing *until* you cry.

- No matter how educated you are, business provides opportunities to learn if we accept the challenge of growth and advancement. Realize that it is likely you will have to learn on the job, especially if you are a first-time entrepreneur, and embrace many opportunities to dive in and figure something out.

- If you think you are too high up to empty the trash, do not start your own business. Entrepreneurs need to be willing to do what it takes to get a business off the ground and out of the basement. If you won't do it, who will?

- Do your research and ask for advisers' opinions, but once you make a decision, stop second-guessing it. Many decisions are neither right nor wrong. Success or failure is often in the execution.

- As many small business engagements are based on relationships and trust, do not hesitate to get all agreements in writing in the form of a contract wherever possible. Spit happens, and you need to be prepared.

- Diversifying your customer base by industry and size can provide a buffer for specific sector spit up. Also, it is prudent to build your relationships deep and wide so that if something starts to go wrong with a client account you have some ability to use your network to mitigate the damage.

- You can choose the "mandate" approach over creative persuasion, but don't overlook the long-term benefits of positive reinforcement or pitching in wherever needed to gain respect from the ground up.

- Use casting ideas as a method for getting people to arrive at their own decisions that complement or support your own views and ideas. Creating buy-in works well in building a loyal and productive workforce, and once you're at the top, getting it done should be more important that who got the credit for it.

- Being the boss can be a lonely job. As the top person, it can take a long time to receive positive feedback or kudos. Make sure to store up enough to keep you going or find the personal acknowledgment and encouragement you need in other places, ideally inside of yourself.

- Unless you have a customer contract in hand when you start your company, do not expect to draw a salary in the beginning. Be prepared to accept that your gratification in the way of cash could come months, maybe years later.
- Growing pains are inevitable, but adjusting quickly to correct unforeseen problems shows your employees you are up to the task.
- Cash is king as companies grow. Plan in advance for your cash needs, and do not overlook the "little" things like credit card limits or meeting people in person before you hire them.
- Embrace "no'" as an opportunity. If you are not hearing "no" enough, you may be missing your big break. You don't have a strategy if you're not saying "no" to any client opportunities.
- Don't let your policies that are meant to be a benefit to employees be a detriment to your business. Put the appropriate controls in place so that you have the ability to say "no" and have the backup documentation to keep it fair and consistent.

It was this approach, along with other benefits, that won our company state and national awards for our work/life policies.

## Additional Resources for The Early Years

### Books

Murray Ainsworth, Neville Smith, and Anne Millership, *Managing Performance, Managing People: Understanding and Improving Team Performance* (New York: Longman, 2001).

Dale Carnegie, *How to Win Friends and Influence People* (New York: Simon & Schuster, 1950).

Steven Covey, *Principle-Centered Leadership* (New York: Fireside, 1990).

Emanuel Rosen, *The Anat omy of Buzz: How to Create Word-of-Mouth Marketing* (New York: Doubleday, 2000).

Walter G. Sutton, *Leap of Strength: A Personal Tour through the Months before and Year after You Start Your Own Business* (Los Angeles: Silver Lake Publishing, 2000).

## Marissa Levin's Top Four Tips

1. Clearly define your own personal values. Make sure you business idea and model are aligned with them.
2. Clearly define your business plan. Make sure you are filling a need.
3. Ensure that you have good personal credit. You will be your best resource for initial funding.
4. Align yourself with good advisers.

CHAPTER

# Ramping Up: A Time to Learn

Sam's son Jerrod had developed into a picky eater, but the rules of the house stood. You had to eat a little of every food that was offered. This particular night, the peas were the object of Jerrod's stubbornness. The typical punishment, "You will sit there until you finish all of those peas," had been levied and the clock ticked on. If you've ever tasted cold, previously cooked peas (I was four and mine was scrambled eggs), you know that they don't age well. 7:00 P.M. 8:00 P.M. 9:00 P.M. Sam was ready to go to bed at 9:30, and Jerrod still sat at the table, the rest of the house dark. There were five peas on the plate, but neither party was budging an inch. At 9:43 P.M., Jerrod finally gave in, ate the peas, and went to bed. Everyone was tired and cranky, but that was the last time he refused to eat.

## Introduction

The difference between kids when they enter elementary school and when they leave it in fifth grade is remarkable. These are the years that we are providing a base from which they will begin their launch into independence, which begins for many when they hit their preteens. Like our children, the way you handle your business at this point is critical as well. We need to be laying the foundation for our infrastructure and culture so that we can weather the challenges that come with growth. Although this time of ramp-up can also be a trial, the lessons learned are vital to our future success. Lessons such as the importance of following through, not disciplining in anger, earning respect, celebrating the small stuff, and getting rid of the "I can'ts" set the basis for our company's management culture. Likewise, keeping your eyes open rather than refusing to see the truth, guarding your time, picking your battles, and asking for support are important for your own personal development and, consequently, the development of your company.

## Following Through

Sometimes, as parents, we make rules with adverse consequences that we hope we won't have to follow through on. Be careful not to threaten something you're not prepared to actualize. I once threatened my daughter that she couldn't play with her friends if she didn't do what I asked her (three times) to do. When the task did not get completed within the allotted time, I had to take away her play date, as painful as that was for me and for the other little girl she was supposed to play with.

Likewise, I learned how much smoother my life was when I set expectations for my children. For example, I realized that they needed some warning before an impending deadline was reached. Before we had to leave a friend's house, they always got a five-minute warning. Prior to my yanking the television plug out of the wall, they were told it was going off in five minutes. I found that preparing them for what was to come and then executing on the threat was much easier when a tangible expectation—in this case, time—was set.

Once you threaten an employee with disciplinary action, from docking their pay to reducing their bonus or even firing them, you have to follow through or you have lost all leverage. Better yet, think twice before you issue such a threat without setting the appropriate expectations.

Ted* was one of my (unfortunately many) sales hire disasters, but he didn't start out that way. We put him through a long interview process that included a personality profile and discussions with two of my outside advisers. Everyone that interviewed him agreed: He was exactly what we needed. He was aggressive but not overpowering, smart, funny, and seemed to grasp the complexity of our business. Our industry was new to him, but we were able to rationalize (and wrongly so) that finding someone that knew our industry would be too hard—anyone can learn it. While we had another strong candidate, he was a lot like me—less hard sales, more relationship. Given that I had a quote from Einstein posted on the wall in front of my desk: "The definition of insanity is doing the same thing over and over again and expecting a different result," I didn't think hiring another Julie was the right course. So we took a chance on Ted.

Shortly after he started working for us, I noticed his car. It was an old piece of junk that was not even maintained very well. When he drove me to an appointment on a rainy day, I discovered that his windshield wipers didn't work. He ended up having to drive with his head sticking out the window like a dog so he could see. Thank goodness his hair was usually slicked back with gel so the customer didn't notice how wet his hair was when we arrived for our appointment. I remember thinking at the time that it was odd; I thought all salespeople drove nice cars. He explained it away somehow, and I did not think anything more about it.

Ted and I worked together to develop his long-term sales plan. We settled on three months of training on our industry and learning our offerings before expecting him to get in front of customers. At the end of the three months, I began to notice some movement but wasn't seeing the progress I had envisioned. He was following up on leads I had turned over to him and while one of those turned into an on-site visit, he wasn't digging up anything new. Given his personality and the way he sold himself, I had expected more.

On the advice of a mentor, I asked Ted to put together his tactical three-month sales plan and submit it to me for review. I gave him one week to complete the plan, which was a generous amount of time given that he was merely following up on my activity and wasn't really out knocking on doors yet. The week came and went, and still I received no plan. At that point, I was getting suspicious. He had been "working at home" in order to get more concentrated time, which also raised my expectations for the output. When I didn't have the report by the designated time, I lowered the ultimatum: Turn in the report or turn in his laptop. Even though we desperately needed a salesperson, I was not getting the output I expected or seeing the progress the company needed. I was hoping that my threat would motivate him to come through, but it was not to be. The second deadline came and went and I still didn't have my plan, though I did receive several excuses about why the plan was not ready. His grandmother was sick. His car broke down (no surprise!). I wrestled over the decision—should I give him some more time or stick to my guns?

I decided to follow through with my threat even though that wasn't the outcome I had intended. Afterwards, I learned that I had waited too long. We found links on his computer to his résumé and e-mails going out to prospective new employers. He knew as well that it was not working, and instead of developing my report, he had been looking for a job. Advice that I had received months before from a friend—"Hire slowly, fire quickly"—kept going through my head. I had taken too long to get rid of Ted, but it finally had been resolved. The other lesson I learned from the experience is that people in sales tend to be good at selling themselves, but you should *think twice* about hiring a salesperson with a crappy car.

I also struggled with following through due to my confidence that I had identified a reasonable consequence of a particular action. Even worse, on occasion I could not come up with a reasonable consequence and so the action (or inaction in this case) would go without one. For example, prior to one of our company quarterly meetings, I asked all employees to read a book, *FISH!*, for discussion at the meeting. I was hoping it would lead to a discussion about our sagging morale and water-cooler grumbling that had recently emerged. The book was a quick and easy read at only 115 pages, and I even went out and bought enough books so that everyone could have one. I also provided a long lead time so there were no excuses.

When we reached the book discussion on the agenda, many people started to look down at the table. It was clear that they had not read the book, and only a handful had actually followed through with the assignment. I distributed a short (and easy) quiz on the book and gave all those who answered all or most of the questions correctly a certificate to a local restaurant. I was left with a lot of extra gift cards; I was crushed. What had I done wrong? Why didn't they read it, and what could I do about it?

While I suspect many staff members did not consider this to be a critical task, I disagreed. I had starting seeing signs that led me to believe we needed to discuss a decline in company morale. Rather than the stereotypical "Floggings will continue until morale improves" approach, I was hoping that the book would motivate people to take it upon themselves to turn things around. That did not happen.

At this point, I turned to one of my mentors who specialized in human resources for assistance. She helped me work through the process of identifying objectives and milestones with reasonable consequences for nonperformance. We began to document these and communicate them to the employees in advance, giving them the opportunity to appeal for a lesser consequence if they felt the chosen one was unfair. That way, when it came time to review milestones against objectives, the results were not unexpected and therefore much easier to stick to. It helped to remove the emotion from the discussion, which is a key to effective discipline.

## Disciplining in Anger

When I was in my early teens, I distinctly remember an altercation between my mother and my younger brother. We were sitting at the dinner table and my brother was sitting with his feet on his chair, his knees up. My mother had asked him several times to put his knees down. At one point, she got so angry at him that she picked up her fork (she thought she grabbed a spoon) and threw it at him. She threw the fork with such force that it stuck into his leg (this is where the "choosing laughter over tears" comes into play again). Please don't alert social services—my brother was not hurt and there was no permanent scar. The funny thing is, my mom and brother both remember the fork lodging in his leg, but it took a while for them to remember what he did to make her so mad. This goes to show that you need to be careful or you might just hit your mark. Oh, and my brother's name is Mark.

In my own parenting, I have had to master the art of counting to 10 when provoked. Sometimes I tick off the numbers with my teeth grinding, but by the time I reach the end of my countdown, I have usually calmed down. If not, I simply start the process again.

Although there have been times when I have wanted to whack an employee over the head with a book, that is not really recommended in a business setting no matter how much they might deserve it. Likewise, smacking a kid the wrong way these days—even your own—could land you in jail. The difference between a tap on the head and child abuse is the emotion and resulting force behind the action. Anger only serves to water down the message in both parenting and business.

Being on the cusp of the Baby Boomers and Generation X, a hard knock for a wrongdoing or a smart comment is not foreign to me. At my grandfather's house, being "taken to the woodshed" had terrifying connotations, especially when the trip involved a switch from the weeping willow tree out back. Today, that would land you on Dr. Phil with him screaming at you: "What were you thinking!?" It's just no longer acceptable. I am not going to debate the merits or damage that can result from spanking your child, but I know that any message or lesson that is attempted through punishment levied in anger is diluted and, many times, ineffective.

In a business setting, we are sometimes presented with confounding actions by employees that immediately have us wanting to reach for the willow switch or, at a minimum, wonder: "What *were* they thinking!?"

Molly* had been our office manager/bookkeeper for six months. One day in a passing discussion with a co-worker, she discovered that her job had actually been offered to someone else before her—that she was the second choice. She became obsessed. Rather than directly asking me, her manager, about the situation, she rummaged through old records to see what she could find. When she couldn't find any information about the prior candidate, First Choice, she did something stupid. When Janet, our human resources manager, was at lunch, she went onto her computer and into her e-mail to find the résumé of First Choice. When she found it, she forwarded it to herself and then tried to delete the trail of what she had done.

I was picking up a report off the printer when I noticed a print-out of the e-mail sent to Molly from Janet. I could not imagine why Janet would be sending First Choice's résumé to anyone, so I went to talk to her. She happened to be at lunch, so I left a note for her to come see me when she returned. When I finally talked with Janet, she did not know anything about the e-mail. This is where it pays to be technically savvy, as I was able to look on Janet's computer and trace Molly's steps. I even saw where she had tried to cover her guilty trail. The anger rose up in me like the tide rising in a hurricane. I was livid. If I had seen her at that very instant, no telling what I would have done and what lawsuit it would have resulted in. Instead of approaching her with the heat still in my face, I retreated to my office to calm down and consider my options. I gave myself a "time out" and conferred with Keenan. I had to separate my emotion from judgment and make sure I was choosing the right course of action, as this would have huge repercussions on the business and on him (he would have to return to doing the books until we found a replacement).

Our company was still small, and this type of behavior could not be tolerated. It was clear what I must do, but by taking myself away from the situation, cooling down, and separating emotions, I was able to approach her just a short time later and deal with the situation professionally and without incident—or at least without a lawsuit.

Paul Silber has built his career on maintaining control of his emotions, though he claims it isn't always as easy as it looks. He has found, however, that when you keep emotions out of the equation when dealing with difficult issues—whether with employees or children—people listen to the message rather than focus on the emotion. One area that he points out as dangerous is e-mail. It has become too easy to blast off a nasty e-mail that makes statements the author would *never* say in a face-to-face situation. To add to the risk, an e-mail can be forwarded to anyone else and take on a life of its own. He cites e-mail as a monologue—a one-way conversation— where you do not have the ability to check for agreement, acknowledgment, or disagreement. That makes it dangerous.

I have experienced that the absence of tone and facial expression leaves written correspondence open to interpretation. You can SHOUT your message by using all capital letters, or indicate sarcasm with a winking smiley face ;-), but that still does not guarantee that the reader will extract the intended meaning of what you are saying.

One important tip that I learned from a customer's mistake: If at all possible, you should *never* configure your e-mail software to send your outgoing e-mails immediately. The best approach is to not write correspondence in anger, but if it will really make you feel better, send the offensive message to yourself or your spouse, or save it in a draft folder to send (or delete) later. Some discussions— especially emotional ones—are absolutely best held in person after the excitement of the moment has worn off.

### Worlds Colliding

Before a certain age, children have no sense of elapsed time. They mark time by events or programs that they are familiar with. In our case, we started marking time using their then-favorite show, *Arthur,* which was 30 minutes long. So a drive to Grandma and Grandpa's house was two Arthurs (an hour). One day when I was walking out of the office to go to lunch, our office manager asked me how long I was going to be gone. Without even thinking I replied, "Three Arthurs."

## Refusing to See the Truth

When we first moved into our neighborhood, we had a neighbor whose son was, you might say, not so nice. He shot at small animals with his BB gun and rode around on the sidewalks on a gas-powered scooter. He was only 11, but the younger kids were scared of him. If you asked his mother, however, she would tell you what an angel he was. For some reason, she either truly didn't see this side of him or refused to see it. Whichever it was, no one could tell her anything negative that her son had done because she would not believe it.

One afternoon our nanny, whom we called Ms. Jean, a wonderful woman who was a mother herself, was driving down our street when she came across this boy riding down the middle of the street on his scooter. It was raining fairly hard, so she rolled down her window and told him that he shouldn't be out riding, that he should go inside. He proceeded to flip her "the bird" and fling other obscenities in her direction. Ms. Jean was incensed.

The next day the boy's mother showed up at my house, screaming at Ms. Jean and wagging her finger, "You don't ever talk to my son like that again!" Ms. Jean was incredulous. The boy had been the offensive one, and his mother was screaming at her. Clearly, she was in an unhealthy state of denial. This can bite us in business as well.

I had known Anne* for years before I hired her. We had worked together at IBM. She had even attended my wedding several years earlier. She was between jobs when we were looking to hire a project manager for a contract with a new customer. It was for an engagement we had limited on-hand experience delivering. Her background appeared to fit perfectly with the needs of the position, and after interviewing her, we brought her on board.

In the beginning, it was as if the project had been tailor-made for her. She seemed to be in her element. I was surprised the first time I received a call from the client at home. He was concerned about the direction she was going and her ability to carry the project through to the end from a technical perspective. At first, I defended Anne. She had many more years of experience than I did—I was sure it was just a blip. I assured him that I would work with her and if I thought the project was in jeopardy, we could discuss alternatives. I immediately called Anne's manager, Greg, at home to ascertain whether he was aware of any issues. He assured me that nothing was amiss but that he would follow up with her in the morning to verify.

The next morning, Anne and Greg had a discussion. Anne had no idea the customer had issues with her and felt like she was on the right path and in control. He told her about the customer's call to me and she was baffled. Afterwards, Greg told me not to be concerned but vowed that he would keep his eye on her. We moved on.

The second call from the client to my home came a few weeks later. There was a real concern among their team members about her ability to carry the entire project forward. It didn't help that she had a couple idiosyncrasies that grated on his project manager. Again, I defended her to the client, but, truthfully, my faith was beginning to wane. I knew this customer well, and his calling me at home *twice* was a sign that something was not right.

The next day I addressed the issue directly with Anne and Greg at the same time. Anne maintained that while there had been some disagreements among the various parties, it was nothing more than normal project progress. She mentioned that there was a big meeting coming up at the customer's site, and we agreed that Greg would attend the meeting with her. Our prevailing thought that was by sending Greg, he could provide the objective insight needed to mediate the situation. His presence was also a sign to our customer that we took his concerns earnestly.

They didn't even make it in the door before the tension between Anne and the customer's project manager was palpable. When she took off her coat, everyone saw (and heard) that Anne was wearing a set of jingle bells around her neck that clinked loudly whenever she walked or even moved. She came to the meeting knowing that the client had issues with her, but chose to wear these bells anyway. Bad choice. To the client, the clinking of the bells was worse than the screeching sound that comes from running fingers down a chalk board. They had reached their tipping point. Seeing that, Greg had her immediately remove the bells.

By the end of the meeting, the problem was clear. The scope of the project had changed, and the skills required to manage it were quickly creeping well beyond Anne's competencies. She had tried to make the best of it, but our course of action was straightforward. She had to be taken off the project.

I did not regret taking the stand to back Anne. I made sure, however, that I did so with caution and with a healthy measure of skepticism. I didn't want to assume that "the customer is always right" to the detriment of my own staff, but I also didn't want to be naïve. Both the relationship with my customer and the relationship with my employee were valuable, and my response to the situation had to reflect that.

On the other side, Sheila Heinze was working through a personnel issue with an employee who was extremely well liked by their customer. Because of the clout this client held, the management team did everything they could—even things outside of the norm—to make this staff member happy. Sheila finally recognized that what they were doing was harmful and setting a bad precedent. What is best for the customer does not mean they get anything they want. Their contract was with SM Consulting, not with the individual. Their eventual course was to work with the customer to replace the troublesome employee on the contract and then counsel the individual out of the company. Ultimately, their client respected their approach and working through that tough issue increased the trust in the relationship.

## Earning Respect

Although some parents try to demand respect from their children because of their position of authority in the family, it doesn't always work. At least it didn't for us.

We were going to be gone for an extended period of time, an hour's drive away. Although the event was during the late afternoon, we weren't comfortable leaving Sydney, who was almost 12, at home alone for that long a period of time. None of our closest neighbors were going to be around, so there was no one to call if an issue came up. We were able to arrange for friends of Madison's to take the girls to the pool with them and then over to their house so they would not be home alone. Sydney didn't like our resolution. She felt as if we didn't trust her, so she pouted and fussed for the entire day before we left. She wanted to make sure that we knew that she wasn't happy about our decision. Her behavior didn't change our plans, but it did have us thinking about a suitable punishment. We went to our event and had a wonderful time.

As we were on our way home but still a bit away, we received a call from our house. Our friends were calling us to make sure we knew that they had dropped the kids off at home. Although it was not dark yet, I called back to the house a short time later to tell the girls that they needed to stop watching TV (which I was *sure* they were doing) and get ready for bed. When I called, however, all I got was a fast busy signal on the other end. Concerned, I called my surrounding neighbors and got a variety of recordings that indicated that the phones were out in our neighborhood. I was not comfortable with this. I called the family that had dropped them off and asked if they could go check on them. When they arrived, everything was fine, but apparently the power had gone out for some time in our neighborhood and taken the phone lines down with them. My daughters hadn't even noticed. When Sydney heard this, she was suddenly thankful that she had *not* been left home alone. When we finally returned home, she hugged me and apologized for not respecting our decision. We had earned her respect.

Whenever my younger daughter gets really tired, she gets mouthy. I often will turn around and look at her and, in my best "Godfather" imitation, ask, "You talkin' to me?! 'Cuz my daughter don't talk to *me* like that! I deserve proper respect." Unfortunately, the accent is so funny that she just laughs and now asks me to do it for her friends. That certainly backfired on me.

In the workplace, you can try to *make* your employees respect you, but in most cases, you have to earn it for it to be truly effective. I can remember talking with the wife of one of my employees in a social situation. She remarked that she couldn't believe her husband was working for a woman. From what she had seen, he did not have any respect for women in technical capacities. What she didn't know is that he and I had already been through the "proving time" and I had earned his respect technically through my knowledge and skills as a programmer. Should I have *had* to earn respect? Perhaps not. Was it deeper and more meaningful because I had earned it? I think so.

Even with customers, I have had to earn respect. Being a young woman in a male-dominated industry—manufacturing—I knew that when I walked into a meeting, I was going to have to prove why I was qualified to be there. I didn't mind, though—I just did it. And the response that I got was respect. Respect earned is respect that sticks with you.

Walking into a manufacturing facility at 24 years of age was an experience. "Hi! I am here to design your new warehousing system." Yeah, right. Being a woman did not make it easier, but at least I had learned not to wear a skirt to a manufacturing plant. Skirts made it dubious to walk on a catwalk or ride a man-lift (a belt with platforms and handles used as a rudimentary elevator). I felt prepared-in-pants when I went to meet with a new prospective customer, Rich.

I was not the first person Rich had met with about this project, which somewhat explains his "What is *she* doing here?" attitude when I arrived. I knew he was not going to be easy. Fifteen years my senior, Rich had been working with another vendor on this particular project for several months. He had been through hours of interviews and design meetings and felt like my appearance meant that he had to start over. It turned out he was right. I reviewed the document the other company had developed and found numerous gaps in their design, which had earned me this meeting. Rich was not the one who had scheduled the discussion, and he was clearly not happy I was there. I did not let that intimidate me. I knew my stuff, and I wasn't going to let his apprehension keep me from pursuing this project.

Once we settled in and he actually listened to what I had to say, he started to see that maybe I did know something. Perhaps my youthful appearance, which was because I *was* young, didn't mean I could not do a better job at this project than his buddies. Point by point, I went through my observations and questions until it became clear that the current design was chock-full of holes. By calmly refusing to let his misconceptions or biases daunt me, I was able to convince them to give us the contract, and the rest, as they say, is history. I secured what would become ACT's largest and most profitable client and gained a long-time personal friend.

I have found that the best way to earn employees' respect is to not ask them to do anything you haven't already done or aren't willing to do. Pete Linsert adopted a similar philosophy, but referred to is as the Golden Rule: Treat others the way you want to be treated. Because I was one of the programming staff that developed the first version of our software, it was clear I understood the application and knew what it was like to walk a mile in my staff's (work) shoes. At least none of them wore stilettos.

Once I moved out of programming and into management, I continued to cater to the needs of the team. If we were working on a tight deadline, I made sure everyone was fed. I stocked the refrigerator with sodas and the freezer with popsicles. I even, on occasion, splurged for Starbucks in the office, which was a big step for me since I didn't even drink coffee. By practicing a form of servant leadership—with nothing being too low for me to do and making sure my employees were being served—I was able to gain deep-rooted respect from my staff that saw us through a lot of difficult times.

Paul's experience was similar. He found that new employees granted him respect based on his title, but that rarely lasted more than a few days. He was able to earn respect by "walking the talk" or emulating the kind of behavior he expected from his employees. He did whatever job needed to be done, no matter how menial, and his employees knew that he was committed. They also witnessed him having to tackle the hard issues: firing an underperforming employee, putting his own personal money into the company to keep it going, and openly answering tough questions candidly and honestly. His consistent and unwavering dedication to making the business succeed earned him respect not only from within his own company, but also from his peers and customers.

Kathy Freeland's experience was slightly different. She had a warm, inviting personality that many of her employees felt drawn to. They also knew, however, that she was one tough lady who was not afraid to make the hard decisions around what was best for the company. It was actually the nature of her company and what it stood for that initiated the respect her employees felt for her.

A couple years after Kathy founded her company, Freeland & Associates, she renamed it to RGII after her son, Richard

Gregory II, who died as an infant. She shared her story with each employee, as difficult as that was. The depth of her commitment to build a company where his name would continue to live on and her willingness to share her story earned her respect. She was creating his legacy, and her employees were compelled to be a part of it out of a sincere respect for her. For Kathy, respect resulted in deep loyalty.

For Terry Chase Hazell, earning respect meant cold hard cash. After six years of raising money from every conceivable source for the company she co-founded, Chesapeake-PERL, Terry had earned a great deal of respect in the local financing community. Her professionalism, as well as her process orientation, was rewarded with praise from investor circles. She was always prepared for every meeting or conversation and tried to anticipate any question that might be asked. This proved helpful as she exited from C-PERL and started her next venture, SD Nanosciences. Even those who did not choose to invest in her former company remembered her professionalism and offered to hear her present her new company concept for funding consideration.

## Guarding Your Time

The current pace at which children are engaging in activities outside of the home is impossible to maintain. Overscheduled children have resulted in an increase in a variety of societal problems, from adolescent depression to early burn-out.

The rule at our house was that each child was allowed one activity per season. Because one night per week was already taken up by their religious education, having games or practices one or two other nights per week was more than enough to keep all of us running. We would compromise for a single event or short-term activity but would try to stick with our guidelines otherwise. It was important to us to make sure we guarded not only our time spent carting kids around, but also our children's time so they didn't get overwhelmed or lose perspective about what is important—God, family, and academics, all while leaving ample time for play.

When our business was growing, I was not always a good guard of our money. I learned the hard way (read: parted with real money) not to get off track financially. We were approached by a marketing company that was selling a television commercial spot for a program highlighting county-based businesses. The idea of having my company on TV was tempting. And the price seemed reasonable—the salesperson told us we only had to pay 50 percent of the production costs. At only $3,000, they assured us, it was a bargain! Lured by the glamour and prestige of having a TV commercial, we decided to do it. While the taping was fun and it was neat to see ourselves on TV, absolutely nothing came out of it. Not a whisper. We should have known better, though. We had a very specific target market that was not represented in the geographic area the commercial was aired. We fell for the glamour of it and parted with a few thousand dollars that we undoubtedly could have used elsewhere.

Another distraction that I have seen trip up novice entrepreneurs is philanthropy. While building your company to be able to provide for a specific cause is noble, unless your products or services are directly related to that cause, getting carried away too early in the business can prove detrimental to your business growth. Jindra Cekan's business is all about making a difference, as she coordinates food aid to third-world countries. My business, however, was not in a position to directly contribute other than the good jobs we provided our employees. Once we began to grow, we had the resources available to give back to our community, but it took some time before we were able to do that. Focusing on that from the very beginning would have been difficult and distracting, though it was always part of my long-term vision.

As mentioned before, our resources are often scarce when we're in start-up mode. Our ability to maintain our energy to build our company is limited when we steal too much time for other interests. It makes more sense to use the time to create a real economic engine that has many times more power to make a difference rather than crippling our effort and diluting our potential for giving back. While I firmly believe that business is the ideal global power to affect real change in the world, the business has to get off the ground before it can be a positive contributor.

In a start-up company, the entrepreneur's time versus the number of tasks to be done is constantly running at a deficit. As discussed in the "Wearing Many Hats" section in Chapter 4, we start out having to do everything because we don't have the money to pay anyone else to do it. At some point, you will need help or your business will stall. Unfortunately, the time when you need the most help is before you have money. You need help to make money and you need money to get help—a typical entrepreneurial paradox.

The key, as you begin to grow, is to evaluate the time you have available against the tasks that need to be done. Are you taking time away from those activities that make money, such as billable work or sales? Ask yourself: Would paying someone else to do this task provide me the opportunity to make more money? Are there projects that my time would be better and more profitably spent on?

Carol Koch-Worrel started building her music business while her son was very young, so scarcity of time was a familiar dilemma. She had the skills to develop her own marketing materials and ads, but she knew those tasks were not the best use of her time. She promptly found a graphic design company that could develop what she needed, and the results were likely more complete and more professional than if she had attempted to fit them into her busy schedule. When a growing business catches you by surprise, it is not always so easy to know when you need help.

The good news was that Margaret Pressler's BurpCatcher product caught on much faster than she could have imagined. The bad news was that she was drowning. She was working part time as a reporter and her three children under age nine were beginning to get jealous of the youngest child in the family—her business. Her receipts were piling up, and she knew she had to get a handle on her business but could not seem to ever catch up. The weight of everything she had to do at any one time hung around like a heavy, dark rain cloud. She rarely slept at night, and it was clear she had to do something.

While she had a general sense of her financial status, she needed a better grip on her bookkeeping or she would not be able to determine definitively if and when her business had rounded the corner toward profitability. She also would not know when she could afford to hire help if she didn't know her *true* financial picture. Her friends who worked in small businesses advised her to purchase QuickBooks, but when she loaded the software and launched the program, she realized she didn't know the first thing about the task in front of her. While intellectually she had the smarts to figure it out, was that really the right place for her to put her already-stretched attention? No. She knew from her years of interviewing entrepreneurs as a reporter for the *Washington Post* that you need to spend money to make money. She took a bold step and decided to hire part-time help to assist her with the books. As a bonus, this person would also have time to help her with shipping products to retailers. While she knew it would take time she did not have to train this person, she also knew in her already-twisted gut that it was the right thing to do to keep her business moving forward.

I decided early that I needed to focus my time on tasks that required my expertise, not just those things that I could figure out or already knew how to do. I posted the saying "Just because you can, doesn't mean you should" on my office wall as a reminder. For example, even though my accounting package had the capability to make all the calculations necessary for payroll, I determined how much time it would take me to perform that process. It didn't take a brick to my head to coerce me to outsource my payroll processing to an outside firm. That decision turned out to be one of the best I ever made. Although I didn't necessarily have the excess money to do that at the time, it freed me up to focus on those tasks that would help me bring in more revenues.

There are also creative ways to get assistance without having to part with much-needed and often scarce cash. Bartering is a common practice among start-ups. Likewise, when a company is young and without cash, exchanging equity for needed help is not uncommon. In general, if you believe something will propel your business, do not hesitate to trade a reasonable amount of equity for it. For example, many companies that license technology from universities offer equity in their company rather than pay the university a license fee. If that product is successful, everyone wins. Likewise, companies can sometimes exchange equity for office space in an incubator, which offers consulting and other technical and administrative support in addition to just office or lab space.

Students at local universities are also underutilized resources that are often free or low cost. I have witnessed entrepreneurs getting logos created by design students and marketing research conducted by MBA candidates. While working with students requires a well-defined project with specific objectives, it is a win-win strategy where the students get practical experience and the business owner gets much-needed services at a bargain.

## Knowing Your Kid

Ashleigh was tall with strong hands, so playing basketball was a natural fit for her. She started playing in the recreational league in the second grade but was already far beyond the skills of many of her peers. Her coach recommended she move to a more challenging league in third grade where she would compete with other players at or above her skill level. As her mastery continued to improve, she persisted in advancing in the leagues. By fourth grade she was on a team that competed across the state, called a *travel* team. When she reached middle school, she was on three teams at one time—the recreational league, the travel team, and the middle school team. It was all she did; it was all she had time for. By the time she got to high school, it started to not be fun. By tenth grade she had burn-out. Fried at 16. Although Ashleigh was a competitive child, her parents let the momentum of the sport carry her too far. Was this really what Ashleigh wanted?

After some time off, she decided that she missed playing sports and tried out for the high school volleyball team. The same skills that helped her excel in basketball were useful in volleyball, and she continued with that through her remaining high school career.

If your child starts to focus on a single sport before high school, ask yourself if she is doing this for you or for herself. Is it really what your child wants or what you want for your child? Do you know what your child wants? Have you asked him or her? In Ashleigh's case, she was very self-driven, but many parents think they know their child better than they really do. Are we seeing what we want or what they want us to see? Are we projecting our dreams and desires on to them?

One entrepreneur's nephew loves working on cars. Unfortunately, his father felt that type of work was beneath his son and had not been supportive. He continually tried to guide him in other directions. Consequently, his son floundered. His strengths were ignored and were not being validated. Unless the father acknowledges that his son should find something to do working with cars, he may never truly shine.

It is critical as well to understand that our employees are different from each other and may require a disparate management approach in order to excel. Graham Weston learned from raising his children the need to recognize how diverse people are and that they need to be treated as such. He points out that great managers like to play chess. Every piece has a different purpose, its own strength. Your job as a manager is to use that strength to your advantage rather than trying to make a piece move in a way that it is not supposed to. Conversely, poor managers like to play checkers. All the pieces are the same and can move the same way. There is no need to worry about treating anyone differently. He cites that having good managers is truly the key to having a thriving culture. A person generally joins a company but quits his or her manager. When the manager does not know his staff and how to bring out the best in them, everyone suffers.

We prided ourselves on having great individuality within our company, but that also meant that there was no one way to motivate or provide incentives for everyone. Some people fed off public recognition, while others preferred a private show of appreciation. Certain people require continual reinforcement, while others would rather be left alone. We had one manager who clearly played checkers, and he did not last long in the management position. He tried to treat everyone alike, the way he wanted to be treated, and found that not everyone responded positively. It is imperative that you know the people around you and understand what makes them tick in order to be an effective manager and leader.

Equally dangerous to many companies is the struggle that comes from not knowing their customer intimately or not understanding what motivates them to buy. That is a fine way to operate if you are an artisan or a hobbyist that derives great joy from building a product or performing a service for the intrinsic value it gives you personally, but not so great if you're really trying to make money. You must have an in-depth understanding of who your ideal customer is and what their likes, dislikes, needs, and wants are to be truly successful in a competitive marketplace.

I have browsed women's trade shows and admired the beautiful clothes and jewelry exhibited there, but rarely will I purchase what I see. For most of these companies, I assume I am in their target market, which is why they have a booth at a conference I am attending. Do they notice that I don't buy? I am sure they do. Ideally, they should be asking me why I just browse or if there is something I was looking for that I didn't find. No one has asked me yet. They are missing an opportunity to get market feedback. Most of the time, the items are beautiful but just too expensive. I rarely spend a lot of money on jewelry. So, although I am a woman of a certain age and income level, there is another aspect to their target market that perhaps they have not considered—their customer must be willing to spend more than the average on jewelry. What type of woman does that? If that is your business, you should be able to answer that question.

All companies should be able to describe a day in the life of their ideal customer in order to truly have an accurate picture of who they are and why they buy. This holds true whether you are selling a medical device, training software, or skin care products. What makes your model customer buy your products or services? What are they actually buying? People buy cars, but they are buying prestige when they choose a Mercedes and safety when they elect to go with a Volvo. Do you know what your customer is buying? Successful companies embrace this and target their marketing accordingly.

Unless you understand the job your product or service provides for your customers (and different customer segments may be buying different things!), you are only guessing at how to market to them. The best way to get to the bottom of this information is by studying your market and asking customers yourself, with a word of caution: Customers do not always know what they are buying or what they need. Case in point: Few people initially saw the need for a personal computer on every desk, but now we can't see how to do without one.

In addition to knowing what makes someone buy your product and what they are actually buying, you need to be able to distinguish between who is purchasing it and who is using it. The software my company developed was essentially an inventory tracking system. The users of it were mainly the people working in a warehouse who maybe had a high school diploma and, at the time, limited knowledge or experience with computers. In fact, I can remember one gentleman picking up the computer mouse and talking into it as if it were a microphone. Obviously, he had never used one before.

What the users wanted was something easy to operate that didn't get in the way of their doing their primary job, which was managing product in a warehouse and fulfilling customer orders. They didn't want to navigate through three computer screens when one would do. They didn't want to be required to enter information more than once if it wasn't necessary. It was for them, our users, that our system was designed, and while they loved it, not one of them could write us a check for it. Winning them over and providing them with a product that they loved wasn't enough and sometimes didn't even help. The people who wrote the check and made the decisions to purchase software like ours were not the people who used it.

Unlike the users, the people who made decisions around buying our product were most often highly educated and had a larger picture in mind when making this type of business decision. They wanted to know how our system fit in with their other systems, how using it would improve productivity and lessen their product liability through accurate traceability. Even the different people making the decisions had very different concerns, all of which had to be considered in the marketing and sales of our product. It was insufficient to understand the motivations and needs of the people who used our product, we also had to understand the internals of who bought our product and why.

## Celebrating the Small Stuff

I had always wanted one and I finally got it—a convertible. Keenan had grown up with an old Mercury Cougar that had been in the family for 16 years. As the third of four boys, the car was well worn when he got it, but as he puts it, "It was such a sweet car." I never owned a *sweet* car and now that my kids were out of car seats, it was my turn.

My first automobile was a 1976 Chevy Vega, and although I have never been obsessed with cars, I have always been into fresh air. Having grown up in Texas, I can stand the heat and actually prefer fans to air conditioning as much as possible. Although my tolerance for heat has lessened since moving north, I still prefer breathing "au naturel" over forced cooled air.

I wasn't looking for anything too fancy or expensive, and it had to seat two people comfortably in the backseat. I had owned a Toyota Camry for years and loved it, so when they came out with the Toyota Solara, which was essentially a convertible Camry, I was sold.

Although my kids didn't like riding in the car with the top up because they couldn't see, they loved taking a cruise with the top down because they could see *everything*. One beautiful spring-time day, we were all riding in the Solara with the top down and enjoying life. My daughter was holding her hands up so she could feel the rushing, cool air pass through her fingers and kept saying "Woohoo!" We all joined her, arms up in the air shouting "Woohoo!" and a family tradition was born—the Family Woohoo. It became our way of celebrating the little things—the warm sun coupled with the cool rush of air and being together as a family that day. Once someone invokes a Family Woohoo, whatever the occasion, it is hard to stay in a bad mood.

Planning for little celebrations in business is important as well. You don't have to spend a lot of money on a Business Woohoo for it to have an impact. In my company, we kept a bottle of champagne sitting on my bookshelf, to be opened when we sold our first software license. For years, we would continue to look wistfully at that bottle wondering if we would ever be able to open it. We finally did, within minutes of getting our first signed license agreement via fax, and whoever was in the office was invited to share in the celebration.

We also celebrated our employees' birthdays. Once a month we would bring in a cake for all those who had birthdays that month, and even sang "Happy Birthday" when we were feeling especially musical. It was an extra special treat if you could get Nat, our quality assurance manager, to sing for you with his high-pitched, sweet, melodious tones.

When the company was small, I would order gift baskets that were tailored to the individual. For example, Sharon* had a thing for crabs, so her basket had cute crab-related foods and trinkets in it. Faye Ann was a chocoholic, so her basket was about, what else, chocolate. Year after year and as we started to grow, it became harder to continue coming up with new and different personalized gifts, so we asked the employees what they would rather have: a basket or a gift card to a book or electronics store. Overwhelmingly, they opted for the gift card, so that was what we did. To keep it personal, we also made sure that we bought a birthday card and had everyone in the company sign it. That little extra personal touch was important and helped to make everyone feel like part of the family.

Kathy also made her employees' birthdays feel special. Each one of her almost 400 employees received a birthday card personally signed by her every year. It is one thing to keep it intimate when you have 10, 20, or even 30 employees, but continuing to make the effort when the numbers reach the hundreds is truly admirable. She cites the outstanding efforts of her executive assistant as a key contributor to retaining that tradition as they grew.

At least twice a year we organized a fun, company-wide event. Our first intercompany laser tag competition was probably one of the best outings we organized. We also started having "Movie Fridays" where we would play a movie on the projector in the conference room at 2:00 P.M. on a Friday provided we had hit certain targets for the month. It was a great way to wind down and celebrate the day-to-day hard work that went into keeping our customers happy.

Staff members at Martek would pass through the office on a Friday afternoon to take up a collection for beer—4:30 was "beer-thirty." Pete claims they celebrated many things in a muted way, but the smallest thing they ever celebrated was a test tube. It wasn't exactly the test tube itself that they cherished, it was what was inside it. They had produced docosahexaenoic acid (DHA)-rich oil, their company's now-flagship product, which they currently manufacture by the truckload. At the time, that little bit was monumental. They thought there might be oil in that thar algae, and when they were actually able to extract their first drops, it was time to party.

They also celebrated innovation. They were having a problem trying to determine how to dry a particular strain of fungal material to extract an essential fatty acid from it. It was long and stringy, like tall grass. One particularly creative scientist discovered that running the strain through a mop bucket would do the trick. He was so excited, he ran around the office with the cardboard-like substance. Needless to say, they needed to buy more mop buckets to complete their research.

In Sheila Heinze's company, she maintains the right to call a "red alert" when she thinks one is needed. In a red alert, managers and employees alike drop everything and participate in a fun activity. They have been bowling, paintballing, and even rock climbing. It has proven to be a great way to relieve stress and put everyone back into a healthy state of mind when work gets too overwhelming and demanding.

Paul implemented monthly all-hands company meetings not only to keep everyone up to date on the business but also to celebrate achievements. At every monthly meeting, they introduced each new employee and recognized anyone who had been promoted since the last gathering. Immediately following the meeting, they held a luncheon as a way to say "thanks for a job well done." Paul has found that by celebrating the small contributions that people make to each other and the company motivates others to do the same. Outside of the monthly meetings, his management team is also empowered to hand out $7 lunch vouchers to anyone within the organization that goes "above and beyond the call of duty" to lend someone a helping hand outside of their standard job responsibilities. The names of the people who are recognized with these vouchers are also posted on a company-wide bulletin board for all to see.

Not all companies are good at celebrating, though. One of Terry's directors told her she had to have a party to celebrate some major achievements. So on Friday afternoon they spread a table full of food—ribs and beer—and hung out in the reception area. She walked around the corner to talk with one of the vice presidents, and when she came back everyone was gone. She found all but three of the beers unopened in the fridge, all the food packed up, and everyone back at work. She asked everyone why they left the celebration and they all had a similar answer. They had work to do, a project to finish, or some other task of great importance to tend to. She had a beer by herself in her office and went home. She felt her work was done.

## Picking Your Battles

When she was in kindergarten, Madison played mostly with boys. She had grown up playing with her friend, Michael, across the street and had just naturally migrated to the opposite sex once she started school. One day she came home from kindergarten and asked if she could wear a white T-shirt under her shirt. At first I was baffled. Why? It wasn't cold outside. Then she said, "Because Jack, Billy, and Michael wear them." She wanted to be one of the boys. Chuckling, I considered her request. It wouldn't really hurt anything to let her do it. Even though I didn't want her to wear that shirt to look like the boys, I decided to pick my battles. I assumed that she would grow out of it sooner or later, so I let her wear it. She was so overjoyed that she went skipping off to school with a big smile on her face the next morning. No harm done, I'd hoped.

Several years later, I took Madison shopping for shoes to wear to my brother's wedding. We had a really nice time together. While at the mall, she had picked out cute little friendship necklaces for her two closest friends, Morgan and Julieann, and was eager to deliver them. I was tired and ready to get home, which drove my first inclination to say *no*. I realized at that moment that she had come a long way from the little girl who wanted to dress like the boys. She was so excited. Since Julieanne's house was on the way and I was not really in a hurry to get anywhere else, I decided that this was not a battle I needed to fight. Tired or not, we took the necklace to her friend.

In business, it is easy to feel that you need to have control over everything. Operating this way is an easy route to an early heart attack. Choosing which battles to fight in your business is easier if you keep in mind which battles you *should* be fighting. In my experience, I have found it critical to maintain control around anything that:

- Impacts the company's culture or values in a negative way.
- Is illegal or unethical.
- Is likely to make a negative impact to the bottom line *over time*.

Other than those items above, you have to let go of the small stuff.

Carol is a licensee of KinderMusik, which has developed curriculum that foster child development for newborns to age seven through music and movement. In her first year of business, she reached the maestro level, which indicates an exceptional number of families reached through her program (read: sales). This achievement encompasses only roughly 5 percent of licensees and is highly unusual for someone in her first year. She attributes her success to continuing to focus on her business as a *serious* business, not as a hobby.

One of her classes full of two-year-olds was especially rambunctious. At one point during a particular class, a train unmistakably passed by, which had all of the children making a variety of train-related sounds. Rather than fight it or ignore it, Carol just went with it. After all, a choo-choo sound can easily be incorporated into music and movement. When the moment had passed, she was able to get right back into her lesson plan for the day without skipping a beat. Had she tried to fight it, she likely would have lost control and had a hard time wrestling it back. She went with the flow and chose not to go against the momentum of the moment. It is critical, at some point, that all entrepreneurs know how and when to go with the flow.

Before I was able to expand our project management staff to meet the needs of our growing customer list, I had to manage a couple of the new projects myself. Since I am not, by nature, an organized person, I opted to create a system to force myself to stay organized. I created a project numbering system and developed a project binder with specific sections and contents. It was the only way I could keep track of those projects given everything else I had going on.

When I hired someone to manage our project management process and our future project managers, I showed him my system and expected that he would adopt it and make his managers adopt it. It didn't happen. In truth, he had been a project manager for a lot longer than I had, which was why I had hired him. While I did have some strong thoughts over the outcomes that we needed from the project management process, it wasn't my job to develop that methodology nor was it my expertise. Rather than force my system on him, I let him work with his team to develop their own. While it didn't include some of the standards that I had implemented, they focused their energies on the tasks where they felt standardization was more important, such as estimating projects and reporting to the customer. I verified that the outcomes met the objectives we had put in place, which they did. In the end, because I let go of that small issue, the project management processes that the team came up with were different from mine but also more effective.

One area that I chose to go to battle over was our flexibility policies. When I founded my company, I did so with the intention of creating an environment where people were regarded as total humans, not just employees. One of the key elements of implementing that ideal was around creating a flexible workplace. I hired several women who worked part-time so they could be home when their kids got off the school bus. I also allowed some employees to work from home on days they had a plumber coming or car troubles.

Not all of my management team shared the same philosophy. Their initial response to an employee who was asking to be considered for a flexible work arrangement was to say "no." Since this was one of the company's, and my, core values, I had to step in. I proceeded to counsel my managers that rather than saying "We can't" as a response to an employee request, they had to find a way to make it work if at all possible, though not to the detriment of the business. Approach it instead as "How can we?" with a "We can't" as an acceptable answer only after a thorough investigation.

## Getting Rid of the "I Can'ts"

If there is one thing about Madison that drives me crazy, it is that she has a tendency to jump to "I can't." The first time I noticed this was when she was in kindergarten and practicing her alphabet. She got to a certain letter and didn't like the way she had formed it. Frustrated, she crumpled up the paper, threw it, and said, "I can't." It was then that I realized that she had a bit of perfectionist in her. I started saying to her, "We don't say 'I can't,' we say, 'I tried to do it myself but now I need help.'"

When she was in third grade, her teacher, Mrs. Howard, reinforced the importance of a positive mental attitude. Every week, she gave the kids a quote and they had to write a paragraph describing what it meant to them. The quotes were almost always about the value of a positive attitude and the idea began to stick with my daughter more deeply than if she had only heard it from us. Having outside advocacy of our ideals brought legitimacy to what we were trying to teach our child.

I was once told that people with a positive outlook are not afraid of being mistaken and that people who perceive things more negatively don't like to be wrong. Successful entrepreneurs tend to fall into the positive category. There is a fine line, however, between being positive and being naïve.

Keenan doesn't like being called negative; he prefers the term *realistic.* With my more optimistic outlook, our working together as partners in the business made for a good balance. I was the one who was looking at a half-full glass, and he was the one asking what we were going to do to keep our cup from going empty. When I would see something to celebrate, he would already be on to the next challenge on our path. We worked out an agreement, however, that he would give me some time to celebrate before he would poke holes in something or worry about how we would get it done. He was not an "I can't" person, he was more of a "How can we?" It was that implementation and problem-solving perspective, coupled with my high aspirations and vision, that helped keep our business going. Without his driving toward implementation I would risk being too lofty without a plan. Without my vision, we would never have taken some of the risks that we did. It was a good balance.

In order to continue to innovate and move your business forward, you have to build a culture of "How Can We?" I actually posted that saying on the walls of our office. It was acceptable and even desirable to foresee the pitfalls in something, but the point was that we need to look for a way to navigate around obstacles, not let them trip us up. I liken this to an off-road bicycle race. The only way a racer can travel so fast through the trees is to focus on the path rather than the trees. Once they focus on a tree, they've hit it.

The attitude required to foster a "How Can We" environment demands flexibility on the part of both the company and the staff. Donna Stevenson discovered early on how important it is that all employees be willing to give and take. She was working on a last-minute proposal with a new manager who had been with the company for only one month. On the Friday before the proposal was due less than a week later, Donna had given this manager some information to review so they could put the finishing touches on the proposal and meet the customer's tight deadline. To her astonishment, the manager looked at her and said quite arrogantly (and loudly), "I am going home and I am not thinking about EMS." She did not ask to talk to Donna in private or offer any excuses. Donna just stood there, incredulous, with her mouth open while several other junior staff members looked on.

The woman left the office thinking that she had just implemented a new no-weekend-thoughts-about-the-company policy. The more Donna stewed over it, the angrier she became. She fumed all weekend. She had worked hard to develop a culture in her organization that was respectful of the individual, but in return, she expected her staff to pitch in when needed. She knew that this woman's attitude so early in her tenure at the company was a bad sign. There was no way the relationship would endure productively. The following Monday, after Donna had a chance to let her emotions dissipate, she fired her. She had to make a statement about what would and would not be tolerated.

## Asking for Support

When I was pregnant, people would ask me if I was planning on getting an epidural or enduring the pain and discomfort of natural childbirth. Admittedly, I never considered *not* accepting the help that was made available to me. When asked, I would retort, "I know of no trophies for natural childbirth." However, some, like my friend Terry, would argue that birthing a baby sans drugs had its own rewards. That may work for some, but I wasn't buying it. I went as long as I could, but eventually succumbed to the pain and opted for the medication to soothe the way.

Though I thankfully haven't required pain medication since, outside support for parenting has come in other ways. Once our kids entered elementary school, I thought I would never get out of my car. With soccer practice and Girl Scouts and religious education and play dates with friends, when was there time to do anything else?! We learned quickly that we had to get a grip on their social lives before their activities obtained a death grip on us. That was when we decided to make the new house rule to limit each child to two activities per season. Even with this activity restriction, we still had to succumb to the dreaded C word—carpooling. What is really a driving co-op, carpools are the ultimate in informal support groups for parents. Unfortunately, carting several kids around also meant giving in to another dreaded (at least for me) hazard of parenthood: the minivan. Not that I didn't appreciate the comfort and convenience of a house on wheels, I just didn't like what it did for my image. At the time I was in my mid-thirties and not really ready to join the "soccer mom" crowd. When you drive a minivan, you don't really have a choice. My husband was actually the one who was excited about purchasing the van—it was his fortieth birthday gift to himself. As midlife crises go, I'm not sure whether this was a good or bad sign. At least it wasn't a muscle car with a hot babe in the front seat. As soon as a sport utility vehicle came out that didn't drive like a truck, we bought one, though it was a few years after that before we got rid of the van for good. All the while, I reserved my four-door sedan so I could have transportation where my passengers weren't sitting on Cheerios and Goldfish crackers.

Not only is an outside support system critical, but support is also an inside job for successful ParentPreneurs. Whether it is a spouse, your own mom or dad, an aunt, or close neighbor—you need someone whom you can trust completely and who has your best interests at heart. I have been fortunate to have a strong support system in my husband, Keenan. He is my partner in raising our children as well as running the business. But even that is not enough—we still need help from the outside. Over the years, we have had a variety of child care situations where our kids were in other people's homes, nannies have come to our house, and we've worked our schedule so we can be home with them. All the while our goal was to make sure they were in a loving, safe environment where they could learn positive manners and behavior and be loved and well cared for. I have a tremendous amount of respect for single parents like Jindra Cekan. She manages to do it successfully by weaving together her own support system from family, friends, and neighbors.

One of the differentiators that set Kathy Freeland's company RGII apart from her competitors was the attention that she as CEO paid to her customers. Every quarter, she traveled to each one of her customers, regardless of whether that customer contracted for one of her employees or 40. As a result of her traveling, Kathy had to weave a network of support to help with her twin daughters while she was away. Her husband, who was also her business partner, played a large role in that support, but her extended family, as well, was a crucial element in her ability to do what she needed to do for her business.

For Terry Chase and Eric Hazell, the choice for Eric to stay home while his wife was raising money for her fledgling biotech company was difficult but clear. Terry truly wanted to stay home with her child, and actually cried most days when she had to leave, but another baby needed her as well. Her business baby was at a very early and delicate stage, and there was no way that it could have survived without her. There was no one else there to care for it, but she knew that her children were in good hands with their father. Since she was self-employed, Terry was able to go to work before the kids woke up and returned as they awoke from their afternoon nap. Daddy took care of them in between. With Terry out of the house, Eric began to feel the isolation of being a stay-at-home-dad and realized that he needed outside support as well. To that end, he founded the Bowie, Maryland, chapter of the stay-at-home-dads support group, DCMetroDads.

My need for outside business support became evident as ACT began to grow. I did not have anyone to talk with about different challenges. At what point do I hire an office manager? After a couple of years in business, the saying "It is lonely at the top" began to course through my head. When is a good time to bring in a salesperson? Should I bring in managers from the outside or try to promote from within? Who do I turn to when I am having issues with my business partner, who also happens to be my husband? I had a lawyer and an accountant I could talk with about certain issues, but I almost always had to pay them. It was time to emerge from my work cocoon and see if there was anyone out there experiencing the same things I was.

I got excited when I saw an event in the local newspaper that was put on by a group of women business owners. The idea of talking with a collection of other women that were, like me, crazy enough to start their own business, was intriguing. What excitement and power would be in that room!

When I arrived at the meeting of the Women Business Owners of Montgomery County (WBO), I was greeted warmly by Donna, the group's president. She made me feel instantly welcome. As I had suspected, the energy in that room was like lightning, and I knew then that I was hooked. Although the group consisted of different sizes and shapes of businesses with varying objectives, we all shared the common bond of entrepreneurship.

I owe a great deal of gratitude to my first mastermind group, which I joined as a result of that first meeting. A mastermind group is a peer mentoring group, and I credit mine for helping me to realize not only how isolated I had truly become but also that relief was available by conferring with others like me. The group held me accountable when I said I was going to do something and helped me see when I might not be going down the right path. Because of the success of my involvement with my small mastermind group, I went on to be an active member of WBO, including running their annual gala fund-raiser and serving on the board as president. While I did not secure new clients through the organization, my association brought me opportunities I never would have otherwise had, such as:

- Being on CNN Headline News.
- Meeting, and getting photographed with, the president of the United States.
- Traveling to Tunisia as an American delegate at an Arab Business Women's Conference.

As my company continued to grow, I began the painful transition from a programmer to the lead technical architect to the CEO. It was painful because I wasn't sure exactly what this evolution would mean or how to do it. I *knew* how to be a programmer—I had been doing that for years. What did I know about being the CEO of a company? I would sit at my desk and be busy without really doing anything. I resisted the temptation to purchase the latest computer adventure games such as Myst for fear that I would become addicted and never emerge to get anything done. Often, I would sit and ponder what I should be doing. That was when I finally realized that I needed a different level of outside help, and not necessarily from a therapist. I didn't have an internal mentor, so it was time to go find one on the outside.

That was when I found Lorraine Warshaw of Business Next, International. I met her through the National Women's Business Center in Washington, D.C. when I became a member of their CEO Roundtable. She was the volunteer facilitator, but it was easy to see why many companies paid her big bucks to consult with them. Lorraine was just what I needed at the time. She was smart, experienced, and very direct. When I was contemplating what to do about only having one, albeit very *large*, customer she told me candidly, "You don't have a business, you have a contract." Ouch. That hurt. But it was exactly what I needed to hear at the time. She motivated me to get busy expanding our customer base rather than allowing our primary customer to continue to consume all of the company's resources. Which brings up an important point about good advisers: They tell you what you need to hear, not necessarily what you want to hear. If you want to hear how wonderful you are, call your mother.

I also began meeting informally with a friend and neighbor who happened to also own a multimillion-dollar business. Sheila Drohan, president and founder of Corporate Fitness Works, met with me every couple of months and for the price of lunch (I tried to pay whenever she would let me!), I would pick her brain about different challenges I was facing in my business. After a year of this, she recommended that I look into joining her CEO peer group, which is organized through The Executive Committee (TEC—now called Vistage). She had been attending the once-a-month sessions for several months and received a great deal of value from the group. Interestingly enough, my lawyer, Sam, was a member of the same group and recommended I look into it within a week of Sheila's suggestion. Coincidence?

What I found in my TEC group was a collection of dedicated, super-sharp CEOs who believed in the peer mentoring process. All of the people in the group ran businesses that were larger than mine, which gave me something to aspire to and learn from. I formed close, personal relationships with people whose companies were 10 times the size of mine, and they were able to help me through the various ups and downs of growing my business with a "carefrontational" approach: confronting me with what I needed to hear, but doing so with care. In the beginning I was afraid that I would take a great deal from the group but not be able to offer anything to the other members. After all, I was still learning! I was pleasantly surprised to realize that my experiences and insight were different from the other members and provided value in different ways. I was also amazed that many of the other CEOs—men included—shared some of the same fears, problems, and issues that I did. That feeling that we were not qualified to be the CEO and that someday, someone would discover that we were imposters in the role was not uncommon. I was not alone—what a liberating thought!

While the time with my TEC group was valuable, I began to feel the need for something more. I needed a group of people who talked only about my business issues—I needed a board of advisers.

In talking with others and researching the role of a board of advisers, I quickly learned about the type of people I needed: people with the skills and expertise that I didn't have. To be well rounded, the group had to be represented by someone with financial expertise, management/operational experience, marketing/industry knowledge, and someone who understands and has mastered the entrepreneurial jungle—who has been where I am and knows how to spot the quicksand. I assembled a group that had all that and more, and they were invaluable in helping me to see not only the issues and challenges in my business but, more importantly, possible solutions. They were my external sounding board, and while they weren't compensated, there was an expectation of financial reward down the line when I created a formal board of directors. Unfortunately for them, that never happened, but my relationship with them has continued. In return, I have paid it forward by providing similar assistance to other budding entrepreneurs as payback for the time my advisers spent with me.

## From School Backpack to Briefcase

- Think twice before you threaten a consequence, and be prepared to follow through with it. Whether it is canceling a customer contract or disciplining an employee, idle threats undermine your authority. Also, I would think hard about hiring salespeople who drive crappy cars.

- Count to 10, punch the wall, or scream into a pillow before disciplining an employee or a child. Penalties levied in anger dilute the message and often lead to unintended consequences, such as lawsuits or fork marks.

- Unless you maintain control of your emotions, you run the risk of letting them mask your message. Let people focus on what you are saying rather than how you are saying it.

- Don't let your relationships cloud your judgment. The customer is not always right, but you need to respect an issue they have with an employee. Investigate complaints with a healthy amount of skepticism and an infinite amount of respect. I also don't recommend wearing jingle bells around people who are already irritated with you.

- The difference between deference and compliance stems from its origin. Ensuring that you earn respect rather than demand it results in a deeper and more meaningful relationship that has more staying power than forced compliance. Using the "Godfather" accent doesn't help either, so don't even try it.

- Your time is one of your businesses most precious assets—guard it as you would your money, because essentially that is what it represents. Don't get caught in the paradox of needing help but having no money to hire help—get creative in obtaining the assistance you need.

- Know your customers—who uses, who buys, what they buy, why they buy, and why they don't buy. Do not assume that you know what they want without asking them directly!

- Take the time to celebrate the small things in your business. If all else fails, make everyone put their hands up in the air and shout "Woohoo!" It is hard not to smile while you're doing that.

- Choose your battles wisely. Unless something keeps you from conducting your business profitably, serving your customers, promoting your culture, or obeying the law, let it go. Don't sweat the small stuff. Contrary to what your ego may be telling you, there might be better ways to do a task than the way you do it!

*(continued)*

- Promoting a positive "How Can We?" culture in your company fuels innovation and nurtures the ability to solve complex problems creatively. Listening to a bunch of whiners saying "I can't" is annoying and not very productive, anyway.
- Don't be timid in asking for outside advice. Seek out organizations that provide support and networking, but make sure you know what your objective is for associating with a specific group to ensure that you spend your time wisely. If you only go for the food, at least admit that.
- Build an outside board of advisers, but make sure you seek out people who are willing to tell you what you need to hear, not what you want to hear. Call your mom if you want to hear how great you are.

# Resources for Growing Businesses

## Books

Joe Batten and Mark Victor Hansen, *The Master Motivator: Secrets of Inspiring Leadership* (Deerfield Beach, Fla.: Health Communications, Inc., 1995).

Marcus Buckingham, *The One Thing You Need to Know . . . about Great Managing, Great Leading, and Sustained Individual Success* (New York: Free Press, 2005).

Stephen C. Lundin, Harry Paul, and John Christensen, *Fish! A Remarkable Way to Boost Morale and Improve Results* (New York: Hyperion, 2000).

John Maxwell, *Thinking for a Change: 11 Ways Highly Successful People Approach Life and Work* (New York: Warner Business Books, 2003).

Bob Rosner, Allan Halcrow, and Alan Levins, *The Boss's Survival Guide: Everything You Need to Know about Getting through (and Getting the Most out of) Every Day* (New York: McGraw-Hill, 2001).

## Support Groups/Web Sites

Service Corps of Retired Executives, www.score.org

Small Business Administration, www.sba.gov

Young Presidents Organization, www.ypo.org

Vistage (formerly TEC—The Executive Committee), www.vistage.com

## Support Groups and Resources Specifically for Women

National Association of Women Business Owners, www.nawbo.org

Women President's Organization, www.womenpresidentsorg.com

National Association of Female Executives, www.nafe.com

Women Entrepreneurs, Inc. www.we-inc.com

*Working Mother* magazine, www.workingmother.com

Women's Business Enterprise National Council, www.wbenc.org

### Terry Chase Hazell's Top Five Tips

1. Find advisers you respect and actually *listen* to them.
2. Don't be afraid to ask for help.
3. Don't be afraid to fail.
4. Truth will win in the end.
5. Always give a good handshake.

CHAPTER

# Growing Pains

Sydney was 11 when she asked me to let her make the dessert for the neighborhood picnic—*all by herself.* She had cooked some minor items solo before—macaroni and cheese (from a box), plain pasta. I had purchased a boxed mix to make a dessert "pizza" that sounded easy enough, so I let her try her hand at it. I helped her to choose the pots and utensils she would need and went upstairs to continue working.

About 10 minutes into her first solo experience as a cook, I heard a scream—"Mommmmm!" Isn't it interesting how parents learn to discern the "my sister is bothering me" scream from the "something is really wrong and I need you" scream? Taking the stairs by twos, I panted into the kitchen to see my plastic Pampered Chef microwave pot with gaping holes and dripping plastic. My daughter was trying to melt butter and while she used the right pot, she put it on the gas stove top instead of in the microwave. The pot was actually in flames and she was fortunate that she did not get burned or set the kitchen on fire. With fast thinking, she was able to briskly move the pot to the sink and douse the fire. The look of sheer terror mixed with relief on her face told me that she had learned a valuable lesson. I took a picture of the pot to put into her memory box, though she won't need the reminder. At least she didn't have to burn the house down to make the lesson stick.

## Introduction

Many people believe that being home with your children when they are babies is the *most* important thing. I disagree. As long as they were loved, safe, healthy, and stimulated in a positive way, I felt the early years were covered. I believe that being present for my children during the preteen and teen years are more critical to their future health and well-being. This is ideally when our children are learning to practice their values and to make good decisions. We can talk to them about those types of issues when they are young but, like business training, the lessons don't really congeal until they are practiced. Being present at this time in our children's lives affords opportunities to provide solid moral grounding and guidance, allowing them to make mistakes while we get out of the details of their lives and combat entitlement along the way. Equally important, being present at this point in our children's development also allows us to provide guidelines to help them choose their friends wisely and find their own special gifts. In business, this parallels the growing years and the lessons are strangely the same.

## Allowing for Mistakes

One of the hardest things we need to do as parents is let our children taste failure. This is hopefully done in harmless or repairable ways. At our house, this opportunity came with homework. Once our kids hit middle school, we began to let them manage their own responsibilities around school work. They were in charge of getting their homework done. One Friday morning, Sydney asked me to write a note to her teacher because she did not get her homework done. She claimed that because she went to her religious education class the night before—which was only an hour—she could not get all her homework done. I refused to write the note. She had to learn. We must do the same for the people who work for us.

Many large, successful companies have recognized that without failure, their company is not taking enough risks and thus likely to stagnate. iRobot's cofounder and chairman, Helen Greiner, was thankful to learn her lesson about failure early. In the early days, iRobot was all about innovation for innovation's sake, a common misstep of science-based companies. One of the first robots they built in working with the Army was extremely advanced technically, but it failed to meet several of the user's specific application needs. The customer thought the device was innovative and unique—maybe even "cool"—but they didn't buy it. Many entrepreneurs at this point will tell themselves and others that the customer "loved our product" while neglecting to focus on the more critical point that they didn't buy it. They will make excuses for the failed sale and miss the real point that Helen picked up: Praise for your product without sales is *no good!* People telling you that they love your product without buying it is good only for the ego, and that doesn't pay the bills. What Helen learned and then incorporated into her company was to solicit the users' input before designing their product so that they are meeting a need that the customer would be willing to pay to have met. Products that are just "cool," in the best case, can turn into a fad if they're not too expensive. Ultimately, however, there has to be a need that is being met—whether it is known or latent—for a product or service to truly take off. iRobot made a mistake but was astute enough to learn a valuable lesson from it and has continued to grow and thrive (Jena McGregor, "How Smart Companies Learn from Their Flops," *BusinessWeek,* July 10, 2006).

Sharon* came to work for me after 10 years of being home to raise her children. She was an educated, bright lady looking to get into a new career. Since she had been referred to us through a current employee, we took a chance in hiring her.

She started out in quality assurance but soon realized her passion was in writing and communications. Coincidentally, we were at the point in developing our software product that those were skills we needed. Sharon jumped in and took on this new role with gusto. She was excellent at organizing and clearly communicating complex concepts and quickly became the go-to person in our company for user documentation.

We had originally developed our software for a specific company, which meant that the documentation we had created was distinctly geared toward their needs. When we landed our next customer, our documentation had to be put into broad terminology for use by any user in any company. As is often the case in aggressive young companies, we sorely underestimated the time required to complete the task and did not have enough resources to put toward it. Sharon bravely stepped up and offered to take this task on, knowing that *not* meeting the deadline was a possibility.

As the weeks went on, I learned a valuable lesson about delegating critical tasks. I failed to incorporate interim milestones to ascertain the progress to keep the project from straying too far off track. This was the first major project Sharon had undertaken as the lead, and I was too busy with my own tasks to provide the needed guidance. I delegated it to her without coaching her on how to complete it successfully or checking on the progress until it was unmistakably lagging behind schedule. Many people had to step in at the last minute to assist with the writing tasks. Thankfully, she had created templates and guides, which made this last-minute effort possible without bringing down the quality of the final product. I had to do a considerable amount of writing on my family vacation, but the lessons we both learned were invaluable.

In some companies a project gone awry to that extent would have resulted in serious disciplinary action. That, however, was not my style. Sharon had stepped up and taken the project on and was not going to be penalized for it; I had to share some of the blame. I let my own frenzied "busyness" get in the way of what I really needed to be doing—managing the business. I did not want to foster a culture of people afraid to take risks with their careers by not stretching themselves. Sharon stretched herself, learned a valuable lesson, and continued to work with us for many more years turning out excellent work products. She was an integral part of our team's success and grew personally from the experience. I grew as well and learned that delegation with abdication is a formula for failure. You must give employees enough lead to accomplish their tasks but also provide a net to catch them before they smack the ground if they fall.

Allowing for failure should not be reserved only for employees—entrepreneurs need to embrace this possibility for themselves as well. My father had a unique perspective on failure. When he was in private high school, one of the priests asked him what he would do if he failed. My father replied, "I can't fail." Astounded at my father's arrogance, the priest challenged him and threatened to flunk him for his comment. My father clarified: "I can't fail if I learn something from the failure."

I have taken this philosophy to heart. Thankfully, my failures to date have been small or at least reversible. I have tried to set an example for my employees by openly admitting and addressing my failures publicly so that others would follow my lead. My hope was that they would in turn face decisions without fear of failure, or if they were afraid, do it anyway.

When we were recruiting a development manager, one of my long-time technical guys stepped up and offered to take over management responsibilities. He was well liked by his peers, so we thought it was a reasonable risk. Unfortunately, it did not work for a number of reasons, but I could not fire him. What message would I be sending to the others in the company? He had taken a risk and failed, but with good intentions—he was pitching in where the company needed help. Though it was hard for him to make the adjustment in returning to his previous role, punishing him for taking a risk would have established the wrong precedent.

There is a general perception that in order to be an entrepreneur you need to be a big risk taker. Most successful business owners I know would disagree. Entrepreneurs must be willing to take risks, but they are calculated risks. We take a look at all of the information and options available at the time, review the worst-case possibilities, and then make a decision. Some of my friends thought I was crazy to jump out of a "perfectly good" airplane, but I was strapped to someone who knew what he was doing. He had a vested interest in my *not* failing at that task—I took a calculated risk.

Managers who are afraid of failure or being wrong often get stuck in "analysis paralysis." They are apprehensive to make a decision until they have all the information they need, but in business we rarely have all the information we need. It is like trying to buy a new computer but waiting until the latest model is out. There will always be a later model that is faster, better, and cheaper, so if you wait, you will never buy one.

Lack of information throws many people for a loop, which renders decision making difficult. This is especially prevalent among scientists-turned-entrepreneurs. Professionally disciplined scientists are trained *not* to guess at anything—to make sure that the data is available to back up any statement made. Otherwise, they say, a statement without supporting data is just a hypothesis and cannot be presented as fact. In preparing these scientists to be entrepreneurs, we have coached them into embracing imperfect information. We illustrated how it is sometimes required to move forward based on best guess or gut feel when all the data is not available. Sometimes you just have to go with what you have and make the best decision you can with the information available at the time. This is often one of the toughest lessons for fact-based professionals.

## Combating Entitlement

How can our children—and people in general—not feel privileged, a sense of entitlement? Doors open automatically for us as we approach them. Walkways move so we don't have to walk, and escalators carry us up stairs so we don't have to climb. We don't have to get up to change the television channel—just point and click. As if that isn't enough, there are now voice-activated remote controls so you can change the channel without really moving. And now we don't even have to get directions because the computer in our car will tell us, turn by turn, how to get anywhere.

Payton was excitedly anticipating her approaching sixteenth birthday. She was going to get her driver's license. She had visions of learning to drive and the ensuing freedom that comes with passing the driver's test and journeying out on her own.

When she asked her parents about taking a driver's education course several months before her birthday, she learned that freedom was going to have to wait. Her parents viewed driving a car at 16 as a privilege, not a right. They did not feel that she was ready to deal with the responsibility that accompanies driving a car. She had to wait—driving at 16 was not a given. This was not the result she had anticipated or preferred but something she had to live with. When she finally got her driver's license at 17, she was better prepared, as were her parents.

My daughter started to think that having the latest and greatest computerized game console was a *right*. When she was little, we bought her a handheld electronic game as a way to help develop her eye–hand coordination. It didn't hurt that it entertained her in the car on long trips. It seemed more active than just watching videos and, with some games, had the potential to stimulate creative problem solving and critical thinking. Little did we know that we were creating a monster.

Once she was old enough to notice the new "devices" that were coming out in the market, the negotiations began. This is when she got her first lesson in the difference between a right and a privilege. In our house, anything electronic is a privilege. Most children go through phases with their attraction to these home electronics (television, computers, Game Boys) and when my younger daughter gets attracted, it can get ugly.

There was a particular show she wanted to watch—a "never before seen" episode of her latest favorite tween sitcom. I can't remember the particular reason, but that night I said no. She proceeded to throw herself on the ground and produce the most annoying whiny cry. She launched into a 10-year-old temper tantrum. I was unfair. All she wanted to watch was 30 minutes. And while we're at it, her friend has a television in her room. Why can't she have a television in her room? And a laptop? Why am I such a mean mom?

After dismissing her upstairs until she calmed down, we had the all-too-familiar discussion about the difference between a privilege and a right. Having air to breathe is a right. Being able to express her emotions, too, is a right, though I also have the right to send her to her room in order not to hear her whining. Eating is a right. Television is a privilege. She found out that anytime she begins to get an unhealthy attachment to any privilege, she loses it for a week until she realizes how unimportant it really is.

When we consistently provide a privilege to our children or employees without tying it to a specific behavior or value, they can begin to feel entitled to it. I never in my wildest dreams thought giving someone a large bonus would be a bad thing, until it happened.

It had been our practice from the beginning to give our employees a portion of our annual earnings as a bonus. Because we had previously enjoyed ample profits, some staff members came to expect their bonus and even plan for it. Being a privately held company, our employees did not have visibility into our financials, but they knew in general that we were doing well. We had great years and shared generously with everyone who had contributed to our success. Our staff had worked hard and deserved every bit of what they were given.

Our mistake was that we didn't create a formula by which to assign bonuses. We calculated bonuses based on contribution to the business versus compensation, but it was admittedly subjective. The next year when we foresaw a dip in our revenues, we tried to set the appropriate expectations with regard to bonuses. We wanted to prepare everyone that the previous year's boon would not be equaled that year. We chose to forgo part of our own personal distributions that year in order to give bonuses that were larger than we should have or would have typically given, but didn't tell anyone what we had done. While most expressed appreciation, rumor had it that some were not so pleased. They felt they deserved more than what they got.

There is such a thing as giving too much when it comes to bonuses. In giving a bonus, you are setting an expectation, and if you are not clear in communicating the conditions around the bonus (more specific than "if we do well, you do well"), disappointment and entitlement are bound to raise their ugly head. That's why it is good to educate everyone in your company on the difference between a privilege and right from the very beginning.

Employees have a right, by law, to their salary. They have a right to be treated fairly. Bonuses are a privilege that needs to be determined objectively so as not to be perceived as unfair. Dispensation of any privilege should be closely coupled with an understanding of the values through which it has been granted. Otherwise, it will become an entitlement.

## Getting Out of the Details

My daughter had a crush on a boy at school and I didn't know it. To some parents, that might not seem like such a big deal. To me, this was a wake-up call. I had always wanted to be the type of mom that my daughters could confide in. I was going to be the *cool* mom. So when I found out about the crush from one of her friends, I was devastated.

When I asked her about it, she got quiet and had a familiar grin on her face, a grin I am sure I sported at the same age when a similar subject came up with my mom. She was embarrassed. I realized then that I was no longer involved in or even aware of the little details in her life. I wasn't about to give up totally, though. I still knew all of her close friends as well as their parents. But I didn't know who her friends had crushes on or who was going out with whom. I still knew where she was at all times, roughly, and retained the right to snoop on her computer at any time. The computers she was permitted to use were in common areas of our house, so there was no such thing as private computer use. Whenever I approached her while she was instant messaging someone I did not recognize, I would simply ask her and she had to tell me who it was and let me look at their online profile. Call it a random inspection. It was part of our agreement for allowing her access to the computer and the Internet (a privilege, not a right). I have tried to strike the right balance of getting out of the details while retaining macro-level control over critical issues. If only it had been that painless at work.

To truly appreciate the following story, you have to understand how intimately involved I was in the creation of my company's software in the early days. I was working side by side with the other programmers and probably developed a good third to half of our initial software release. As the company grew, I knew I needed to get out of the details, but it was harder than I thought it would be. Having a technical team I could trust helped, but I could not yet envision what I should be doing instead.

I had been counseled that if I were going to grow my business, I had to stop working *in* it and work *on* it instead. I got that, but I did not know how to do that. When you're the doer, it is much easier to do a task yourself. You know you can do it better and faster. While it is also more comfortable for you to continue tending to the details, it doesn't get your company away from being You, Inc.

We had just released our first major software version that I was not involved in, and it was killing me. I was working late one night at the office when the support line rang. Since I was the only one there, I answered the call. The person on the other end of the phone worked for a customer I knew well, but I was not familiar with the voice. That was a first. Even more amazingly, at least to me: I didn't know the function that they were having a problem with. I had become so accustomed to being the one with all the answers that I didn't know what to say. I used a phrase I hadn't uttered in years: "I'll have to research this and get back to you."

The growing business also meant we needed to start building a management team. It was time to get my name and Keenan's name off of all the boxes on our organization chart. We knew our first manager was going to be a key hire, so we tried to go about it the right way—we solicited the input of the people who would work for him or her. Our employees were involved in drafting the description of the responsibilities for this position (a mini version of a job description) as well as participating in the actual interview process. Everyone seemed pleased with the candidate we ended up hiring, or at least they were content for the first 30 days.

Admittedly, I wasn't quite sure how much to pull out of this new manager's department. Keenan had been managing that department prior to that, and he was ready to pull out of the business altogether. In fact, we had just let our nanny know that we no longer needed her services because he was going cut back to part time so he could be home when the kids got off the school bus. Besides, this new manager had more management experience than I did, this being my first management job, so I gave him more leeway than I probably should have.

By the time the complaints from long-time employees reached my ears, it was too late—the damage had been done. The morale in his department was at an all-time low. I realized then that I had pulled out too far. I recognized that I had failed to apply the same logic that I had employed with my daughter: Get out of the details while retaining macro-level control over critical issues. One of the critical issues I had lost sight of was communication. This manager's philosophy was that information sharing was very hierarchical. Our chain of command was put in place more for guidance than for strict control. There was a clear mismatch in our company culture and the way he operated.

Another discord came from how loosely our company was controlled at the time and what he was comfortable with. We had yet to develop a performance planning and evaluation system (that came later) and we were still working on developing how our management team was going to work together. I believe he was used to having everything already set up in a controlled manner and did not have the patience to go with the flow as we developed those processes for ourselves. I am sure he would make a fine manager in a company with a different operating philosophy and already-defined processes.

What I also concluded from that experience was that the culture of my company was one of those critical issues that I could not pull out of. I had to retain control over that. Rather than focusing our hiring solely on the best skill for the job, we had to also pay attention to the candidate's fit within the culture of our organization.

Another realization we came to was that we must get our processes in place. We needed guidelines in order to achieve consistency in management and execution. It was time to look at formalizing our human resource tools and internal processes to aid in the control over the macro-level issues.

## Creating Consistency

We learned early that consistency and routine in our children's lives were important. A consistent bedtime and recurring chores helped them maintain some sense of order in their lives. As they got older, the need for constants became even more apparent. Their lives began to get more hectic with activities as the expectations placed upon them from school and approaching adulthood continued to increase. Maintaining a routine grew to be crucial as the social life and extracurricular activities of a preteen began to encroach on schoolwork and home life.

While some children can focus on schoolwork later in the evening, we knew our kids' most productive time was right after school. When they came home from school, they were to get a snack, relax for a little bit, and then dive into homework. On nights they had additional activities, conforming to the plan became even more important. The more we deviated from the scheme, the harder it was to return to it and catch up—just like attending church or working out.

When we attended Mass on a regular basis, there was no resistance from the troops to get up, get dressed, and get moving. When we fell out of that routine, getting the kids motivated on a Sunday morning was met with resistance. Likewise with exercise—I notice when I am diligent in my routine, it becomes easier to keep. I miss it when I don't do it. Being sick or otherwise releasing myself from that habit makes it all the more difficult to pick back up. Maintaining consistency is essential.

Providing a constant, predictable result in business requires that we develop a process that ensures uniformity. Mary Cantando relays a story about the value of teaching your children about developing processes. Her youngest son, Matt, was so excited when he bought his first new house. Because he had the limited funds of a 24-year-old, he decided to install four ceiling fans himself rather than adding that onto his mortgage. One weekend Mary and her husband, John, headed to Matt's place for the "Great Fan Installation." Thankfully, he'd had the good sense to buy four fans that were identical in style and size—a first step that Southwest Airlines has proven to be a good one. By utilizing the same model aircraft on all their routes, they maximize the strength of their maintenance procedures because they can leverage them across the company. It also cuts down on the spare parts inventory since they don't need three different doohickeys for three different models of airplanes.

Matt hoped he and his Dad could get all four fans installed on Saturday morning; then they would have the afternoon to purchase and install a screen door. That was not going to happen. They unpacked the first fan in the guest bedroom. After many expletives, they finally got it up, but the light wouldn't turn on. They took it down. They got it up again, but the fixture wobbled when the fan was turned on. They took it down. On the third try, they finally got it right. The total elapsed time: four and a half hours.

At this rate, it looked as if it would take the entire weekend to install the four fans. However, because the fans all went up the same way, they were able to develop a process to streamline the installation of the second one; that took just under two hours. The third one, then, took less than an hour. By the time they got to the fourth fan, they had streamlined their process so much that they had it up in about 45 minutes. Given the productivity benefit of processes in ceiling fan installation, can you imagine how much more valuable consistent processes could be in a business?

I learned an important lesson in business consistency before I even started my company. I was asked to head up a proposal effort for a large project opportunity that was in an area we were trying to break into. It was different than anything we had ever taken on before, which meant we were essentially starting up a new business. We were in competition for the project with a large consulting firm that had been performing this type of engagement for years.

One differentiator that our competition touted to their prospective clients was their process. Being new at this, we did not yet have a process, though we tried to present ourselves as if we did. When the client asked if they could interview our proposed project team, I did not think anything of it. I knew the team was sharp and could answer any question that they posed. What I did not anticipate is that they would be looking for uniformity in those answers. Prompted by our competition, the customer was specifically interviewing our team looking for evidence of an undeviating process. We failed miserably. I vowed at that moment to do it right someday.

When I founded my company years later, I could still feel the bruise of that experience. I became vigilant about setting up standards for our software development and checklists for our internal processes. No software would be accepted by the testing group without a completed developer checklist. No functions could be sent to the client without going through our documented test cases. Developing software "on the fly" was a thing of the past. The result was a consistently high level of quality in our software that our customers valued.

What I did not realize in the beginning was the importance of setting up other types of processes within the company as well. As a self-proclaimed computer geek, the technical stuff came naturally. It was not until I started building my management team that I realized it was time to formalize our human resource (HR) processes as well.

Since this was not my area of expertise, I hired an outside consultant to help us with the task. The first thing she asked to see was our job descriptions. Yeah, those things. We didn't exactly *have* job descriptions, except for the responsibilities we had outlined for our recent management hire. At least it was not hard for her to decide where we needed to start.

What I learned was that my gut instinct, which told me that no one should be surprised when they get fired, could be rectified by putting a formal HR process into place. It would also provide us with consistency among managers and thereby lessen our exposure and risk of lawsuits.

We were concerned that implementing job descriptions would constrain our staff from doing whatever needed to be done. Our consultant taught me that the job description was just the beginning—it was how we set certain position-specific expectations. We could still encourage initiative and teamwork, working outside of your job description, through our measurement system. That was the task we tackled next. We needed to develop a process for evaluating the staff where we could make sure we encouraged and rewarded the appropriate behaviors.

The process that we undertook was very educational. We started by looking at the characteristics of our most successful employees. What we found were behaviors that were consistent across them all and those became our competencies, which were the basis for our evaluations. Among these competencies were teamwork, drive for results, initiative, and adaptability. What was not covered in the job description was reinforced through these competencies. When new employees came on board, we introduced them to these desired behaviors so they would know how they were being evaluated.

Another key element of the process was setting individual goals, which we called a professional development plan. This plan included a list of competencies targeted for development, professional development objectives, and career goals. We also included individual business goals with detailed action steps, time frames, and how success in that goal would be measured.

As we were creating objectives for individuals, we needed to ensure that their targets were tied to departmental goals, which in turn needed to be clearly connected to our corporate concerns. That meant that our corporate priorities, which we called our Top Five, had to be clearly communicated. Department goals, in turn, had to be derived from the higher-level ones. It was a sometimes painful exercise, as the management team often disagreed on the direction or priorities. Our ability to dissent as a team was critical (see the next section, "Encouraging Productive Conflict"), and the results were better than they would have been had I developed the Top Five alone. The outcome of this process guaranteed that we were all marching in the same direction and contributed to our ability to produce consistent results. Holding people accountable was the last piece of that puzzle.

As discussed in the "Following Through" section in Chapter 5, encouraging specific behaviors or actions requires execution of consequences. We had to ensure that managers were holding both formal and informal reviews according to our schedules and identifying appropriate repercussions for missed deadlines. This was a challenge for me personally because I was often managing people that were older than I was. While this was also generally difficult in a small and growing company because of the lack of time, it was clear that it was necessary in order to manage the growth and pro-duce the consistent results we required.

## Encouraging Productive Conflict

If we continually solve our children's problems for them, they will never develop problem-solving skills themselves. Since my daugh-ters are so close in age, the noise of their fighting is a common din in our household. The younger one wants to play and her sister won't play with her. She wants to see a page in the craft book they're both working with. They can't agree on which movie to watch and there is only one television available. Keenan and I have tried to give them the tools to deal with conflict without solving the problems ourselves. The lessons have been hard and too many times result in screaming and crying, with someone getting hurt. It is certainly delayed gratification, but we are making progress.

One of my recent summer goals was to teach my children how to do their own laundry. My sole direction to them was to work together to get their laundry done. Ha! If only it had been that easy. Every time they came to me with a problem or a discrepancy in who was doing more work, I calmly told them to work together to find a solution. When it was clear that I wasn't stepping in, they would har-rumph off and discuss (okay, scream about) the issue together.

As the day progressed and the laundry was actually getting done, their conversations became less combative and more cooper-ative. At one point, I even caught them counting the pieces of laun-dry that each had folded to make sure they were even. Although that is not how I would have directed them to solve the problem, it was working for them and for me as a result.

When my brother and I would fight as children, my mother would often just let us duke it out. He would tackle me, pin my arms down, and let spit drop out of his mouth until it almost hit my face and then quickly suck it back up. Sometimes the suck came too late and I would scream. My pleas for help were met with resist-ance from a mother teaching her children to be resourceful and to solve their own problems.

Conflict in the workplace does not necessarily involve screaming or tackling. Any time two people disagree, there is a type of conflict present that is not necessarily bad. Through the years I've witnessed firsthand a variety of styles and approaches to conflict in the workplace—some that worked and some that didn't. One employee we had (for a short time) indicated that she thought bullying people was the best approach to get what she wanted. Funny, that didn't come across when I interviewed her. It also did not bode well for her in our culture of teamwork.

## Worlds Colliding

Running late for a meeting, as is often the case, I grabbed a pair of pantyhose out of my drawer, put them on, and ran out the door. About halfway through the meeting I was facilitating, my pantyhose started creeping down. The more I moved, the worse it got. It didn't help that my previously flat stomach was no longer smooth. When I finally got to the bathroom, I realized I had grabbed a pair of maternity pantyhose. Since I still had hours to go and going "au naturel" at this point wasn't an option, I ran to my office, gathered the waist of the pantyhose, and stapled them. Thankfully, my jacket hid the bulge.

Another gentleman seemed to really like conflict—or like being right—and would badger someone with logical arguments to his point. He rarely let up until they would either succumb or pretend to concede to get him to move on. One afternoon he and I were standing in the hallway and I made a comment about a decision our customer had made with which I did not agree. He had a different perspective and did not hesitate to share it with me. Before the conversation went on too long, I cut him off: "There is no harm in my thinking the way I do, so just let it go." That ended that conversation. Not all unproductive conflict ends so easily, however.

Paul Silber relayed a specific occasion in his company where he had to turn fruitless bickering into a productive solution. The dispute developed because of a perceived product quality problem. The production manager was always defending the quality of the device and attacking the sales manager for doing a poor job of teaching their customers to use it. At the same time, the sales manager was attacking the quality of their product and defending his sales team. They evolved into "warring camps" that were merely tossing grenades at each other while failing to either look for the source of the problem or get any closer to a resolution. They called a meeting to get all of the stakeholders together, some of whom had to fly in from out of town. Sitting together in a room, the team was able to focus on the issues, come up with solutions, and stop pointing fingers at each other.

Paul has found that two of the people he valued most in his organization were his chief operating officer and his laboratory director. Both of those individuals constantly challenged many of the ideas he came up with or the directions he wanted to take. Their questioning was not negative. Alternatively, he found that it helped him to double-check whatever rationale he might have had for making a particular decision. In some cases, challenges from his managers caused him to completely change a decision he had made, but at a minimum acted as a sanity check. He eventually started interviewing prospective employees to determine their willingness to address conflict by asking for situations where they had done so in the past.

Terry Chase Hazell experienced negative conflict through an employee who harbored a passive-aggressive attitude. He withheld important information and even "forgot" to tell her about an appointment with a very important partner at which she was expected to speak. Somehow he remembered to attend the meeting. He was often unable to take delegation and would always point to her alleged inadequate instruction as the reason he could not complete a task. Early in her career, she spent time "helping" him adjust to her instructions, denying that a real conflict existed. She was afraid to address the behavior because its passive nature was so hard to specifically describe. However, dozens of management books and advisers later, she spoke with him about this behavior and the passive nature of their conflict. He was completely surprised. She was direct with him, and the result was satisfactory for all involved. He chose to leave the company.

Terry sees the same behavior in her teenager. Because of her experience at work, she recognized it immediately and addressed it rather than ignoring it or offering to "help" more. She told her to get her dirty clothes off the floor, and the result is her clothes are hanging from her bed, dresser, chair and every available shelf. When questioned, she will refer back to the instruction: "You said *off the floor.*" Terry takes that conflict head on.

Most people, however, do whatever they can to avoid conflict. That was the camp that I was in when it came to managing employees in the beginning. Thankfully, I learned, but not without some bumps and bruises.

When our company was still very small, we were not good at documenting employee expectations or conducting regular performance evaluations. In fact, it wasn't until we had already passed the $2 million mark in revenues that we realized we really needed these tools. Unfortunately, not having these critical documents made any performance-related discussions with an employee extremely difficult. I have learned that no one should be surprised when they are fired from a job. Unless they just do something outrageous, it should be made clear to them along the way what they are doing that isn't working and given a fair chance to correct it.

I don't even like to buy cars, so owning my business was an opportunity to embrace conflict, both personally and professionally. Thinking about a forthcoming clash made me so sick to my stomach that—and I hate to admit this—my husband had to fire one of my employees. It was, in fact, the first person that I would have ever fired, except that I didn't actually fire her—he did. She was an extremely nice woman who had been with our company for less than a year. She was a programmer, but her skills were shallow and she had very few critical problem-solving skills. She knew the programming tool we used but didn't really understand much more than the basic mechanics. It took so much of our other programmers' time to help her with her assignments that her net contribution was negative—she was actually a drain on our resources. It was clear she had to go for the better of the whole company. I knew that if she didn't leave, I would lose other, more experienced programmers instead. The problem was that she tried hard and was so darn nice.

To make matters worse, she had baked a cake (from scratch!) for my daughter's fourth birthday a few months earlier. While I now know that should not have ever come into consideration, I couldn't help it. She had touched my heart.

Leading up to the day, I resolved myself that I was going to do it. I was going to suck it up and just do it. The morning of the firing came and, suddenly, I could not get out of bed. I had not slept the night before from thinking about what I had to do and worked myself into a frenzy of nerves. I could not fire her. Keenan, who did not really work with her, had to do my dirty work. The funny thing was, after Keenan lowered the boom, she looked at him and said, "Julie couldn't do it, could she?" She knew. My secret was out—I wasn't fooling anyone! When I heard that, I vowed that would *never* happen again, and it hasn't. As hard as it was for me, I had to learn to embrace conflict. I could not let Keenan become the "hatchet man."

I am sorry to say that I have had the unfortunate experience of firing other people since and will never get used to it. At least I am able to do it, though. I believe if you ever get to where you enjoy firing people, you should stop managing people.

So how did I get over my fear of conflict? My fear never went away. I started to do what I needed to do in spite of my fear. As an adviser so deftly pointed out to me, logic does not overcome fear, only experience does. I had to reposition my business in my mind as just that—a business. Although we had a very warm, familial atmosphere in our company, I couldn't approach it as such. I had to look at it as strictly business.

As the company continued to grow and my role in the company began to change, I started to embrace conflict so much that I felt like there wasn't enough of it happening around the office and at meetings. Not that I wanted a free-for-all, but I wanted even less to have a company of people nodding their heads up and down like the bobble-head figures that sit in the back windows of cars. What I discovered by reading and talking with friends and mentors is that although conflict is unavoidable, there is a way to approach it so that it is productive, as opposed to destructive.

Greg, our chief operating officer, had the right approach. When we were working on revising the way we measured our employees, he provided a strong argument for tracking and evaluating people based on the percentage of their hours that are logged against a customer project, or their *billable hours*. He came from a consulting company for which that method worked well. For our management meeting, he made his case with detailed pros and cons in a very unemotional argument. After our discussion, I decided not to go in that direction for a number of reasons, and Greg accepted the verdict gracefully. He never again brought up the issue or seemed to begrudge implementing the decision I had made. That is a sign of a true professional.

The basis for productive conflict arises from the respect or trust that each member has for the others. Each person's preconceived notions about the other person's intelligence, motive, or background experience plays into how well (or not!) they interact with each other.

One area in which I did not have any problem with conflict was in fighting for what I believed was a technically correct approach to a problem. It was with one of our customers, Ernie, that I was most often able to practice that form of conflict. At 6 feet 4 inches and 280 pounds, Ernie was a commanding figure. He was also technically savvy. Very few people inside or outside his company stood up to him. Anytime we discussed design issues where I did not agree with his approach, I voiced my disagreement. I approached the issues in a nonpersonal, nonemotional, and logical way. I think he appreciated the fact that I contradicted him because it showed I cared enough to get it right. We also had a mutual respect for each other and an underlying trust that we were both ultimately working toward the same goal. All are critical characteristics for productive conflict.

Some women I have spoken with turned to entrepreneurship as a way to avoid conflict with their boss or job—disagreements over hours, job responsibilities, the right approach to take with a customer or product, and so on. In my experience, conflict is not something you can avoid in business, nor should you want to. When approached correctly, conflict can actually help your business thrive by opening it up to new ideas and defying conventional thinking. Truly effective innovation is impossible without challenging the norm in some way. The bottom line is that constructive and respectful conflict is a useful tool for identifying problems, getting all possible solutions out on the table, and then developing the best plan of attack.

## Choosing Your Friends Wisely

When our children are little, we have total control over their play dates and, as a result, their friends. We see who they interact with on the playground and can decide it is time to go if we're not comfortable with the chosen playmate. Elementary school is generally a tight-knit group with small classes, so it isn't hard to get to know who your child is spending time with if you so desire. As parents, we have dominion over their social lives—at least until they reach middle school.

In my daughter's middle school, three different elementary schools converge into one. I quickly discovered that I no longer knew the parents of all Sydney's friends. While she tended to hang around the same pack of girls—all good girls—the group did start to expand. I refused to let her go over to someone's house unless I had talked to and knew the parents. While that wasn't a popular position from Sydney's perspective, I believe strongly in the power of the people we associate with. The people we hang around have a profound influence on our development. Until children develop a "creep filter" for themselves, it is incumbent upon us as parents to help them understand what to look for as they learn how to choose friends based on solid criteria. For example, friends that make you feel bad about yourself are not true buddies. Friends should help you to be the best person you can be and encourage you along the way. It seems like the maturation of this filtering ability varies from child to child, so it is important to know your kid.

It would be nice if by the time we become adults we have fully developed a filter for finding the right sort of people to spend time with. For our business, given that our time is one of our scarcest resources, this is critical. Unfortunately, the filter isn't always active or acknowledged.

Some people pride themselves on being great judges of character, but the interview process can interfere with our natural filters, making it hard to hire the right people. There are books and seminars on how to interview a candidate, but somehow when we get wrapped up in our growing business venture, we lose sight of that wisdom. One reason could be the pressure we feel from waiting until we really need the resources to look for them. We are often under the gun and so desperate to have a position filled that we forget that we need to hire slowly. As managers of a growing concern, we also fail to recognize that different people and skills may be needed as our organizations grow and change. This is especially characteristic of companies that enjoyed early success in building a strong start-up team. We absolutely fell into this trap.

In the beginning, with a few exceptions, I brought people into the business that I knew or with whom I had worked. While we did hire a couple folks that did not fit in or otherwise work out, we were moving so fast that it became obvious fairly quickly and we moved them out of the business before they began to bring it down. As a result, the core group we started with was outstanding. As we began to grow, I started thinking about the type of person I should be hiring based on some preconceived (and later discovered as *false*) notions of how the business should be run. I also received advice from outside consultants and advisers who did not really know my business or understand the underlying dynamics of our culture. I ignored my instincts and followed what others said that sounded correct.

While I knew that I did not have to personally like everyone I hired, I sometimes hired people *because* I did not particularly like them but thought they could do the job. My last sales manager was a perfect example. My intent at the time was to prove that I could make an objective hiring decision. We even administered a personality test that had been recommended to us by an adviser. He emerged as the type of salesperson we needed—aggressive and persistent. He pursued us, and we took that as a good sign. Unfortunately, I learned quickly that I should have trusted my personal filter and that of my team. He was a bad choice who began to spread morale problems and negative vibes through the company like a contagious disease. For some of our core team, catching that ailment proved to be terminal.

I realized from a personal development side that the people I spent time with mattered a great deal as well. Everyone remembers where they were on 9/11/01 and what lifelong lesson that day taught them. One of my wake-up calls from that day is not typical of what you would expect. I was at a meeting of my TEC (The Executive Committee) CEO roundtable with guest speaker, author Tom Hill. Ironically, he gave a presentation on making the most of our lives prior to the news breaking about the devastating terrorist attacks. The one thing that he said that I will never forget and changed my life was: "You are the average of the 10 people you spend the most time with." Wow. What a thought. Who was it that I was spending most of my time with? My husband and kids? They were good. But when I began to examine more closely my affiliations and with whom I was spending my time, I saw a void. Generally speaking, I tended to hang around people who had different life goals and dreams than I do. My friends were good people with whom we had a great deal of fun, but there were sparse opportunities for professional advancement and personal growth. We had few real deep or broad conversations of any nature, much less of a professional nature. Mostly, we just talked about our kids or neighborhood gossip. While this was fine, it was time to expand my network. I needed to seek out others who were, as Tom put it, on a rung higher than I was on the ladder of life.

The key was to find those people who not only had achieved what I wanted to achieve, but did it in a way that was consistent with my values. After all, I didn't want to align myself with people whose methods and approaches were in conflict with my own. Slowly and intentionally, I have been seeking out the right sort of people to add to my list of friends and am happy to say that while I probably don't get to spend enough time with them, my current set of friends represents a group of people that not only support me in what I do but inspire me to do even greater things. As a result of the support and mentorship I have received from my friends,

I enthusiastically work with other women to help them reach their goals and be their best.

Marissa Levin has been fortunate to populate her company with people she considers her mentors. She cites each of her vice presidents as someone she has learned valuable lessons from. Her VP of government affairs has taught her the ins and outs of marketing to and doing business with the government. Her VP of technology has shown her how embracing the right technology can—and has—advanced her company. She is adamant that acquiring people with the right set of skills that complement her own and compensate for her weaknesses has been a critical factor in propelling her business beyond her imagination.

## Not Taking It Personally

It is difficult for parents not to take their children's behavior personally. Our hope is that even if they act rotten when they're with us, they resemble an angel around other people. What parent doesn't feel a twinge of embarrassment when their child says or does something we don't like, shows bad judgment, or is just plain rude? We take it personally.

When my daughter was fairly young, we were walking through the grocery store and came up behind a rather large woman. My daughter blurted out before I could stop her "Mommy, that lady is fat!" I cringed. I wanted to run away and hide. Rather than avoiding the situation, I explained to her (loudly enough that the woman could hear me) that her comment was rude and uncalled for. Poor kid, she was just being honest and calling it like she saw it. The woman was gracious enough to turn around and smile, no doubt noticing my scarlet face and guilty expression. What are you going to do?

Madison is old enough now to be responsible for putting away her own laundry. I fold it but leave it on the bed for her to put away. When she does, she shoves as many garments into her dresser drawer as she can fit. Often, this means that she goes to school looking as if she has slept in her clothes. Should I take my daughter's appearance personally? Many parents do. I don't have time to iron her clothes and put them away for her. My philosophy has been to teach her to do it herself. Unfortunately, that may also mean that other moms in the neighborhood think that my children's sloppy dress is a negative reflection on me. Oh, well. I can't own that, though it does require a tough skin to adopt that stance when there is a risk that others see it differently. I can't let it bother me that others might see me as a Slacker Mom. I know I am not in areas that I believe count more than wrinkled shirts.

For entrepreneurs, it is equally difficult not to take the bumps in the road personally. After all, our business is our baby. If our business appears wrinkled, it is certainly a reflection on us as the owners, isn't it? Things that don't go the way we want feel personal.

When Steve quit the first time, I had a hard time not taking it personally. I had connected with Steve over the Internet before it was common to do so. He was one of our first employees. He and I developed a bond—we had the same perspective on technical solutions and quickly developed a mutual respect for each other's technical abilities. We used each other as a sounding board when working through technical design issues, and it was through my confidence in him that I was able to pull out of the technical details of our software development. When I did pull out of the details, however, Steve felt like he had lost his confidant. I felt guilty for previously abandoning him and angry that he was leaving. I took his leaving as sign of a lack of faith in me. I was totally wrong.

Steve was actually leaving for personal reasons. He was burnt out. The commute—which was an hour both ways some days—was killing him. He also thought he wanted to return to more in-depth development as opposed to his current role developing requirements and providing customer support. He believed he was doing what was best for him and his family, and it had absolutely *nothing* to do with me.

I've learned since that people ultimately need to (and *will*) do what is best for them personally, while I need to do what is best for the business. A friend was thinking about leaving her job but felt like she owed it to the company to stay and asked me what she should do. I told her that if the company had to eliminate her position, while they might feel really bad about it, they would do what is best for the business. It isn't personal, I told her, it is just business. As hard as that is for entrepreneurs to accept, erecting an emotional buffer between you and your business may not change what happens with your business, but it can add years to your life from the reduction in stress.

After letting my sales manager, Ted, go, I was alerted to a multitude of dubious charges on his company credit card. For example, he charged $100 against his personal cell phone bill. When questioned, he replied that he did it because he had seen that line item in his budget and thought he should use it. Per our company policy, he was asked to submit proof that the reimbursed calls were business related, but the evidence never surfaced. He had also charged an expensive meal with his buddy that, when confronted, he rationalized as a potential partnership. The company his friend worked for had never entered our radar or our discussions until I inquired about the charge several weeks later. I felt more and more abused as additional questionable expenditures were uncovered. I was hurt and angry. This was personal. It was *my* money this man was spending. I had to work diligently to personally forgive him or risk letting my ire fester into a grudge that would torture no one but me. He was gone; I had to let it go. Again, I had to continue to remind myself, it was just business—but it wasn't easy to let go.

## Communicating Effectively

One morning I was standing in my closet after a shower and remotely heard my younger daughter screaming at me from downstairs in the kitchen. I could not make out what she was saying, though it was clear it was not an emergency. Since I was not yet dressed, I yelled down the stairs for her to come upstairs and talk to me. As she continued to screech, my frustration grew. The energy that was being wasted on her ineffective communications was maddening.

When I finished getting dressed and went downstairs, we discussed her unproductive behavior. What was so important? She wanted to know which cans of food she could take from our pantry into school to donate to their canned food drive. I was relieved that it was not something more critical and pleased that she wanted to help. However, I had issue with her methods. I pointed out to her that although coming upstairs to talk to me may have seemed like a large effort in the beginning, the time and energy she wasted by yelling across the house was worse. It only served to frustrate both of us and not resolve the issue at hand.

This type of frustrating and unfruitful communication also happens in the workplace. I have witnessed many problems in businesses where the underlying root is ineffective communication. Not recognizing or acknowledging the more critical base cause of the issues serves only to accelerate the rate at which other seemingly unrelated problems emerge. Continuing to treat the symptoms of the problem ignores a cancerous issue that can take down not only businesses but friendships and marriages as well. For example, I have seen many wars started over an e-mail communication.

While e-mail is a great time saver, it should not be used as a substitute for dealing with complex or emotional issues face to face. How many e-mails have to go back and forth before someone should pick up the phone to resolve an issue? As mentioned in the "Disciplining in Anger" section in Chapter 5, e-mail is a one-way communication. Think of it as a Pony Express on speed, with the trails of the e-mail pony just as nasty and annoying as the trail a real horse leaves. Stepping into either is messy. In general, because there is no exchange of body language or facial expression, communicating via electronic means is often fraught with misread tone or intentions. Adopt a rule that when any e-mail has more than four threads to it, or it has been replied to a reply to a reply many times, you will pick up the phone to resolve the issue at hand rather than adding to the trail.

Instant messaging (IM), another electronic medium for communication, has found its place in business as well. It has proven helpful when conferring with a geographically dispersed team. When our client requested that our support staff install IM software on their computers, I was hesitant. The interruptive nature of this type of communication is one of the reasons I hesitated personally to adopt it. I get enough interruptions internally from my own thoughts, and e-mail is already a big enough temptation. We succumbed and implemented it on a trial basis.

IM turned out to be very helpful to our project manager, Peter, in providing production support for our client. It saved the time of crafting e-mails and was useful in tracking people down when they were mobile. For example, some of the folks that we needed to coordinate with traveled frequently. If Peter had a quick question, he could IM them for the answer. They were more likely to respond to that rather than to an e-mail, especially when they might have had a huge pile of unread e-mail to wade through from being out of the office.

The downside, as expected, was the intrusive nature of IM. While he was instant messaging someone, he might get four or five other IMs he was not ready to deal with. Making himself unavailable made it look like he was blowing off their pending requests. It's like having someone on call waiting and hanging up once you're done with the primary caller. You could not gauge the emotion behind the response or lack of response. Sometimes, however, the silence on the other end said a great deal.

You cannot *not* communicate. That is a powerful statement. Even by refusing to communicate, you are sending a message that the issue at hand is either not worth talking about or there is something you are hiding. That is a tough line to walk, especially when communicating too much can be just as harmful.

Pete Linsert has discovered that people who are not used to or comfortable with uncertainty do not deal well with completely open communications. For example, if you share too much with your staff about the ambiguity of a certain project, prospect, or your chosen direction, they might surmise that you don't know what you're doing. It is sometimes dangerous to let them see you cogitate out loud too much. Furthermore, whereas you may not panic in a particular situation, you cannot predict or govern anyone else's response. As uncertainty is a given in most any business, you have to be careful how much information you share and how you share it.

The day Keenan and I were scheduled to fly overseas for a combination business/10-year anniversary trip, we discovered that office equipment had been stolen. To make matters worse, the goods were taken from a door with a lockbox on it, which made it appear like an inside job. I was crushed. I knew in my heart that it was not one of my long-term employees that had perpetrated the crime. We did, however, have several new people and on-site contractors whom I did not know as well and for whose innocence I could not vouch. I had no proof with which to accuse or dismiss anyone, so I had to address the group as a whole. I called everyone together into the conference room and relayed the news of the theft. I offered that if anyone in the room had the equipment and returned it, we would not press charges. I left that meeting feeling more drained than I ever had before. It was a difficult situation that resulted in weeks of whispering at the water cooler.

Several weeks later, the whispering stopped. We received a call from the police department that one of the items had been received at a local pawn shop. The person who had brought the equipment into the shop had been required to submit his driver's license. His identification was without question. A vendor (and one of my neighbors) had been in our office a year earlier to repair our air conditioner and had apparently made a copy of the office key we gave him. Since so much time had passed, we had forgotten that he had also been given the access code for the locked room. We were all relieved, and I expected that the cloud of suspicion would automatically dissipate from the office. Oddly, it did not. Some of the long-term employees felt that I owed them an apology. I knew that I did what I had to do at the time and did not feel like an apology or even an explanation was necessary. I could not tell them whom I had suspected, but not being able to relay that led them to believe that I might have been suspicious of them. By saying nothing, they felt I was saying volumes. Unfortunately, some employees seemed to never be able to recover from that incident. I realized that what I say as the CEO, and as a parent, can have more weight and power than I previously thought.

As a parent or as a boss, many of us underestimate the weight of our words. A mild suggestion can often be taken as a strict directive. This happens many times with anyone in a position of authority. The manner in which we say something, too, takes on greater meaning. You must have control of this to be an effective communicator.

When we were first starting up the company, I would make suggestions to my colleagues about how they might want to approach a specific system function or lay out a screen for our software. Sometimes they would take my advice, sometimes not. That was fine. As we began to grow and I pulled out of the day-to-day software development, I would still dive into a specific function or screen and make suggestions or provide design advice. With newer employees who had not worked side by side with me, my suggestions or advice were perceived as mandates. Even when I would suggest a certain vendor to consider for an outsourced project, some people took my recommendations as directives, even though they were not meant as such. I had to govern how I framed my ideas and suggestions and what I actually said as well as how I said it to make sure it was construed as intended.

As important as it is for us to say the right things in the right way, truly listening can be more significant in business and parenting than talking. As our children begin to develop logic and a growing feeling of self-sufficiency, it is important that we begin to treat them as emerging adults. Part of this involves actually listening and considering what they have to say before we cut them off or fling our opinion at them. In business, too, we need to practice our active listening skills.

Often, a communication issue stems solely from someone's need to be heard. We all want to feel like our thoughts and ideas have merit and are at least worthy of consideration. When we feel heard, we feel validated, even if our ideas are not adopted. For many of us, it is sufficient that what we have to say is genuinely heard and acknowledged. This can be done if the other person is *actively listening* to us.

One of the key principles to active listening is to be fully present with the person who is talking. If it is face to face, maintaining constant eye contact is crucial. To truly hear what someone else is saying, you must focus on *them* rather than thinking about your response, considering the 100 other things that you have to do that day, or going through your e-mail. This is a hard thing to do and something that I have struggled with personally.

I claim that my mind is *random access*, which is geek-speak that means it jumps all over the place at any given moment. I suspect that if there had been any focus on attention deficit disorder when I was a child, I would have been pegged early. I clearly have learned to adapt to my wandering mind, but it is not always so easy.

Early in my career, I learned that I had a bad habit of interrupting people while they were talking. I have no doubt this is something I have been doing since I was young, but the first time I remember being called on it was while I was in consultative sales training for IBM. I was attending a class on a technique called Solutions Selling, where as the salesperson I had to be able to listen to what the customer is saying and repeat back to them their problems with a twist toward the solution that my company provided. As my boss, Jan, was relaying her specific needs and concerns to me in a role-playing exercise in front of the whole class, I cut her off. The instructor stopped the program right there. He pointed out that I had just interrupted my customer and asked Jan how she felt about being interrupted. It was not good. Humiliated, I began to consider why I harbored this damaging habit. Upon reflection, I realized (or rationalized) that because my mind cannot stay focused and I was afraid I would lose the current thought in my head, I felt the need to blurt it out before she was even done speaking. It was a good thought, too, but not good enough to repair the damage that my rude behavior had inflicted. Since that time, I wish I could say I no longer interrupt people while they're talking, but the truth is that it is something I need to work on every day. I have started carrying a small notebook with me so that I can jot down my ideas that I believe to be so important so as not to lose them. Interestingly enough, if I just let the other person finish, my thoughts are sometimes no longer relevant.

Paul, too, claims that before he became an entrepreneur he had poor listening skills and a bad habit of interrupting others in the course of a normal conversation. As an entrepreneur and a business leader, he has learned the critical need to be an effective and active listener. He has found those skills beneficial when interacting with his kids as well and an important capability he has worked to teach them.

Once you have heard someone, it helps to reiterate to them what you heard. This not only provides confirmation that you were really listening but also validation that what you heard was correct. This is especially critical when dealing with an employee or a teen who has not felt heard in the past.

Once I started conscientiously focusing on what people were saying, I began to hear what truly matters to them. I have found that this is a required ingredient for effective leadership. Knowing what people care about allows you to lead them from a base of their own values while also addressing their concerns. It helps you to frame your response around them and their concerns, rather than making it about you. This works not only for employees but for our children as well.

## Celebrating Uniqueness

My older daughter's emotions seemed to level out around the third grade. Not that she did not have temper tantrums, but they were not so easily ignited nor as frequent. When my second daughter hit the same age, we patiently waited for her transition. It never came. I realized then that there were distinct differences between the two girls' personalities, and what works for one does not necessarily work for the other. For example, for a long time we would take away television rights as a punishment. For Sydney, that would usually do the trick and correct the undesirable behavior. Unfortunately, that type of consequence had no impact whatsoever on Madison. She did not care about TV—she could take it or leave it. What we found motivates her is the ability to play with her friends. She would do whatever you want in order to earn play time with a buddy. Although that does not even always work, we continued to experiment to find something that was effective.

We used to marvel that even with sharing the same parents, living in the same house under the same rules, our children still have more differences than similarities. One of our jobs as parents is to help our children find and use their unique gifts. It is up to us to recognize the differences and help develop them into strengths. Everyone has them, some just take longer to identify or develop. The key is to expose kids to a variety of ideas and opportunities so as to awaken the gifts within.

Both my children began playing soccer in kindergarten, but it was more like "herd ball": a group of four little six-year-olds from each team running up and down the field with the ball. Forget about playing a position—everyone just wanted to kick the ball or pick it up. As our kids have grown, we have tried to introduce them to a variety of activities to determine the ones at which they can excel or at least enjoy. Over the years they have tried many different sports such as soccer, basketball, lacrosse, tennis, gymnastics, and softball as well as Girl Scouts, art classes, theater, and playing a musical instrument. Hopefully, by having a chance to sample different things, they have found a few interests that they will continue to pursue. The objective has been for them to learn about themselves and find their gifts.

In teaching experienced businesspeople how to transition into entrepreneurship, one of the hardest lessons to convey is the importance of finding what delineates your company from the competition—your company's uniqueness—and exploiting that through your marketing. It is not that it is difficult for teams to identify what they believe potential distinctive qualities are, but finding differences that customers value and will pay for seems to be the most laborious part.

Many companies, especially those in the information technology industry, claim that their quality and customer service are incomparable. If so many companies tout those features, how unique can they really be? If you really do have something in these areas that your company does differently than the competition, then find quantitative ways to present it. Does your software have 25 percent fewer problems than the other players in your industry? Although this type of information will be hard to obtain from your competition, you must be able to provide some concrete way to illustrate that your quality truly is above and beyond the rest. Do you receive 15 percent fewer customer service calls? Can you report 99.9 percent customer satisfaction or 100 percent repeat business?

It took a call from an angry customer to indicate to Graham Weston that merely putting computers in service for customers to rent space on was *not* enough to build a thriving business. They went through several iterations of their differentiation before someone asked, "What is your customers' greatest fear?" The answer was simple: having their servers unavailable, especially for an extended period of time. Through that exploration, they were able to find the true value that attracted and kept customers: their fanatical customer service. Because this is a difficult difference to quantify, they knew they had to make their service stand out so much that it became "remarkable"—great enough that their clients will think to remark about it to others without being asked or prodded. Graham noted that the only way to do that was to have people who are passionate about their jobs. At Rackspace, they strive to make people *want* to give incredible service through their creative persuasion, described in Chapter 4.

In addition to finding your differentiation, you have to diffuse it throughout the culture of your organization. When a customer's server is down, they needed to react to that event with the same sense of urgency as the customer themselves. This level of caring had to be proliferated through every level of the company. Their web site includes an attendant that pops up to ask you if you need help. They eliminated the automated attendant on their phone system so customers can talk to a real person. What they found was that although there was added cost and difficulty to scale live receptionists as their business grew, their clients most decidedly did *not* want to talk to a computer when they were having a problem. Everything they did in their business reflected their differentiation and was designed to support it.

Once you have what you believe to be your unique offering, try it out on current or potential customers to see if it passes the "so what?" test. If they do not see the value in it, move on and find something else. Try asking your customers why they do business with you. Better yet, have someone else query your customers so you can know what they *really* think. What do they see as your value-add, your differentiators? Once you identify what those are, highlight them in every marketing piece you develop.

Let your potential customers know what is so special about working with you.

When Mary Cantando was running an IT services firm, she assigned one of her graphic artists to design a T-shirt as a holiday gift for her customers. She asked her to take their company name, "PDR," and conduct a contest among their clients to develop a phrase, starting with those letters, which represented a client's view of the company.

The winning submission, which came from a client named Joan, still brings a smile to Mary's face. It was a caricature of a cowboy in spurs wearing a 10-gallon hat. Beside him were three words starting with the letters PDR: "Purdy Dadgum Reliable."

What made this phrase so great was the fact this was truly how Joan felt about Mary's organization: that they were reliable in that they would deliver what she needed, when she needed it, no matter what.

As Mary thought back on her experiences in selling to Joan, she realized that, after they completed their first project for her, they never really had to sell to her again. In effect, all they did was take her next order. That doesn't mean that they didn't have competition; every IT consulting firm in the state was vying to work for Joan's Fortune 500 company. In fact, Mary's biggest competitor consistently underbid them on proposal after proposal, but somehow they always won the contract because Joan was so convinced of their reliability.

Their reputation for reliability spread as Joan referred more and more of her colleagues to Mary's company. They began winning contracts with other divisions of her company, and then with other of their sites around the world. By asking their customer what was so special about them, Mary was able to grow not only within that account but also through their referrals to other companies.

We determined that our experience in and knowledge of our customers' industry was what put us above our competition. We made sure that we highlighted that knowledge in every piece of marketing material we created, from our web site to our brochures, and even in our proposals. This focus, however, made branching into new markets difficult. We had to identify industries that were similar enough that we could claim superior knowledge and experience or find something else to set us apart. The approach we selected was to partner with companies that provided varied services and industry expertise to bolster our offerings in new industries. We exploited our uniqueness but then also used the strengths of others to expand our reach.

## From School Backpack to Briefcase

- Give your employees ample opportunities to excel, but realize that there is a chance that they will fail as they stretch their abilities. Implement the safety nets necessary to allow for those mistakes without seriously jeopardizing the business. Start small and then use increasingly larger, controlled failures as personal and business growth opportunities. Hopefully, nothing will get burned too badly.
- Don't let your own "busyness" interfere with your business.
- Being afraid to fail can put you into analysis paralysis—not being able to make a decision until every question is answered, which will likely never happen. Decisions most often must be made without all of the needed information, which means you need to take calculated risks and, sometimes, just go with your gut.
- Successful entrepreneurs rarely take all-out risks. Instead, they analyze the available information and venture into what they consider *calculated* risks.
- Clarify the difference between a right and a privilege early. Be fair and consistent in assigning privileges. Don't put in automatic doors if you want employees to learn to open doors for themselves.
- Not getting out of the details of your business will stifle your growth and keep it from growing beyond your own personal capabilities and efforts. It might not be comfortable at first, but it is required to move your company away from You, Inc.
- Delegate tasks without abdicating oversight. Stay on top of critical issues and project timing. Even if you can do tasks faster than the time it takes to delegate, it is a critical requirement to give you time to work *on* your business instead of *in* your business.
- Many growing businesses overlook the importance of consistency and processes in parts of the business that are not within their core competency. HR processes are a common afterthought. When you

*(continued)*

begin hiring outside of your close personal network and building your management team, a consistent HR process will become crucial to being able to grow successfully and keep everyone marching to the beat of the same drum.

- Do not underestimate the damaging power of hiring the wrong people. A negative seed in your business can spread dysfunction like a contagious disease. Hire slowly, fire quickly.

- High-performing work environments encourage productive conflict. Letting people "duke it out" like adults can be productive if proper boundaries and techniques are applied. Contrary opinions can open up new possibilities; just draw the line at dangling spit.

- Surround yourself, personally, with the right people. Always seek out those who have accomplished what you want to accomplish and from whom you can learn and grow. Being around successful people begets success; just make sure their methods are consistent with your morals and values.

- It isn't personal, it is just business. It is admirable to approach your company with heart and compassion, but don't let it get too close or you risk tainting your judgment.

- Good and effective communication is imperative to building a successful business and becoming an effective leader. You cannot *not* communicate.

- When you are in a position of leadership, you must carefully consider what you say and how you say it. The weight of your words when you are in a position of authority increases like my waist after a Thanksgiving meal. Make all of your communications intentional.

- Find your company's differentiation and exploit that. Tell a story no one else is telling, or tell it in a compelling new way. Whatever your distinction is, it has to be something your customers value and will pay for. Not everyone can be the best at quality and customer service, but if you are, provide your customers with evidence to back it up. When in doubt, have someone else ask them what makes working with you special.

# Additional Resources

The Arbinger Institute, *Leadership and Self-Deception: Getting Out of the Box* (San Francisco: Berrett-Koehler Publishers, 2000).

Harry E. Chambers, *The Bad Attitude Survival Guide: Essential Tools for Managers* (New York: Perseus Books, 1998).

Alan S. Horowitz, *Unofficial Guide to Hiring and Firing People* (Indianapolis: Macmillan, 1999).

## Marketing and Differentiation

Harry Beckwith, *What Clients Love: The Field Guide to Growing Your Business* (New York: Warner Business Books, 2003).

Seth Godin, Purple Cow: *Transform Your Business by Being Remarkable* (New York: Portfolio, 2003).

Jack Trout, *Differentiate or Die: Survival in Our Era of Killer Competition* (New York: John Wiley & Sons, 2000).

## Communications

Susan Scott, *Fierce Conversations: Achieving Success at Work & in Life, One Conversation at a Time* (New York: Berkley, 2002).

## Delegation

Kenneth H. Blanchard, William Oncken, and Hal Burrows, *The One Minute Manager Meets the Monkey* (New York: William Morrow, 1989).

Donna M. Genett, *If You Want It Done Right, You Don't Have to Do It Yourself: The Power of Effective Delegation* (Sanger, Calif.: Quill Driver Books/Word Dancer Press, 2004).

### Graham Weston's Top Five Tips

1. In order to build a customer service-based business, you have to make people want to give great service.
2. Your management team is the key to your culture. People join a company and quit a manager.
3. Position your differentiation around your customer's biggest fear.
4. Find out what is unique about each person that works for you and capitalize on it.
5. Recognize that in a rapidly expanding business, many people's jobs outgrow them. Not everyone can scale.

CHAPTER

# Emerging Independence

Online social networking web sites such as MySpace and Face-Book have evolved into must-have virtual meeting places for teens. Photos of parties and friends abound, many of which, if seen, would raise a few parent's eyebrows. It is a place where the kids can put on any persona they want, be anyone they choose, and rant about their lives and the people in it through their blogs. To them, it is their own private party place.

Tammy Middleton is one of a few Internet-savvy mothers with teens. She monitors her daughters' use of MySpace and other similar web sites. She created her own profile and required her kids to make her their "friend" so that she can see the private comments, pictures, and information that is being provided and shared. She can make sure that the pictures being posted are appropriate and that no personal information is being shared that might give online perverts a path to find them. By occasionally commenting on their profile, Tammy makes sure her daughters realize that they are not really alone in this cyber party space.

While some parents may think that this is invading their teens' privacy or let their teens convince them this is the case, it is a misperception to think there is anything private about these types of web sites. Without the appropriate controls or guidelines for whom you connect with, any stranger can invade what they may believe is a secret and protected space. As a parent, I want insight into their so-called secret spot where pedophiles have been known to lurk. Keeping an eye on them at this level helps to keep them safe and reminds them that they are not really alone.

## Introduction

As our children enter their teenage years, we parents are often exposed to our last opportunity to provide a constant and profound influence over them. Contrary to what teens would have you believe, their judgment is not yet completely developed, which is why it is important to ensure the boundaries are clear before you let teens (or your business!) fly solo. Although teenagers can start to understand why fair is not always equal, you must make sure you focus on being a parent, not a friend. If you are fortunate, you can convince your teen that you are all on the same team as a family as you strive to train them as your replacement—to be responsible, contributing adults.

## Making Your Presence Known

When my kids went away to camp, I would leave little reminders that I was thinking about them. Small notes I call "love notes" got tucked away in their suitcase where they might not see them until they had been gone a couple days. The notes let them know that although they can't see me, I am still there.

Parents have found a new way of letting their college-age children know they are present through instant messaging (IM). Many parents have found that being able to send their kids short notes, reminders, or tidbits of gossip via IM throughout the day or week helps them remember that although they are gone, they have not been forgotten.

Making your presence known to employees and customers is equally important for different reasons. First, it is important for employees to know that someone is aware of the work they are doing and "in touch" with the pulse of the business. This can be done in several ways.

Providing positive feedback or periodic minor corrections demonstrates that the efforts of those serving your customers or developing your products are not going overlooked. This does not always have to be done in formal ways—many successful managers practice "management by walking around," offering real-time feedback on the spot. It should be someone's job responsibility to know what is going on in your office, not just at the formal status level, but at the underground, water-cooler level as well. It is hard to maintain that level of knowledge without a physical presence. This creates a challenge with an increasing mobile workforce.

At any one time, we had at least a couple of employees who were telecommuting. We found employees who continually worked from home began to feel disconnected from the rest of the organization. We made a point to schedule these folks into the office on a weekly or biweekly basis for informal training we called "Brown Bag Lunch Seminars." Through these seminars, we provided information on a range of topics from personal wellness to an overview of a specific project. In addition to being educational, these sessions enabled remote staff members to reconnect with their colleagues and supervisors.

The metrics we used to measure success also had to be adjusted to accommodate telecommuting. We had to focus on productivity, results, and output as opposed to time spent punching a virtual time clock. Had we been a government contractor, this would not have been possible due to their project timekeeping requirements. However, this shift required a different type of management training and for some, a transformation of their philosophy. Those who had been used to measuring success based on time in the office with former employers were now forced to break projects into milestones and manage to those instead. No rewards for face time alone. It was a whole new world for some, but one worth forging.

Additionally, we had to alter the way we communicated in this new remote frontier. Because of the variety of flexible work options we supported, we had to shift our expectations and methods for communicating with each other. Tin cans and string don't work over long distances, but picking up the phone rather than waiting for an e-mail response does wonders. We discovered that not everyone checks their e-mail constantly. Rather than making obsession with e-mail a job requirement, we had to realize that a phone call (with a *real* phone instead of a tin can) can often do the trick when an immediate answer is needed.

Our customers and potential customer had to be constantly reminded of our presence as well. I was keenly aware of the multitude of companies that had a technically superior product but lost out to competition with an inferior design concept. The difference, in many cases, was in the marketing (or lack thereof). It is a common gaffe of technically focused people I counsel to assume that a superior product will sell itself. In general, this is not so. If no one knows about your product or recognizes why it is superior, nothing else matters. It will not sell.

Getting the word about your company into the market is no easy feat, especially when the company, concept, product, or service is new. Setting up a web site has become a no-brainer first step. It illustrates to potential customers that you are "real," but how will people find you on the vastness of the Internet?

Unless you have *recent* experience in optimizing web sites for search engines, it is best to hire someone to do it for you. Another opportunity to increase the visibility of your website is to partner with other organizations or sites to cross-promote your product/service and link to your web site. There are many sites that will do this for you at no charge, while others require money to secure a listing. I have tried both and have had inconsistent results. The bottom line is that you need to know who your target customer is in detail (not just "women" or "computer users") and then get links from those web sites your customers are spending time on.

If you use your web site to attract business, you need to know how many people are visiting your web site, where they are going, and how they found you. There are many different software packages for tracking web site traffic, and most likely the company that hosts your site offers this option. You can then use the information derived from this service to tweak your web site content and format to ensure you're making the most of your online investment. For example, we noticed in analyzing our online traffic that people who entered our site from a specific page rarely went anywhere else on the site. When we compared that trend to the navigation patterns of people that entered on other pages, we noticed a discrepancy. Upon investigation, we found that links were missing on the problem page. Once we added the new links, the usage patterns became more consistent across the site.

The other important aspect we learned about our web site is to design it around our customers' needs rather than making it about us. Customers may not always be able to grasp the connection between what you can do and the problem they are facing. People are much more quickly drawn to something they can relate to—their problem—rather than the features you are providing. Spell it out for them as simply as you can and watch them stick around.

There should also be something on the web site that makes them come back—news from their industry that is continually updated, free tools, or white papers (informational articles you write and post on the Internet). A free newsletter that you provide that they can sign up for on your web site also provides you with the opportunity to capture their contact information and continually stay in touch.

One of the most often overlooked and easiest ways to promote your business and keep it front of your current and potential customers is to do it personally. Many entrepreneurs discount their role in building their own company's brand. Talk to everyone you meet about your business and ask for referrals. You don't have to perform like a car salesman on a TV commercial to be effective. Be prepared with what you will say when someone asks you what you do. Tell them about your business in a clear and concise way. They may not have any personal connection to it, but they may know someone that does.

Carol Koch-Worrell cringes when she sees the big signs on her Suburban advertising her business, but she knows it is necessary. She takes her license for teaching children to love music through Kindermusik seriously. It is no hobby. She is continually amazed at other licensees who do not understand the power they hold for making their business successful. For example, she chastises others who do not recognize why they should carefully consider what they wear when going out, even to the grocery store. When your business requires that you sell products or services to members of the local community, your appearance and demeanor in public matter. You are always selling—every person you encounter is a sales opportunity. When you are not looking and feeling your best, you are less likely to reach out to talk with others to create spontaneous business opportunities. If you are dressed in sweatpants, you are more likely to hide in the frozen food aisle when you see someone you know rather than approach them. Likewise, if you happen to sell makeup but often go out without it, you may be missing a chance at a sales connection.

When I first started attending networking events through local business organizations, I was skeptical about what good it would do to be able to describe my business. After all, how many people at these types of events could use bar-coded inventory tracking that specializes in large-scale food manufacturing? I actually developed an alternate elevator pitch for just such an occasion.

---

### What Is an Elevator Pitch?

Imagine you are in an elevator (or at a cocktail party) and someone asks you what you do. What do you say? You do not know this person, but you want to provide them with a description of your business. Being concise is critical—you only have so much time before you get to the next floor, but you want to tell them enough to pique their interest. Maybe they or someone they know could use your product or service.

"I specialize in bars—not the kind you drink in, the kind that make up a product code. Bar *codes* . . ."

My target market was not generally represented at these events. My purpose for attending was to identify services I could use to help my business grow, not find customers. Imagine my surprise when an opportunity surfaced from such an event. One of the women at the event had a cousin who worked for a large food manufacturer. She had recently heard him complaining about some of the problems we had helped other customers fix and recalled that when she heard my spiel. By making my presence known and, more specifically, by describing what my business did in nontechnical terms, I was able to identify opportunities that I might not have otherwise found.

Our company also enjoyed marketing success from establishing ourselves as experts in our target market by writing articles and speaking at conferences. It is much easier than you might think to become a speaker at industry events. When I was researching our target market, I discovered *the* trade show put on by the main industry magazine and was able to locate the editor's contact information. I have advised many entrepreneurs that if they don't like cold calling, they just need to get over it. You will have to do it, and it can pay off as it did for me in this case. I called the editor to find out how they selected speakers for their events. By the end of the conversation, he had not only asked me to speak at their event but—and here's the good part—they would pay me to do it. I was also able to avail speaking engagements into having my articles published in the magazine. This relationship went on for several years and evolved into opportunities to speak internationally with all expenses paid *and* an honorarium—all because I dared to ask and made my presence known.

Once you have customers, it is imperative that you keep in touch with them as well. You need to not only remind them that you are there but also ensure they believe that is a *good* thing. As your company grows and your customer list expands, this can become a challenge.

In my company, we strived to conduct quarterly customer satisfaction surveys to find out how our customers felt we were doing.

Even if we hadn't been doing anything more than answering the occasional support call from them, the survey gave us a reason to contact them and remind them that we were available should any new needs arise. Our customers also seemed to appreciate being asked for their thoughts and opinions, which resulted in a bonus from the process—their continued loyalty.

Additionally, these surveys provided our management team with information about who among our customer support team was doing exceptionally well or needed some adjustments to their work approach. Thankfully, we rarely received any negative feedback on our employees' performance, though we did receive interesting insights into our newly adopted marketing messages. In response to a question about whether they would consider our company for future work, one customer replied that they weren't sure what new types of products or services we were now providing. This afforded us the opportunity to engage them in a discussion about our new offerings. Once we clarified our strategy and provided details of our new endeavors, the client was able to identify several potential projects for us. Their confusion prompted us to refine our marketing campaign and adjust our messaging. By keeping in front of our customers and reminding them we were there, we were able to halt a faulty perception that could have kept us from expanding our services within that organization or attracting new customers.

Research has shown that it costs less to grow your presence within an established customer than to acquire a new one (see discussion in the "Teaching Your Baby to Feed Herself" section in Chapter 4). We implemented a "keep in touch" program that involved an e-newsletter that was sent electronically once a month to those customers we were supporting. It contained tips on new software functions that were being released, trade shows we were attending, or articles we had published. Every edition also requested feedback. Even if the customer didn't read the entire newsletter, seeing our name on a consistent basis and knowing that we were interested in what they thought was invaluable and assisted us in building a loyal customer base. I would also keep my eye out for articles or professionally written book summaries that I thought might be interesting to one or more clients. I would then send it to them without anything "salesy"; rather, a simple message that I had found this and thought of they might find it interesting. That type of outreach went a long way toward subtly keeping our presence known.

If you are in direct sales, especially if you represent consumable products like skin care, makeup, or hair products, you should be making your virtual presence known by putting your name on every single product you sell. You don't want your clients to wash their face or put on their makeup without thinking of you. When their products are running low, they won't have to search for your name or phone number—it should be right there. Regardless of the product you sell, you should also have options to get in touch with your clients on a regular basis via multiple means. That means mailings (also called "snail mail"), promotional announcements, and e-mail newsletters should be going out to your contacts (not just your clients!) on a regular basis. If you are worried about inundating people with e-mail or junk mail, don't be. Let them decide whether or not they want to receive ongoing information from you—don't decide for them. Give them a method for stopping the communication and move on. There will always be those who don't want it, but for those who do, provide them with an additional service. For example, Carol provides educational content on the various stages of child development and how her program supports them in her e-mail newsletter. By focusing on information her clients are interested in and not making her newsletters about her, she creates value that keeps them coming back.

Even more difficult than keeping in touch with contacts is creating a new market or addressing a need that customers do not know they have. Marketing a new product is hard enough, but it is even more arduous to educate customers into realizing their need. Plugging into latent or unconscious needs has proven profitable for companies that can do it, such as Apple (iPod), eBay, and Google. The cost is high, however, and the risk is great. Only through fostering a culture of innovation can a company be successful at creating new markets.

# Flying Alone

I moved to Maryland after college but the rest of my family stayed put. My mom was the second of 10 children, which made for a large extended family. Most of them resided in the same town where I grew up—Dallas, Texas. I stayed close to my family in spite of the distance, which meant that my daughters had been making the Texas pilgrimage since they were eight weeks old. It wasn't unusual for my kids to fly in an airplane two to three times per year, with at least one of those trips to Texas. Trekking through airports was not foreign to them—even foreign airports—but they had always had at least one parent with them.

I had been talking about sending them to Texas alone for years. My mom (they call her "Nanny") had been working on them as well. Madison was ready to go as soon as she understood what it meant, but her older, more cautious sister was the hold-out. A couple of times a year I would ask her about going to see Nanny without Mom and Dad and get the same answer: "no." When she was 12 and Madison was 10, she finally relented. She had decided she was brave enough to give flying as an unaccompanied minor a try.

The girls knew the air travel routine well. Getting to and through the airport and security was uneventful, though Sydney now knows what it is like to be frisked due to a metal belt that was permanently attached to her shorts. Even once we got to the boarding area, both girls were fine. It was Mom that was the mess. I didn't cry when they were escorted onto the plane, but my eyes misted when the plane took off. My babies were growing up. This was monumental for them and for me.

My melancholy mood lasted only as long as it took me to get out to my car and put the convertible top down. It was a beautiful day and I was heading to the beach to spend some one-on-one time with Keenan. Although I caught myself wondering what they might be doing once or twice, I can't say that I ever worried. They had flown so many times before, they knew what to do. We had reviewed safety procedures before they left, and I felt confident that they were as safe as if I were on the plane with them. I spoke to them shortly after they arrived. They were on their way to Nanny's house to get in the pool. They never missed a beat. Mission accomplished.

Letting a company or even a department "fly alone" without its leader can be difficult for managers and entrepreneurs. Unfortunately, there are many entrepreneurs who never make it to the point that their companies fly alone. Some have *never* been away from their office without checking in. Now with instant access to people through cell phones, the Internet, and Blackberries (also called "crack" berries due to their addictive nature), it is even harder for entrepreneurs to truly get away. The result often is extreme burnout.

If he had to do it over again, Paul Silber reveals that he would have taken more vacations. He did not take a vacation for the first four years of his business and began to feel it. When he did finally start taking a break and letting his baby fly alone, he found that stepping away from work was actually extremely productive. In his times away from the office—on the beach, in the mountains, or just at home *not* thinking about work—he conceived some of his best strategic ideas. Once his mind was clear of the clutter of the day-to-day minutiae of his business, he could begin to see the bigger picture more clearly, the forest through the trees. Getting away brought much-needed clarity of higher-level business issues and strategies. It also worried his managers. They dreaded what new project or change would be initiated when Paul returned from his vacation. Most of the time, however, the strategic changes that he brought back from his time away ended up being key elements of the company's future success.

When my company consisted of just me, I did not mind taking business with me. I would prefer to address an issue immediately rather than let it get to a point of exploding when I returned. I even helped a customer reinitiate our application while driving a golf cart. A colleague was putting, so I had to do it *quietly*.

My first true vacation came about five years into the business. At that time, Keenan and I really needed the time away. We decided to join some friends on a trip to Jamaica. We found out quickly that calling from the island was not easy and there was no way, at the time, to dial in to get our e-mail. We had no choice but to lose contact with the office. We were able to call the office from our hotel room, at $3 per minute, to give them the hotel phone number in case of emergency. Otherwise, we were isolated, and that was not a bad thing. We came back refreshed and renewed at a time when our business and children needed every bit of reserve energy we could muster. The long weekend away with good friends and warm sun replenished our reserves. We found that only taking out of that reserve and not contributing to it will eventually drain you and leave you unable to do *anything* well.

There are several key contributing factors that helped me get to the point of being able to leave my business without checking in:

- I quit marketing *myself* and marketed *my company* instead.

   Early in my business, I recognized that if I ever wanted to have a life, I had to get my clients to quit calling me directly when they had questions or problems. In order to do that, I needed to hire competent people who could and *would* take ownership of our customers' projects and problems. I had to refuse to answer a question, even if I could answer it quickly. Instead, I referred our customers to their project team and let my staff find their own answers.

   I also had to stop saying *me* and start using the words *us, our team,* and our company name, ACT. Once I stopped acting like a sole proprietor, it became easier to grow out of being one.

- I built a team I could trust.

   We entrepreneurs sometimes have a difficult time hiring the right people and putting them into decision-making positions because it signifies giving up control. We either hire people exactly like us, which can be deadly, or hire good people but do not give them the right environment in which to succeed. We need to hire people who not only work well within the culture of our company but who also complement our skills and fill in for our weaknesses. By giving them responsibility with accountability we are also building the context in which our business can thrive.

I was fortunate to have worked in my company with some of the best people I have ever had the privilege of working with. While we experienced bumps in learning how to delegate and what it meant to fit new people culturally into our organization, our core group of employees was unmatched in their professionalism and commitment to our customers. I trusted them completely.

- I empowered our team to make decisions without me.

In order to get out of the office, I had to allow my team to make decisions and be willing to live with the consequences. We tried to lay the foundation in our company for a culture of responsible decision making. In order to do that, my staff had to be clear about what the company's priorities were. The more I learned to refuse to make decisions for other people while I was in the office, the more I was able to trust them to make decisions while I was out of the office.

Letting your children and your business "fly alone" at the right time is a significant accomplishment for any business. It is as much as reflection on them for earning our trust as it is on us to be able to train them to someday take our place.

## Training Your Replacement

Mary Cantando had been a hardworking entrepreneur (is there any other kind?) since her children were young. She never learned to love cooking, so she did what any other savvy entrepreneur would do—she outsourced it. When each of her three children turned 12, she taught them to cook a few different dishes. Each had responsibility for planning and cooking the family meal one night a week. It was also their responsibility to put the items they needed for their meal on the family grocery list and to get a sibling to substitute if they were not going to be available to cook on their assigned night.

One thing that Mary had not anticipated was that they would figure out which was the easiest meal to prepare and cook that week after week. So, rather than Tuesday being Suzi's night to cook, it became chili night. And Thursday, Keith's night, became taco night. Mary didn't really care because it was one less night she had to cook and her children learned the responsibility of being part of a family. As they got older, cooking dinner became something they enjoyed together. Mary was preparing her children to be adults by imparting skills that would serve them well for the rest of their lives.

Based on my personal experience and input from other working parents, I have concluded that many of us have a different perspective on our role as parents. Whereas our parent's generation and those that espouse a more traditional view of parenthood are more concerned with caretaking, working parents tend to focus on teaching our children how to be independent. We teach our children to fish rather than just putting the fish on the table. It is often the only viable choice—each member of the family needs to pitch in to get everything done. We view our children as "adults-in-training" from the time they are very small. We are, in essence, training our replacements.

## Worlds Colliding

Paul worked very hard to keep his work from intruding on his family time and vice versa. Some days, however, were harder than others. Many times he would come home from work in what his children call "CEO mode." At those times, he would make rapid-fire decisions and expect everyone to be super-productive. Once someone called him on it, he was able to take a deep breath, exhale while letting the work go, and take the time to enjoy his family.

In each step as you extract yourself out of the details of your company, you should be filling in behind you with competent, trained people. In order to do this, you must be completely transparent with many aspects of your business, such as the criteria you use to make decisions. If you are concerned about working yourself out of a job, don't be. The ultimate job security for an entrepreneur or a good manager is obtained by building a business that runs without you. In order to do that effectively, you must be constantly training your replacement.

When a company is growing, a lot of time is spent training people. From that first organizational chart with one or two names on it, we are progressively working to fill the boxes with others. Finding a number two—a second in command—is a particularly monumental step for entrepreneurial companies, especially when founded by one person. As critical as it is for the future growth of any company, it is equally as challenging.

Donna Stevenson and her husband Cecil have had to go through the process of identifying and hiring a second in command twice. The first search was precipitated by Donna's pregnancy. She knew that she was going to be out of the business for some span, and, at the time, Cecil was not in a position to run the company alone. What they discovered through that process is that they needed to identify someone who was entrepreneurial. They needed a person who was willing to take risks, who could see the bigger picture. They wanted someone who could not help but think about the company as his or her own and be willing to accept equity in lieu of a large salary. The process was successful, in part because there was a hard deadline (delivery).

The second search for their number two came several years later when Donna was separating from the business to start up her own baby, PRISM Compliance. This time, the deadline for finding a replacement was neither as clear nor perceived as urgent and consequently took a lot longer to accomplish. Our search for a number two at ACT was not that dissimilar from Donna's.

Once we recognized that Keenan was abdicating his throne as chief operating officer (COO), which was our number two position, our search began. The first step was to lay out the duties that the COO would perform. To do that, we researched how other companies defined that role while also looking at the tasks Keenan was performing. In addition, we realized that we needed to consider the responsibilities that I continued to hold as the CEO that I needed to let go.

The next step was to find candidates who not only had all the right skills but also possessed a high level of energy. It was difficult to find someone who carried the same level of passion and energy for the business that I did, and I realized: That may never happen.

This was my baby, and anyone else would just be babysitting. What I quickly realized is that one of the worst things we could have done was to hire someone just like me, anyway. This is where it pays to know yourself as the CEO—what your strengths are as well as where your weak spots lurk. We needed to bring in someone who compensated for my weaknesses and was able to do the tasks that I did not want to do or did not do well.

When we finally found Greg, we knew we had found a great fit. Unlike me, he was detail oriented (which we needed), but he and I also shared important qualities. He brought an in-depth knowledge of our customer's industry and a good presence in front of clients. He was smart, polished, and jumped right in. We had found our future number two.

A common novice mistake that I fell into was not to let go enough to allow him to be successful. My tendency was to continue doing what I was doing before and not delegate tasks to him. Bad idea. He got frustrated and I wondered why I hadn't felt any relief. After he brought this to my attention, I was more aware and began intentionally letting go.

Another common misstep that companies, big and small, take is to become too reliant on specific people. I have heard in our company and from other entrepreneurs too many times, that we just can't lose so-and-so. If you believe that losing one specific person has the potential to cripple your business, you've already stepped off that curb and are in front of traffic. While it would be nice to think that our employees will stay with us forever, there are a lot of outside forces we cannot control. There are several behaviors that cause us to fall into this destructive dependency.

First, we can slip into overreliance on certain people by selling our customers on those specific people. If customers believe they are buying the services of John, it is likely that only John will do. After all, we've highlighted John's unique characteristics, skills, and experiences to sell them on him. If something happens and John is no longer able to service that client, how can we then go back and convince them that we've found someone just as good? A better approach is to sell the capabilities of our business to potential customers. If John truly is the only person in your company who can perform the proposed tasks, then it may be time to look at strengthening your company's bench.

A company's bench, or backup resources, can be made strong only when there is cross-training involved. As people work independently on projects with no review process or other cross-pollination, pockets of excellence develop. The results obtained by that group cannot be repeated without involving the same people. That is unacceptable.

Another condition that invites this to occur is a lack of formal process in our organizations. Although this was addressed in a previous chapter, it bears some repetition here. When our companies are grounded only in the abilities of individual people, we are only as strong as our ability to retain those people and attract others like them. That is fine, but if we can build a company with a strong foundation in processes, we are in a better position to not only foster repeatable success but to also build assets that someone else would be interested in buying. That is made much easier if we make sure we construct the appropriate boundaries.

## Setting Boundaries

When I was growing up, we had what we thought were fairly strict rules about where we could go and what time we had to be home. There were serious expectations around our behavior, and crossing those boundaries would result in severe punishment.

My grandparents had a large steel bell on a post in their backyard. Our only instruction when we set out to play at 10:00 A.M. was that we had to be able to hear the bell ring, telling us it was time to come home. It is amazing how far the clang of that bell reached. We systematically tested the outer limits of our "playground" over the summer. As long as we were within the bell's range, we were within our boundaries. We knew what the consequences were, so we dared not risk being unable to hear the bell because we had all met the end of the willow switch before.

As parents, Keenan and I have set similar expectations albeit without the clanging bell or such harsh punishment as the willow switch provided. With our children, we have found that we need a different set of boundaries that are not so physical. The neighborhood we live in is family friendly, so we do not worry so much about where they are. They don't go very far, anyway. We do, however, watch where they go on the Internet. We keep our computers in common areas of the house and will not allow a computer in a private area such as a bedroom. It is not because we do not trust our children that we impart such strict rules. Rather, it is our knowledge of the dangers lurking on the Internet that has driven us to demand full disclosure and exposure—little things such as making sure we know who they are talking to while instant messaging and looking at their profiles to make sure they are safe. For example, I have had to show my daughter why giving out her phone number through any electronic means is a risk she should not be taking. One visit to Google with our phone number and showing her the map that displays where we live was enough to convince her that it was not necessary or even smart. Likewise, some of her friends post their cell phone numbers on the profiles, which can provide the same illicit access to personal information they might not want to share with the whole world.

Additional boundaries we place around our kids are geared toward teaching them respect, honesty, and responsibility. It is natural for children to test their boundaries, and we need to rebuke them when they do. We correct them for not addressing an adult or a peer with respect. They know that it is worse to lie about something bad they did than the wrong deed itself. Taking responsibility for themselves and for their actions is rewarded. They know what to expect from us, and we try to be consistent in our implementation of it. This is equally important in a business situation.

Early in my company, we did not set many boundaries. We used to jokingly relate to new employees that we had only three company policies:

1. No photocopying body parts.
2. No fish in the microwave.
3. No taking the last cold Diet Dr. Pepper.

As strange as they may sound, each rule resulted from an incident. Although they weren't in any policy manual we had, these were unspoken rules that were passed down from person to person and perpetuated through our culture. If nothing else, they communicated that humor was an asset in our office.

No doubt if you have ever smelled the inside of a microwave after fish has been cooked in it, you understand where that rule came from. Our first office was only 800 square feet, and the kitchenette—if you could call it that—was smack in the middle of everything (next to the single bathroom, but that is another story altogether!). One day, one of our employees brought in leftover fish from her dinner the night before as her lunch. It didn't take more than 30 seconds of cook time for everyone in the office, and probably some in the one above us, to know what she was having. It reeked. Burning popcorn was added to the list of microwave no-nos shortly thereafter.

We were well into our growth before we realized the need for a formal employment manual. In the beginning, we pulled most of our employees from within our known network—former colleagues, friends, and neighbors. We knew these people and shared a similar work ethic. It wasn't until a couple of years into our company when we began hiring outside of this realm that we realized the need for an employment manual that spelled out company policies. It is not uncommon for small business owners to overlook this important document as something 'bureaucratic," and it certainly hadn't bubbled up in priority for us until we began to need it.

As is common in many young and growing companies, we were trying to do more work with fewer resources. Everyone was, at some point, required to do more than their share of work with the expectation that they would be compensated fairly for their efforts, though not necessarily with money. Because people tend to come from different backgrounds, we did not all have the same understanding or expectation of what was *fair*.

One of our employees came from a larger company where he was often given one hour of comp time for every hour of overtime he worked. As a small company, we were not in a position to do that. Besides, when there were slower weeks that perhaps allowed him to work less than 40 hours, we continued to pay him his full salary. This discrepancy in expectations led us to the development of our employee manual. There, we highlighted any behavior that was not tolerated and detailed what the consequences could be. From a legal perspective, this document was critical.

Rather than develop our own from scratch or pay a lawyer thousands of dollars to create an employment manual, we were able to find samples on the Internet and adapt them to our own business. The resulting manual was sufficient for a time, but as we grew and changed, we reached a point that we paid a lawyer for a template containing a more complete set of policies. All new employees were required to sign off that they had reviewed the manual, which ensured that our expectations were read and acknowledged. As we continued to grow, we augmented the document as situations arose or we encountered questionable behavior. For example, we never thought that we would have to worry about employees trying to use an "optional holiday" after they put in their two weeks' notice. Sure enough, we found a need to add that provision.

Sienna* had forgotten about that part of our policy when she gave her two weeks' notice. She e-mailed her resignation to me while I was out of town, which was also one week before she was going away on vacation. She had originally planned to use her optional holidays over that period, but once she had resigned, she was forced to tap into reserved vacation days to cover her remaining work days. She had counted on being paid for those days but quickly needed to adjust her expectations.

We also began to see signs that we needed to create a policy around use of company computer equipment, including the Internet. While this is now a standard provision at many companies, we had not even thought about it. At the time, we could not even get a digital subscriber line (DSL) to our office, so we used the Internet only as needed. We had a dedicated line to reach our customers, so the impetus to update was lagging. When we were finally able to get high-speed service into the office, we discovered that when one employee listened to a radio station over the Internet, the frustration with the diminished network throughput was palpable. We had to make a policy about banning streaming anything during office hours. It wasn't a popular decision, but one that was required for the good of the team.

It was a different catalyst that drove Donna to develop her company's employment manual. Three years into their business they hired Cecil's brother, right out of college. Being the brother of the boss, he took certain privileges as rights. As the other employees began to notice his liberties, management knew they had to find a way to deal with the situation productively. They felt that the best way to address the problem impersonally was to create an employment manual that detailed expected and acceptable behaviors as well as spelled out various rights and privileges. Unfortunately, that did not have the desired effect and they ended up having to coach the brother into venturing out into Corporate America to learn from others how it is done. When he rejoined the company three years later, he was a different and more respectful person.

Setting boundaries in business and with kids is an important way to make sure your expectations are communicated. It provides a method for fair administration of the rules even though not everyone may like them.

## Wanting to Be Liked

"I hate you." Words I know I said at least once (or more!) to my mother and wanted to avoid at all costs with my children. It is not uncommon, however, for parents to hear those words from their child at some point.

After Austin's* first year in middle school, Joe* realized that his youngest son needed more help than the local school systems could provide. He had always been a social child, but he also had an increasing problem with impulse control. The chaos of moving from one classroom to another in middle school was a difficult distraction for Austin. It was not uncommon for Joe to receive two to three phone calls a day from his school regarding some behavioral issue. The whole family was suffering, and it could not go on. It was critical to Joe and his wife that their son not only make it through middle school but be adequately prepared for high school.

Consequently, they hired an educational consultant to help them explore their options for Austin.

Based on Austin's unique profile and needs, the school recommended by the consultant was a boarding school over 400 miles away from home. Joe was concerned about Austin's reaction and imagined that the distance would be a scary proposition for him. After all, he was only 13 years old and had never been away from home alone. Joe and his wife struggled with the decision to send him off to school. They knew there was a possibility that he would never forgive them, but they felt strongly that their son needed them to make decisions for him as parents more than as friends. With heavy hearts, they decided he had to go.

Joe agonized over the best time to break the news and opted to tell him a scant three days before they were to visit the school. He figured that the less time he had to sulk over it, the better. To their surprise, Austin's reaction when they told him it was a boarding school was to say, "I think that is a good thing." His next question was whether or not it was co-ed and when he found the school was only boys, he became less than enthused. Still, he was suffering enough to acquiesce to his parent's judgment and that of the consultant.

As difficult as it was to take their son so far away to school, it was even harder to leave him there. Joe claims that leaving Austin at school was the second worst moment he has ever experienced in his life. It was a long journey back to the airport that first time they left him, but a drive they'll never forget. When he called week after week pleading with his parents to let him come home, they stood firm. They needed to give the school a chance to bring out Austin's best.

It took several months for Austin to adjust to his surroundings and integrate himself into his new environment. Over time, he began to shine and eventually graduated at the top of his class. Unexpectedly, he was also given an award by the school's board of directors as the student who most exemplified the goals of the school. Neither Austin nor his parents could have imagined his progress and accomplishments. Had he stayed where he was, he might have been lost. They took a chance on making the tough and unpopular decision, and it paid off.

I once asked my daughter if she thought I was strict compared to her friends' mothers. Her reply was, "Yes, but that's okay." I've struggled with wanting to be my daughter's friend and wanting to be her mother, which by definition is *not* one and the same. In order to be a good parent to your children, you must be prepared to make decisions that are not popular and are—in the words of my mother—for their own good. Many of us are faced with similar tough and unwelcome choices not only for our kids but for our businesses as well.

When I first read Patrick Lencioni's book *The Five Temptations of a CEO* (see Resources at the end of the chapter), I immediately identified "needing to be liked" as a trap I had fallen into. When I started my company, I was elbow to elbow with my staff, developing our software. As the company began to grow and I needed to move out of the day-to-day operations, I felt like I was losing friends. It was lonely at the top. I realized that it is no fun to discipline or, worse, fire a friend and I have had to do both.

Cheryl* and I had worked in the same group at my former employer, though I never worked on any projects with her. We were, however, friends outside of work. When we were looking to expand our development group, she was in the process of transitioning out of IBM. She held a master's degree in computer science and had been at IBM longer than I had, so I concluded with our common base and her educational background, she would be a good candidate to bring into our business. After she interviewed with the development team, we decided to bring her on board.

She had been working with us for a while when we reached a point in our growth that I needed her to step up and take the lead on a project. I figured with her educational background and longevity with the company that this would not be a problem. While this had not been originally discussed when we hired her, the needs of the business had changed. We no longer needed her to continue doing what she was doing—we needed more leaders. Unfortunately, she had a hard time with the idea of taking charge of the project and was unwilling to commit to it. We had to let her go, and with her went our friendship. Unfortunately, she was neither the first nor the last with whom that happened. I learned that in order to be an effective CEO I had to be able to make the tough decisions, which might mean that some people won't like me or I might lose a friendship. That was challenging for me. I felt guilty, like I was letting them down.

What I later realized is that guilt only served to cloud my judgment. Like the guilt I would feel with my children when I was away on a business trip, I would lean more toward trying to be their friend to make it up to them rather than being their parent. As it became clear that we were fighting an uphill battle in expanding into our chosen new markets, I continued to press forward for the wrong reasons. I did not want to let my employees down—I felt like I owed it to them to keep going. I let my guilt cloud my business judgment, though only for a brief while. When we stepped back from the emotion of the situation and looked at the realities, we saw that we could not continue on. We were not doing anyone any favors by pressing ahead.

I have also learned that you do not help people by keeping them in a job that they are not suited for. Chances are they already know they are in the wrong position and are just as miserable as you are. I have struggled over firing people that later relayed their discharge was the best thing that could have happened to them. By setting them free from a job that did not fit or fulfill them, they were allowed to find their true calling or at least work that was a better match for their skills, interests, and capabilities.

Kathy Freeland knew it would not be easy when she realized that bringing her husband's brother into the company was not her best hiring decision. To make matters worse, her husband, who worked with her in the company, was going to have to let him go. Thankfully, the discharge did not come as a surprise. His brother had been feeling out of his element and consequently was relieved when told he wasn't the right person for the job. From that point forward, terminating people became much easier for Kathy's husband.

When I started my company, my need to be liked drove me toward a consensus model for decision making. Using this approach, I wanted to get everyone's input and come to consensus rather than stepping up and risk making an unpopular choice on my own. What I found is that in addition to becoming extremely frustrating, assuming this approach also belabored every decision. Nothing happened quickly. I evolved our business decision-making model into one that we practiced with our children.

The tactic we took with our children was to solicit their opinion and thoughts on a matter, but then make sure they understood that the ultimate decision was ours. For example, when we were considering moving, we asked for their thoughts and concerns but made it clear that we would make the ultimate decision based on what was best overall for the whole family. By soliciting their input we often increased their buy-in of the final decision. In the end, however, we had information or insight that they did not and made a decision that was sometimes not popular.

Likewise, I had to make decisions in my company that were not necessarily accepted by everyone. A specific decision that was often revisited and even discussed at company happy hours revolved around our technical architecture. One particular developer was adamant that we needed to update our architecture, that by doing so our business would grow. From my perspective, I saw more pressing problems. While I did not disagree that taking the step to upgrade our architecture was a task we should consider, there were bigger issues that I felt were thwarting our growth. I used our customers as my gauge on the areas in which we should invest in our software product. At the time, not one customer or prospective customer listed our architecture as a deterrent. We had not lost any business or potential customers because of it. Our positioning and customers' priorities were the real issues behind our sputtering efforts to bring in new clients. We were positioned in between the plant floor and business systems, which provided us with no critical entry point. Our customer's loved what we did, saw the need, but always had some other need or project that was more pressing.

When you accept the responsibility for making decisions in your company, you are taking a risk that someone will not agree or like the decision that was made. If you approach your decision making with consistency, you have the opportunity to make decisions that are at least construed as *fair*.

## Fair Is Not Equal

The front seat of our car is a constant subject of the discussion about what is fair. Both kids love to sit in the front seat, but Sydney is the only one who is old enough. We will let Madison sit in the front seat on occasion when we are traveling a short distance and not on any major roads. To Sydney, this is unfair. It is unfair because she had to wait until she was 12 to sit in the front seat (Madison was 10). After a particular encounter, she funneled her frustration by sitting down and compiling a list of all the things she deemed were unfair. When Keenan found the list, he took each point and countered it with something that she got that Madison did not. A bigger room. A roomier closet. The privilege of using IM on the computer. After she reviewed the list, I tried to explain to her the burden and the benefits of being the older child. Younger brothers and sisters tend to get access to privileges at an earlier age than we do. In return, we tend to receive additional perks. It *was* fair.

One of the chores that my children share is cleaning out the cat box. When they were begging me to get a cat (we ended up getting two!), they promised they would help take care of them. Yeah, right. Trying to get them to do this particular not-so-glamorous task is often a struggle. We try to keep it even between the two of them by having them put their name on the calendar when they do it. Unfortunately, the name does not always get there. On occasion, it does not end up equal, either. Any parent could easily take out the words *cat box* and insert whatever it is that their child deems unfair. The same conversation takes place all over the world, with every child.

Sydney had been sick with strep throat followed by a nasty virus for over a week that left her dizzy and worn out. She was miserable. I asked Madison to clean out the cat box for the week and, of course, was met with the "That's not fair!" reply. She was right—it was not really fair. It was not her fault that her sister was sick. But it was not her sister's fault, either. No one could be blamed—it just *was*. I explained to her (for the umpteenth time) that fair does not mean everything is equal. Was it fair that I cooked dinner all the time (okay, so I didn't do it all the time, but I was trying to make a point!)? Such a hard concept for kids to get, yet we must continue to try.

What we continually teach our children is that fair is not the same as equal. Privileges are not doled out on a one-for-one basis where we keep score. Our children are different and may not be able to handle the same things at the same age. Chores, as well, should not be tallied side by side. For some reason, this is the innate definition of fair for kids. It can be like that with employees as well.

Terry Chase Hazell purposely did not give all employees the same privileges. She was clear that employees earned special privileges and felt that was fair. The office assistant was willing to come in on weekends or work nights if Terry asked. In return, she knew she could call in if she had a family event and get the time off without a problem. Others who didn't give the company flexibility didn't get it. Some of her staff thought she had *favorites*, but she preferred to think of them as *performers*. One year she had a management team with four stars on it. That team was hot, and they got privileges that made others envious. One had car trouble, and Terry ended up giving him her company car to drive so he wouldn't be distracted. Another had a parent pass away and he was given three weeks paid time off without deducting from his vacation time. Still another star employee was having nanny troubles, and Terry allowed her to hire an assistant to give her more work-time flexibility. They paid full MBA tuition for the other. She invested in her high performers, and they deserved it. She felt they had earned it. That team made great progress, and the company—even those who had been envious—continued to benefit from the contracts they won.

Our struggle with fairness was driven by a fluctuating labor market. When we started to hire programming staff members, the labor market for technical people was tight and competition for talent was high. We were required to offer at or above-market salaries and benefits in order to attract talent. For a small start-up company, allocating the cash needed for a killer benefits package was tough. Instead, we adopted a strategy where we paid salaries at or slightly above the market and then focused on free or near-free benefits such as flexible work schedules and the ability to work from home. These benefits, we discovered, were often more valued than the monetary ones. It was our willingness to see our employees as total human beings that bred loyalty more than the money. Not to say that anyone was willing to work for free, but it was important to find the right mix for each individual rather than approach it as a "one size fits all." We just had to make sure it was fair.

As the years went on and the labor market opened up, salaries began to drop. We were able to hire people with similar skills but with lower salaries during that period. They were paid what was fair in the market at the time, but it was not equal to where others had started. We chose not to cut the salary of those employees that we hired when the market was tight, they just got smaller raises. When we had a profitable year, however, they were given their share of bonuses, and perhaps even more given that they had not had a substantial raise in some time. While it may not have been equal dollar for dollar, we felt it was fair. After all, is it fair that teachers are paid less than computer programmers? Does it make sense that we put a higher value on entertainers than police officers?

It is also necessary to manage people differently, as discussed in the "Knowing Your Kid" section in Chapter 5, which can be construed as unfair from the outside. For example, some employees enjoy public recognition for their accomplishments, while others would rather walk on hot coals than be the center of attention. Does that mean they should just deal with it or should you opt, instead, to recognize them in private? Making fair decisions in a company establishes a base of trust, which goes a long way toward creating an environment where teams can work together to achieve great things.

## The Team Approach

When her youngest child was five years old, Sheila Heinze's mother decided to open a flower shop. She had previously been a social worker, which had allowed her more time at home raising her seven children. As anyone who has owned a retail establishment can tell you, it does not lend itself to flexibility. The new business required a shift in household balance and a great deal of teamwork from all of the siblings to be successful. Sheila has been able to draw on these experiences as the child of an entrepreneur to build up her team.

Trying to convince my own children that we are all part of a team has been a constant effort. Anytime they start to pick on each other, I remind them that a family is a team and we need to be supportive of one another, not tear each other down. As I tell my daughters, there are enough people in the world who don't care what happens to you that, as a family, we have to support each other. "We are all on the same team."

Donna is one of the lucky ones. She received proof that her five-year-old son really bought into the notion of family teamwork. She had been telling her kids that if everyone pitches in and helps with the chores around the house, Mommy does not have to do it all by herself on the weekend and will have more time to do fun things with them. One morning, she came downstairs and her son had organized all of the shoes in their mud room without being asked. She was beside herself. This was an extraordinary amount of initiative for a child his age. As a result, she made sure she did something extra special for him that weekend. He saw the power of what teamwork could do—give him more time with Mom.

Our customer Ernie believed strongly in team building and went out of his way to create a sharing, caring environment to support group development. One year, he rented a house on a lake in North Carolina and had all of his direct reports as well as their close vendors in attendance, which was where I came in. During this session we had discussions that bounced between tactical and strategic, personal and corporate. He even rented a pontoon boat that we took out for a cruise when the team needed a boost of energy. The result was a team that bonded together not only professionally but also, and more importantly, on a personal level. There was a true feeling that we were all in this together.

In a workplace where this sentiment is practiced, egos have been cast aside, each person trusts in the positive intentions (motivations) of others, and people generally feel listened to. We had to build some of these systems into our culture or risk falling prey to an environment where everyone was out for himself. Where ego is in play and there is a lack of respect for each other, people tend to adopt a "cover your butt" philosophy. From what I had seen, this was ineffective and *not* what I wanted to come to each day.

The reality of building a business is that constructing the team is often the most difficult part. One of the challenges to building an effective team is that everyone comes into a company with different assumptions and experiences. If those are not recognized, voiced, or otherwise addressed, it can lead to an underlying lack of trust. One of the best books on this topic is *Leadership and Self-Deception* by the Arbinger Institute (San Francisco: Berrett-Koehler Publishers, 2000). In this book, the idea is presented that the way we view other people can cause us to have adverse reactions to their behavior. By clearing out our assumptions and checking our attitudes, we can find a better way to relate to those around us in order to build more trusting, less destructive relationships. The concepts in the book work for both parenting and business, illustrating once again the parallels between the two.

Another book that I used extensively in my own business team building and awareness was *The Five Dysfunctions of a Team* by Patrick Lencioni (see Resources at the end of the chapter). In the book, Patrick sets up five key ingredients for a successful team and places them in a hierarchical pyramid. At the bottom is trust, next is commitment followed by conflict, team-based accountability, and a focus on results. While there are a lot of books available on team building, this one seemed to work best within the confines and culture of our organization. They key is to find a model or a rhythm that works within your organization and implement it with consistency.

## From School Backpack to Briefcase

- Make sure your employees recognize your commitment to and involvement in the organization. Do not underestimate knowledge gained at the water cooler or coffee pot.
- Customers must be constantly reminded of your presence. Keeping in touch with current and potential customers opens up a whole realm of additional information and opportunity.
- Realize that you are one of the best sales people for your business. You must maintain a professional appearance and talk about your business

any chance you get. You never know who might know someone that can help you in your business or be a potential customer.

- Develop a 30-second, clear and concise statement about your business—an elevator pitch—to use when anybody asks what you do.
- Take a vacation. Your business will be better off. Make sure your business is ready by (1) marketing your company instead of yourself, (2) building a team you can trust to hold down the fort, and (3) empowering your team to make decisions without you.
- Making yourself the most expendable person in your company is good. Refusing to train your replacement and those of your management team will stall your company's growth and ensure that it will never grow beyond your personal reach and abilities.
- We often wait until boundaries are crossed before actually setting them. Prudent business managers make sure those boundaries are defined from the very beginning and save time, energy, and possibly a lawsuit in the process.
- Don't fall into the trap of needing to be liked, at least in your business. While it is nice to be popular, letting that guide your decisions renders you unable to make the tough decisions that are needed in successful businesses.
- Gaining consensus around decisions is fine but a difficult decision-making model to uphold for growing companies. Define the decision-making process in your company, and don't be afraid to make decisions that are unpopular.
- Being fair to your employees does not mean that everything is equal. People don't all get paid the same, but they are compensated fairly.
- The team approach is critical in business and often one of the hardest aspects to master. At the base of an effective team is trust, but equally important is a team's ability to engage in productive conflict, share the same level of commitment, hold each other accountable, and focus on results.

## Resources for Businesses' Emerging Independence

Jim Collins, *Good to Great* (New York: HarperCollins, 2001).

Jon R. Katzenbach and Douglas K. Smith, *Wisdom of Teams: Creating the High-Performance Organization* (Cambridge, Mass.: Harvard Business School Press, 1993).

Patrick Lencioni, *The Five Dysfunctions of a Team: A Leadership Fable* (San Francisco: Jossey-Bass, 2002).

Patrick Lencioni, *The Five Temptations of a CEO: A Leadership Fable* (San Francisco: Jossey-Bass, 1998).

Kathleen D. Ryan and Daniel K. Oestreich, *Driving Fear Out of the Workplace: Creating the High-Trust, High-Performance Organization,* (San Francisco: Jossey-Bass, 1998).

## Sheila Heinze's Top Five Tips

1. A good support system is imperative to growing a business while raising children.
2. Fair is better than equal. You can't give everything in your life equal time, but make sure the time allotted is fair.
3. Let go by teaching your employees how to make decisions and allow them make mistakes. Delegating must be intentional and it is not easy for most entrepreneurs.
4. Don't second-guess your decisions—trust yourself. You will make mistakes, but you can recover and become stronger as a result.
5. Balance is not equal—it is being in the right place at the time you are needed.

CHAPTER

# Exercising Your Exit

Ashleigh had a good head on her shoulders. Not that she didn't make mistakes similar to other teenagers, but her mom, Tammy, wasn't concerned about her ability to handle the responsibilities of going away to college. Ashleigh was confident, too, in her ability to handle the independence of college life away from home. She had been working different jobs for a couple years and felt that her parents had given her enough leeway in her social life that the independence university life offered would not be very different from her final year in high school. Although cooking was a life skill she had yet to truly master, she enrolled in the campus meal plan so who needed to cook?

Academically, Ashleigh felt primed as well. She was an honors student and had taken a class at the local community college during her senior year in high school. She was registered for a full 15 hours in her first semester, but remained undaunted by warnings from those who had gone before her that she might do better with a lighter load to ease into college life. Even history class, she was told, is harder at the college level than she might think. Convinced she could handle the burden, she refused to be swayed.

When the time came for the family to drive her down to school in order to move into her dorm, everything went as they had planned. The goodbyes were hard, as expected, but the thrill of embarking on a new chapter in her life kept Ashleigh looking forward. The excitement was palpable and all was good. Tears were few, at least in the beginning.

The first call was actually an instant message (IM) that came the day after she arrived and still several days before classes started. Her new roommate seemed nice, but they weren't "bonding" as Ashleigh had hoped. The freshman mixers were lame, and it wasn't as easy to make friends as expected. A couple of days later and the night before classes started, something had turned her laundry green (later discovered to be new towels) and her roommate just wasn't warming up. Tammy reassured her that things would get better.

The first day of classes was likewise more arduous than Ashleigh had anticipated. The vocabulary used by her professors seemed leagues above what she had become accustomed to in high school and that history class was not the "easy A" she had counted on. On day three of classes she instant messaged her mom that she wanted to drop history and take music appreciation. She subsequently e-mailed her mom a letter to review that she had written to the head resident assistant requesting to move into a different dorm room. As luck would have it, the roommate of a friend from her hometown had failed to appear, and Ashleigh saw that as an opportunity to improve her own roommate situation. She didn't want to come home because she felt like she would burst into tears if she saw her parents. The weight of the transition had sunk in.

As much as Tammy wanted emotionally to make everything okay for Ashleigh, she had to let her go. She provided tidbits of motherly advice but mostly left Ashleigh to figure out how to make things work. It was hard not to run in and try and fix everything for her daughter, but Tammy knew that the best she could do for her was to let her work through it on her own. She had worked for 18 years to give her solid roots, and now it was time to let her fly on her own wings.

It took Ashleigh only a month to break in her wings and fly on her own. Although she hit some turbulence while adjusting to the modified air flow that college life embodies, the fact that she was in full control of her own decisions, successes, and failures had her loving her first solo flight.

## Introduction

We have many points in our lives and in our businesses when we are letting go: putting our child on the bus to go to kindergarten for the first time, hiring a manager to fill in where we had been dabbling, realizing you don't know everything that is going on with your preteen or with your development manager, or allowing your teen to drive your car . . . anywhere.

As hard as it is to do, at some point we must let our children venture out on their own. Kick the birds out of the nest. I have a print hanging in my kitchen reminding me of this, with a quote from Hooding Carter: "There are two lasting bequests we can give our children: One is roots, the other is wings." The same applies to our businesses. At some point, business owners will likely have to let go of their business as well and may find it just as difficult. As discussed in the "Deciding to Take the Plunge" section in Chapter 2, the ideal scenario is to start your business with the end in mind. Know what you want to get out of it so that you can make decisions along the way with your exit strategy in mind. For many entrepreneurs, the ideal end is found in the sale, although that is not the only way to make a successful exit.

## Business Exit—The Sale

Paul Silber was able to sell his company and reap the benefits, though it took a little longer than he had planned. When he started his company, In Vitro Technologies, in 1990, he did so with the knowledge that he was not interested in running a publicly held company. That left two options: to run it until he was able to pass it on to his children or to position the company for eventual sale. He had been taught early in his entrepreneurial career to always run your company as if positioning it for sale even if that is not your intention. His observation, which paid off in millions of dollars, was that the characteristics that make a company attractive to potential buyers are the same attributes that make a company a strong performer in any market. Those distinctions include a strong management team, intellectual property position (if you are in a technology field), customer base, growing revenues, profits, and brand recognition.

---

### Paul's Advice for Preparing to Sell Your Company

View your business as a potential buyer would. Make sure decisions you make are good for the long haul because the sale might not go through and you will be stuck with your decisions.

---

As he got closer to selling his company, he did find that he became more intolerant of mediocre performance in his management team. Where he had let behaviors or performance issues slide before, when he looked at his company as a potential buyer would, he recognized that those had to be corrected more quickly.

Although Paul had developed a "thick skin" after so many years of running an organization, he admits that selling his company was the most emotionally challenging process he had ever gone through in his professional life. It was a difficult experience with a lot of negatives. First, he was frustrated by dealing in the minutiae of the due diligence process, answering hundreds of repetitive questions from attorneys representing the buyers. What he didn't know is that "ask them the same question 50 times" is a torture mechanism used to break the unsuspecting entrepreneur down. He wasn't giving in, though.

He also worried about his employees. There were many who had been with him from the early days, and he valued their loyalty. He cared for his company as he would for a child, except that he would never sell his children, no matter what the offering price. When the sale of the company went through for $30 million plus a potential additional bonus of $5 million, Paul agreed to stay on for at least a year to ensure a smooth transition. Even with the money in his bank account, he continued to be concerned about the future of his baby, now owned by a company from the United Kingdom. For Paul, the end worked out as he had planned, even if it was a few years past his original goal.

When Kathy Freeland started her company she, too, had a long-term exit strategy: Build a company of value and, when the time was right, sell. Although she did not have a specific time frame in mind, the exit strategy was part of her strategic plan for RGII. The intent, consistently, was to focus on building value into the company so they could come out with something someone else would want—a company that was greater than the sum of all of its contracts.

Her original goal was to exit from the government's 8(a) program, which spans nine years, at $100 million in revenues. Kathy cites the changes in the marketplace, customers, and competition as key factors that kept their strategic plan morphing with the economic environment. Although the company did not reach that milestone, they were able to grow to over 300 employees and approximately $40 million in revenues at the time they sold their company in 2003.

The management team at RGII did not focus their revenue strategy or the types of contracts to pursue based on their goal of selling. Instead, they focused on continuing to build a company that was as strong as it could be until the time and opportunity presented itself to sell. Long-term growth was always the focus, and that paid off.

When they were approached in 2003 by Computer Horizons Corporation, Kathy was at first apprehensive. She felt the same way any parent would feel when considering letting their baby go. As she began to get to look at the landscape of the marketplace—where they were a small fish in a big pond—she perceived that the company's prospective new parent could provide resources and reach that they would need to continue to grow the business. With this merger, they would be in a position to pursue those large contracts that they had previously opted out of based on inability to scale or to produce sufficient past performance. This was an opportunity to provide the legacy of RGII a sustainable future.

Along with the sale came an agreement for Kathy to stay on and run the company for a period of three years. In doing so, she was able to personally ensure that the transition went smoothly, that her baby was in good hands. While she anticipated a sense of loss when she left at the end of her three years, what she found instead was an extreme sense of accomplishment. She had done what she had been tasked to do. The company was in a strong position when her contract ended, and she felt cautiously optimistic with the management team that had been brought in to take her place. Additionally, her goal of keeping her son's memory forever alive had been met and was now soaring off to new heights. Realizing her dream made all the hard work worthwhile.

Both Paul and Kathy constantly focused on building value into their company. Rather than looking for short-term opportunities, they approached their business with a longer-term perspective. Kathy was not looking for it—her suitor came to her. While Paul was putting out feelers for a buyer, the company that approached him was not previously on his radar. They simply focused on prudent decisions for their businesses without doing anything special for a buyer. They both hit the jackpot.

Graham Weston, although he has not yet executed his exit, has continued to focus on building value in his business but without the intention of specific size or value. When he started, he and his partners thought perhaps they could reach $30 to 50 million in revenues. In reality, they had no idea of market size. They felt as if they were pursuing a business opportunity that made sense. He compares this approach to raising kids: You have no idea how they'll turn out, you just do your best and hope for good things. Now that his company has surpassed $200 million in annual revenues, with 1,150 employees, he claims he feels like his child is a Nobel Prize winner. And he hasn't even cashed out yet.

Jan B. King had not been thinking at all about exiting her business, Merritt Publishing, when she was approached by a prospective buyer. A guest speaker at her CEO networking meeting remembered her company when talking with another business owner months later in a different city. The other entrepreneur was looking to buy a company like Jan's, so he put the two in touch.

At their first meeting, the interested buyer pulled Jan aside. He asked her if she was interested in selling and, if so, had she given any thought to a price? Because the company was at that time employee owned, she had to have an idea what amount would be required to satisfy all of the shareholders. Although she had not previously been thinking about selling, she knew exactly what she would sell the company for. Her business coach had taught her the importance of keeping a number in mind—what would it take for you to walk away? She certainly did not envision needing to use it. She suggested a figure to him right there, which turned out to be the final deal price nine months later.

From a market perspective, the timing of the purchase turned out to be perfect. The intent was for Jan to stay on and continue to run the West Coast operations. Two weeks before the papers were signed, the buyer changed the plan. Instead, they agreed to give her several years of paid salary in exchange for an agreement that would keep her out of publishing. She remembers the day of the signing vividly. It was a Friday, and afterward, everyone else went back to work. She went home. She had the worst weekend she had ever experienced. She expected at least some of her former employees to call her to see how she was doing, but none of them did. Suddenly, she was unemployed. No one was returning her calls. No voice mail messages to follow up on. A sudden plummet in the number of e-mails she needed to address. This was not going to be easy.

Instead of dealing with what had happened, Jan searched frantically for something else to do. She felt a desperate need to keep busy. She located a nonprofit that needed her help, so she took it on and ran it for six months. Unfortunately, she could not deny the loss she was trying so hard to cover up and it kept coming back. Finally, she conceded and addressed the grief she was feeling. She immersed herself in designing her new life, whatever that was going to be.

My story is similar to Jan's, and I admit that I did not practice what I preach when it comes to planning an exit. I waited until I was burned out to decide it was time to get out of my first business.

Just like the stock market, you never want to be caught selling low. Looking back, I was running on fumes.

The critical lesson I learned is the importance of planning your exit. It seems odd to think about when you're just starting, but as Stephen Covey recommends: "Start with the end in mind." When you know what your ultimate goal is, you can develop your business plan to get there and make decisions along the way knowing what you want to get out of it in the end.

Through the 10 years with my first business, there were many opportunities along the way that had I been building my company with "big" in mind, I would have jumped on. For example, as the company was beginning its initial growth spurt, we had the opportunity to hire a very experienced senior manager who would have really driven us to accelerate our growth rate. At the time, I knew I was not in the business to "build another Microsoft," as I would tell people, which meant that I was on the slow, managed growth track. I claimed I was not ready to pay the level of salary that he needed, but the truth was that I was not ready to kick it up to where he would have wanted to take us. The business, for me, was more of a "lifestyle" business—built to accommodate my lifestyle choices. In this case, my choice was to grow slowly so I did not lose my ability to be with my children when I needed to. That does not mean I was not serious about my business, just more cautious of the opportunities we pursued.

When I began to think about exiting the business, we had started to decline in revenues, though not significantly. We still had some strong customers and ongoing contracts. About that time, I came in contact with a company that was growing and needed the types of people and skills that I had on staff. We had the experience, the internal processes, and the industry knowledge that they needed to grow their new practice. It would have been a perfect match. Unfortunately, they determined that their needs were much greater than what I had to offer. They were looking to hire four times more people than we had at the time and felt like we were just not large enough. My heart sank with my hopes of a quick exit. At least I got an entertaining site visit to Belgium out of the exercise and some hard lessons learned.

From there, I continued to try to turn things around, but my heart was not fully in it. My father had always taught me not to give up, and I felt like I owed it to my staff to push ahead. After all, they had put their livelihood and their trust in me personally, or so I believed. Unfortunately, my employees recognized that I had lost the passion and drive needed to keep the business growing before I had even admitted it to myself. After one of my key employees, my chief operating officer, resigned, I knew it was time to go. He was the only other person in the company who was assisting me with business development. I did not have the energy to search for his replacement—I was that burned out.

Reviewing our financial statements, which were still strong, we planned to cash out at the right point. Thankfully, I was able to leverage my relationship with a long-time partner to assume our existing support contracts. Yes, I actually walked away from significant contracts, but they were a small percentage of the total amount we were able to get out of the business. This partner eventually purchased our software assets as well. The point of turning everything over to them was a bittersweet moment. I felt as if I were giving my baby up for adoption. I was sure they would take care of it and knew it would live on, but it was still difficult. At least I still have visitation rights.

I found that immediately after my exit, I did not know what to do with myself. My identity had been wrapped up in my company for so long I wasn't sure who I really was. I felt I needed to keep busy and found it hard to relax. I also realized I was experiencing the stages of grief over the six months following. With the assistance of a good friend with great listening skills, I was able to finally enjoy my time off and experience a rejuvenation of interest and energy. I also received help from a book by Gail Blanke titled *Between Trapezes: Flying into a New Life with the Greatest of Ease* (see the "Recommended Reading" section at the end of this chapter). In the book, Gail deftly makes the point that you cannot grab onto other opportunities unless you are willing to let go of the old ones. It made a lot of sense to me at the time and was instrumental in nudging me to release my fingers from the bar so I could be ready to grasp hold of the next one that came my way.

## Walking Away

I exited my second business much sooner in the process than the first. Our second business baby was Sydison Foods, which was named after a combination of our daughters' names. It was conceived while we were still trying to determine the ultimate fate of ACT. Keenan was struggling with a variety of food allergies and frustrated at his inability to find any healthy, convenient snacks on the market that he could eat. All of the products that were currently available on the market, with a very few exceptions, tasted nasty. He once made me taste a breakfast bar that was made out of chickpea flour. It was so disgusting I had to spit it into the trash. He struggled to find nonperishable food to keep in his car for when we were running errands or on a trip. His solution was to start making his own snack bars.

One morning at breakfast, the idea hit him. If he were having this problem, so must a lot of other people. Why couldn't we start a company making healthy, convenient snacks for people with food allergies? We had spent over 10 years working with food manufacturers, so we knew about that end of the business. With that, our new baby was born. This time, Keenan was more actively involved in the conception of our business baby.

Over the next 18 months, we were engaged in conducting a feasibility analysis for our new offspring. We found the opportunity to apply a good deal of the lessons that we had learned from growing ACT to our new endeavor. We wanted to confirm the market, learn more about the sales side of the food business, and fully understand the supply chain and who takes what at each step of the way.

We traveled to trade shows and commissioned a customer survey through a national association to understand if there was truly a customer need as Keenan had experienced. Through those mechanisms, we learned a great deal about what the consumers wanted as well as the dearth of products currently on the market. Interestingly, some of the customer needs and interests were not what we had predicted. We learned a lot by asking our potential customers what they wanted and needed.

To determine the size of the market, we searched the Internet for industry reports and ended up purchasing point-of-sale data. Unfortunately, the data was not encouraging. We could not help but wonder, was it because there was no need or because the available product tasted like the inside of a dirty tennis shoe (not that I have personally compared the two)? We decided we really needed to create an advisory board with strong industry background to help us interpret the data we were finding and help chart our path forward.

We were able to commission a strong advisory board from the people that we had met through our former company. We also continued to network at industry events. One of our advisers was the president of a $100 million organic food company who was a panelist at a conference we were attending. Keenan went up to him after his panel and talked to him about their products, which he used. In the process, he also explained the nature of our new start-up. It turned out that he had helped grow his current company, which was in the process of being purchased, and was interested in helping us get our business off the ground. Before I knew it, Keenan had asked him to be an adviser for us and he agreed. Who would have thought? All we had to do was ask.

As we learned more about how the market worked—the size, challenges, and small profit margins—we began to realize that this was not the best opportunity for us. This is where our focused flexibility, which I discussed in Chapter 2, came into play. Our original "differentiator" was the main ingredient we used. There were no other snack foods on the market using this unique type of flour. In his research, Keenan also found reports that this flour was helpful for diabetics, though its use as such was protected by a patent. We decided to switch our research to pursuing all-natural snack foods that help lower blood sugar levels for diabetics. Once we took this alternate path, we knew the scientific twist was going to be a stretch for our capabilities and would require a change in our advisers. We were subsequently able to recruit an internationally recognized expert in diabetes to our board to compensate for our weaknesses. Unfortunately, however, roadblocks continued to develop. In the end, the patent holder's unwillingness to negotiate a favorable license agreement led us to abandoning the idea all together. We had to walk away. This go around, it was not hard. Although we had put some money into our analysis, it was significantly less than it would have been had we gone to market with a product that failed. While we had also put a lot of time into the process, it was not a waste, as we continued to learn from it.

Terry Chase Hazell claims that she cannot put a price on the experience she gained starting and running Chesapeake-PERL, but she also knows that you sometimes get to a point where you need to walk away. In the days leading up to her board meeting, Terry was clearing her personal items off her computer and out of her e-mail. She knew what the resolution was going to be and had been, in fact, one of the architects of it. Six months earlier she was beginning to feel burned out and told her board that she was *done*. They needed to find a new CEO. She agreed to stay on in the interim while they searched for her replacement.

When that day finally came, she was exhilarated by what lay before her, but sad all the same. She had spent six years of her life—a couple of them without pay—building this company out of a business plan that had been all but lost in a filing cabinet. The plan had been there for over a year when she was having lunch with one of the company founders and he said, "You should come run the company." She liked the technology, liked him and the other founder, and had just received a master's degree, which had given her an itch to start a company. Her cofounder was shocked at her quick exit from a paying job but no doubt pleased when she was able to build the company into something of value. After raising over $6 million in outside capital and on the brink of profitability, Terry was ready to let her baby go. Perhaps her willingness to release it lay in the nature of her relationship with the company she built. She adopted a newborn—worked with someone else's initial idea—with full intention of someday letting it go. It turned out not to be as easy as she had anticipated. She had grown to really care for her baby.

She compares the emotions through her exit as similar to graduating from high school but without the cap and gown. She was excited, sad, and worried about the future but confident in her accomplishment. She remembers telling friends they would keep in touch, but inside knowing it wouldn't really work. She retained her seat on the board, which essentially gave her visitation rights. Unfortunately, that did not last long, as she found that being involved without having much control was too difficult. She resigned from the board a few months later.

Several months after her departure, Terry was having a long talk with the chairman of her former company and the strangest thing occurred to her. When they spoke about the company, it was "we" but the "we" clearly did not include her. She was happy and sad all at the same time. When she relayed the story to her dad, he empathized. It was the same feeling he experienced the first time she had left after visiting him and said she was going "home to the family." He realized that the "family" she was referring to did not include him.

Sam Roberts had been frustrated for months. As the managing partner of the law firm he had founded 15 years prior, he was feeling underappreciated. He spent too much time managing the practice and not enough time doing what he enjoyed—helping others by practicing law. Furthermore, he felt like the energy of many of his partners had vanished. They seemed disengaged and distracted. His company had changed, and the value system had evolved until it was now no longer congruent with his own. He found himself in a place he did not want to be.

"I want my freedom."

The words left his mouth before he was certain what he had said. He was talking to one of his partners and just blurted it out. Immediately after he said it, he felt a sense of relief. He did not previously realize that was where he was headed, but it was suddenly upon him and he was glad. Two weeks went by and he had not heard a word from any of his partners on his departure. He decided to bring it up again, and they finally responded—in a letter. His first reaction was that of hurt—these were his children and they weren't blocking the door to keep him from leaving. They were willing to buy him out as expected. They also cut him off, which he felt was a mistake. They had no idea how much work went into managing a firm with 15 lawyers and over 4,200 clients, but they would soon find out.

Sam's final two and a half months at the firm he had created—his baby—were extremely stressful. So stressful, in fact, that he lost 24 pounds over the course of eight weeks. He saw the remaining partners making bad choices, but like a father watching his child make a mistake, there was nothing he could do. He concedes that while it took guts to start his company, it took five times the moxie to walk away.

He asked for three things in addition to his buyout: (1) to leave with his dignity, (2) that the bank be informed he was leaving, and (3) that staff members were given a choice to either stay at the firm or go with Sam as he started his new practice. He continued to focus on the idea of his new firm to keep him moving forward. The people he would have wanted to come with him from his old firm are the ones who opted to join him. He was allowed to take his clients with him, and most indicated they would remain loyal. He created, once again, a practice that he got excited thinking about. Rather than expanding as he had before to provide a full suite of legal services, he was going to keep the new practice small and focus on the parts of law that he enjoyed the most: corporate and wills. He would refer any clients who needed litigation or real estate lawyers to other firms.

He also planned for his second time around to limit his company's growth and pay more attention to, as Jim Collins talks about in *Good to Great* (see Resources at the end of Chapter 7), the people on the bus. Their office space was even intentionally limited in its capacity so as to remind him of his objectives.

Looking back, Sam sees that there were signs that this change was coming even if he didn't acknowledge them. Once he made the decision, he was amazed at how well everything fell together, which convinced him further that he was on the right path. He called this transition a reorganization of his priorities and could not be more pleased with his newfound freedom. He is now free to focus on doing what he loves best. Without all of the additional responsibilities on his shoulders, he is even taking time to pursue other business ideas and interests. It was not until he let go of one that he was free to find the next one. And this one, he is convinced, will be better than the last.

## The Succession Plan

As Pete Linsert was approaching what he considered to be retirement age, he knew it was nearing the time they had planned for his exit from the business. He had been brought on to raise money to get their business, Martek Biosciences, to profitability. That objective had been achieved a few years earlier. The company was rapidly morphing from the 15-person entrepreneurial start-up company he had joined to a growing but mature corporation. His job was less relating to employees on a personal level and more conferring with committees. The previous atmosphere of innovation and discovery had been replaced with process-based execution. As a publicly held company, he had lawyers constantly advising him on what he could say and what he could *not* say. Politics replaced the excitement of the early days. In short, his job was not as interesting to him anymore and not necessarily the best use of his strengths. He had done what he came for—he led the company to close on almost $500 million in outside investments and, with that, achieve solid profitability with a positive cash flow. It was time to move on.

The management team had actually prepared for his retirement a couple years before it was announced in their 2005 annual report. That was part of their succession planning. Once they knew it was coming, he began to transition his responsibilities and duties to other members of his management team. He even quit attending meetings. He had agreed to stay on as chairman of the board for a period of time to ease the transition. With all of the preparation, the passing of the baton still left him with mixed emotions. He compares his feelings in passing on his position to the ring in the *Lord of the Rings* trilogy by J.R.R. Tolkien. In the stories, there was a ring that had great power, but with it came incredible burdens. To pass on the ring and shed that power was a pronounced relief, but it was also hard to release. He has let go without regrets and is already looking into his follow-on start-up venture. The next time around, he is planning to find a business opportunity that can be bootstrapped—financed through organic growth—in order to avoid what he calls the "biotech curse—the huge amount of time and equity dilution of continual money raising."

## What Next?

There are other ways to exit a business that have not been discussed. Implementing an employee stock option plan can be constructed to buy the owner out of a business. This method generally takes time to get bought out and generally results in a cash-out, providing the business continues to perform. Additionally, businesses go bankrupt, the owner dies, or they get wiped out by a natural disaster. It has been estimated that in 2003, 315,000 businesses filed for bankruptcy, which is 19.5 percent of all bankruptcy filings. (Jim Hopkins, "Study Puts Business Bankruptcy Rates Higher," *USA Today,* June 15, 2005). Owner death can be mitigated by purchasing a type of life insurance called key man (or key *person*) insurance. It has been difficult to quantify the number of bankruptcies caused by Hurricane Katrina. Some experts cite that a great number of people left the area and many aren't even bothering to return and file for liquidity. There is nothing on which to file. Regardless of how an owner gets out of his business, it cannot be denied that he was touched by the process of the exit. Although others may see these some of these exits as failures, you can learn just as much or more from a troubled ending then you can from a successful one.

Many people, once they have tasted what it is like to chart their own course and be their own boss, find it hard to go back to work for someone else. Most of us agree that we would not make good employees, anyway. For example, I know that if I worked for someone else and saw an opportunity they chose not to pursue, I would get frustrated. If I felt in my gut that taking the company in a specific direction was right but could not convince them, I would feel stifled. After all, control was a significant driver in my business ownership. It would have to be the right situation for me to consider abdicating that control.

There are some people, however, who decide that the risks of entrepreneurship outweigh the benefits for them. They would prefer to leave the grueling work of self-employment behind. It goes back to the reasons they got into business for themselves and what they learned in the process. It is possible that they determined what they are really good at and it was not running a company.

Those who have been fortunate enough to exit with ample cash so that not drawing a paycheck is an option may choose to continue to make an impact in a variety of ways. Some do this through mentoring and investing in other small companies and others choose philanthropy. Few truly retire. The rest suffer from what has been labeled "serial entrepreneur's disease" or SED (which, unfortunately, sounds similar to STD). Those with SED enjoy the rush and the rewards that come from building a company so much that they can't imagine doing anything else. Generally, the second (or third or fourth) business has a greater probability for success, anyway. Coming back older and smarter may also change your perspective on what type or size of a company you look for the next time around. I was so burned out that it took a year to consider anything in the high-tech field again. Now that I am over that, I find I am more fastidious in looking for demonstrable market need when assessing potential new business opportunities.

Terry chose her first company based on the "cool" technology and her strong relationship with the founders. She chose the second company because she saw an excellent financial opportunity. She was also able to find a business that she could mold to fit her entrepreneurial strengths and avoid her weaknesses. She didn't know what those qualities were when she started her first business. She plans to raise more money and start building a strong team earlier. With her last business, her initial hire was a scientist to help in the lab. This time she wants to hire another businessperson first so she doesn't have to carry the burden alone for so long. She is looking, perhaps, for a better balance.

# Recommended Reading

Gail Blanke, *Between Trapezes: Flying into a New Life with the Greatest of Ease* (Emmaus, Pa.: Rodale Books, 2004).

John Hawkey, *Exit Strategy Planning: Grooming Your Business for Sale or Succession* (Burlington, Vt.: Gower Publishing, 2002).

Andy Nadeau, *Focus Factor: Strategic Planning for Entrepreneurial Companies* (Bloomington, Ind.: AuthorHouse, 2002).

Martin Staubus (ed.), *Transitioning Ownership in the Private Company: The ESOP Solution* (Foundation for Enterprise Development, 2001).

CHAPTER

# Having It All—Myth or Reality?

Sheila Heinze came from a family of successful, entrepreneurial parents, which has played heavily into her own success. Her company, SM Consulting, has been recognized four times as a Fortune 100 fastest-growing company, and with 480 employees and over $70 million in revenues, she is at the top of her game.

Things changed for her personally, however, when she adopted two children over a period of three years. She purposely held off on having children until she felt her oldest child—her company—was in a position for her to be away for a period of time. By building a solid management team and working her way out of the details, she was able to take several weeks off to travel to China to pick up her daughter and then spend time getting to know her. After she returned to work, however, she didn't like the feeling of being "out of the loop" and worked her way back into the critical fold of her company's operations. Several months later, she found herself angry that she couldn't spend as much time with her family, until she realized that she had created her current reality and was the only one who could fix it.

She began working herself back out of the details in preparation for the arrival of her second child. This time, upon her return, she remained at the appropriate level. As a result, she is much happier with the direction her family life is taking and pleased with the progress the company is making. She admits that she hasn't fully figured out her own personal balance, but scheduling her time with her kids as if it were a client meeting and working from home a couple days a week, she is on her way. In her opinion, balance isn't something that is consistent on any one day. It is being where you need to be when you need to be there. Some days that is at work, other days it is with her kids. She has yet to reach a conflict between the two that she cannot solve by revisiting her priorities.

## Overcoming Stereotypes

When I think of what image the idea of "having it all" conjures up for many women, I recall the old commercial where the woman is wearing a dress topped off with pearls, coming in from work singing, "I can bring home the bacon, fry it up in a pan, and never let you forget you're a man." I am sure this is some men's idea of heaven. My reality, however, is precooked bacon from a box that gets heated in the microwave. As for my husband, he's quite secure in his masculinity.

A woman that I was mentoring sent me a CD with Helen Reddy's "I Am Woman" (hear me roar) song on it. Listening to it made her feel empowered. She felt that song was sung specifically for her, as the theme song for her generation's fight for equality. The results of that battle, which is still being fought on many fronts, have been hard won. I find the struggle has been taken for granted by many of those who reaped the benefits without the fight.

Being on the cusp of the Baby Boomers and Generation X, I have not personally been confronted with in-my-face gender discrimination. That does not mean it does not exist, I have just never personally witnessed it. An alternative theory that some have posed to me is that it was there and I just did not see it. Working in male-dominated industries, I have become accustomed to being the only female in a meeting or at the table. Is that because other women were unwelcome? I don't believe so. It is more likely that they were not present by choice rather than by force. After all, wearing a hairnet, a hard hat, and steel-toed shoes is a personal choice that not everyone (regardless of gender) would opt for. While the gender barriers have not been completely erased, I do believe we're continuing to make progress. There is much left to do, and my vision is for a day when we no longer need to recognize *women* of achievement, or "the first woman ___" because it has become so commonplace. Instead, let us be recognized simply as *people* of achievement.

For men, the traditional model is transforming as well. The previous ideal for a man was the strong, infallible provider, leaving the childrearing to the lady of the house. Today, men are becoming less tentative in sharing their "softer" side. Hollywood is leading the charge by creating sensitive, vulnerable lead characters on TV and in movies. The lines are blurring, making it less unusual to go against tradition.

Pushing stereotypes and convention aside is one of the hallmarks of an entrepreneur. They are not concerned with how society defines success. They do not focus on what having it all means to others. They are too busy creating their own reality. They are successful because they define their own vision of success and view having it all as very personal.

Marissa Levin believes that women trying to "have it all" according to some stereotype are indeed killing themselves in the process. She strongly advocates the value of defining a more personal vision of what success means rather than letting others define it for you. Once you have done that, you must then clearly define your values. If these two aspects of your life are not aligned, she postulates, there is no way you can be free of internal conflict. Rather than looking for balance, she strives for synergy—making all of the pieces of her life work together. She defines her "all" as being healthy, having a healthy family, enjoying a "manageable" level of stress, and leaving time to enjoy her children. Her definition, while personal, is not unique and represents some common themes among the entrepreneurs I interviewed.

Early in her business, Mary Moslander was having trouble sleeping one night. She was tossing and turning over cash flow. Would she have enough money to make payroll? Was she doing the right thing? Should she go back to work for someone else? Her husband, awakened by her restlessness, listened as she vented her fears.

"Mary, you can't quit now. You've got the three H's."

Puzzled, Mary asked him to explain. He relayed his observation that she had never been happier and healthier, while also being at home. In her previous job she had worked long hours, which meant she was not home very much. She also had been plagued by constant, recurring bronchitis. When she considered his comment, she realized that she had not been sick since she had left her job and started her own company. Coincidence? She knew at that moment that she *did* have it all, even though the uncertainty of her company's survival was what had awakened her. She wasn't sure whether her company was going to survive, but she realized that everything would be all right either way.

Pete Linsert is adamant that possessions and wealth have nothing to do with a genuine and lasting feeling of having it all. He views it as accomplishing something good and doing it in the right way. Like most entrepreneurs, he is driven by what he can give rather than what he has received. His approach reminded me of one of my favorite quotes from Sir Winston Churchill: "We make a living by what we get, we make a life by what we give."

Mary Cantando points out that there's a huge difference between "having it all" and perceiving that you "have a great life." She observes that many of us perceive our lives as always in scarcity. We never have enough time, money, friends, or clients. She prefers to perceive life as abundant. *Of course,* there is enough time, money, and clients—you just have to turn your head slightly to see them and they are, absolutely, there.

The second half of "having it all" for Mary is appreciating what she has. She sees so many people who have all kinds of things— successful businesses, happy families, and great homes—but struggle to make it through the day. She maintains her happiness not only because she has a great life, but because she appreciates how rare that is. She's a healthy, happy, well-educated American, which automatically puts her in the top tier of all people on the earth. She notices that many people focus only on what they don't have, which forms the root of their unhappiness and struggle.

Terry Chase Hazell agrees with Mary but explains it in a different way. Her belief is that "having it all" is a state of mind and not really attainable by any type of job or situation. It has to come from within. She considers the reaction she would get by telling her 16-year-old self about her 36-year-old life. That would be one impressed kid: You have three cars you can drive whenever and wherever you want, you can stay up as late as you want, go out with friends without permission, and even stay out all night if the mood strikes. Looking backward or forward from a different point in your life, you may easily see that you had it all. She believes the problem lies in the fact that we spend so much time "out of sync" with our current reality and our desired situation. We refuse to live in the present and, as Mary puts it, appreciate what we have when we have it.

Paul Silber is keenly aware of what he has. Having it all to him is having happiness and health for him and his family. Personally, it also implies having a few close friends. Fundamentally, it means waking up and looking forward to whatever the day holds in store, whether that is going into the office or working in his garden. It alludes to having the ways and means to pursue whatever he is interested in, like reading a good book or going for a long walk, and continuing to learn about the world, about which he feels he still knows so little. It also means the absence of factors in his life that would cause significant worry, such as financial, family, or health pressures.

For many years, being an entrepreneur did not always help him to "have it all." To the contrary, through the early stages of his entrepreneurship he experienced great financial risk, a lot of emotional and mental stress, and never enough time for family, friends, or himself. Over time, however, the balance has shifted much more to the positive. By putting a strong management team in place he has more time for family, friends, and himself, and with the sale of his business, he has eliminated the substantial financial risks that he shouldered for so many years. The bottom line, he believes, is that it is possible to have it all as long as you establish realistic expectations about what "it all" really entails.

For Margaret Pressler, having it all is difficult given the infancy of her business. To her, there are so many wonderful facets of her life that she doesn't want to give anything up. Since there is nothing she is doing that she would be willing to trade out, she works more diligently to make it all work. She has noted, too, that her definition of what "all" is has changed over time as other opportunities present themselves. For example, she made the choice to step back from a column assignment with the *Washington Post* because it was taking up too much time. Although the column had received great reviews and was well received, her business was becoming more demanding and she could not do both. She felt she had to make a choice and at the time, there were other more pressing priorities in her life.

She has also had to learn to adjust her perspective. On nights she worked late, she didn't get to see the kids until right before they went to bed and felt guilty as a result. Her husband reminded her that being away one evening here and there will not make a difference in the large scheme of things, especially when she is home by 3:00 most days. She needed to stay focused on the bigger picture: She has created a great product that provides a benefit to people. Her children see her pursuing a dream that they feel a part of. While she is not able to spend as much time with them as she did before she started her company, she is still available more often than if she were working full time for someone else.

Linda Frost sees having it all as being at peace and believes she has accomplished that. She is comfortable with who she is, where she is in life, how she has raised her children, and where she is headed in the future. For her, it is about, as Mary Cantando pointed out, making the most of what you have. At the same time, she is also aware that there is still so much left to do, to see, to experience, and to learn that she does not want to stop at what she has already achieved.

For Kathy Freeland, having it all is very personal as well. She sees it as having her health, her family, her spiritual life, and her ability to have all of her mental and physical capacities, along with the love of family and friends. Balanced life to her means all those things are in check. She notes that being financially stable is an add-on and has its place. It is a contributor to her sense of well-being while also allowing her to pursue her philanthropic desires as well. Her goal is to live every day in balance. She focuses on being her best at all times, every day, and she requires this of her employees and children as well.

While some days are all work, Kathy makes a point to shut the office out to accommodate family time and then turn work back on later if needed. She diligently manages her time such that she can fit all her priorities in. The weakest area, she concedes, is her workout schedule. That is the only element that gets out of whack. She remains physically fit, so she does not believe her occasional missed workout impacts her overall sense of well-being.

Self-fulfillment is a big component of what having it all means to Donna Stevenson. It is having the flexibility to attend to her personal interests—her children, serving on nonprofit boards, and giving back to the community. She, too, experiences the difficulty of trying to be in perfect balance at any one time, but she feels she can make it work over time. Her minimum time frame for judging her balance is a quarter (three months). She observes that it runs in peaks and valleys. Some days are mostly business, other days are all about kids. Each day she has to ask herself: "What is the most important thing I need to do today?" and prioritize from there.

Doing what she loves to do and having the family she wanted to have is, in Jan King's mind, everything. She loved her career, and the thought of not having a child was simply not an option. She believes people can and should try to do everything they want, but realize that they might not be able to do it all at the same time.

Sam Roberts's idea of having it all is being able to get out of bed every day knowing that he is going to make a positive impact in someone's life. It is the freedom to choose what he does and when he does it. Having it all, for him, requires the ability to choose with whom he associates and, equally important, it must provide opportunities to have a good time. He lost sight of having fun for a long while, but has made it a priority in starting his new law practice. Although he did not include money when asked about what it meant to have it all, he conceded that financial security was a base need we likely all share. Given that he had already obtained a level of financial success, it was not top of mind.

## Show Me the Money!

Linda has been adamant about teaching her children and grandchildren that money is not everything. Her posture is that she only needs enough money to live on and pay bills and that she does not need to make a million dollars (although her businesses have done *quite* well). While making money has its own rewards, she explains to them, it can cause a lot of headaches as well. She believes the adage is true: You can't buy happiness.

The other entrepreneurs I spoke with also downplayed the role money contributed to their overall happiness. Perhaps that is because it is easy to say that having it all does not include money when your base financial needs are being met. Some did indicate that their perception of having it all included the absence of having to worry about money. However, most everyone I spoke with has at one time or another panicked over making payroll or chosen to forgo a reasonable salary in order to keep their business afloat. They toiled hard to make sure their business would not only survive but flourish, and financial security followed. Although money was not the object of any one spoken need, almost all of the items described are enabled from a base of financial security. Without it, detractors such as stress and its resultant health issues would creep into the picture and murk up the clear waters of the good life.

Whenever I say that I am not driven by money, my husband cringes. It is true, though, to some extent. I am driven by the opportunities and freedom that money provides, but not wealth accumulation for its own sake. After all, making an impact and having your health are great goals, but if you can't feed your kids, your perspective changes. I have always been a great believer that things work out when you follow the right path. You cannot be foolish, but the money takes care of itself if you do the right things. Once we made the decision that it was time to cash out of our company, we were able to effortlessly find buyers for our office furniture and another company to take over our lease. Additional opportunities continued to open up for me once I let go of my passionless endeavors and focused where my real energy was taking me. It was not about the money—we left what many would consider to be a large amount of it on the table—it was about much more than that. Besides, consistently managing the company's cash flow from the beginning provided us with that flexibility. Having paid off our mortgage and put away money for our children's education, we found the long-sought-after freedom from financial worries we had been working for. Money was no longer a problem.

As mentioned earlier, Paul spent two years without a salary while his wife stayed home with their young children. He lived frugally by not eating out and renting rather than buying a house. Kathy, too, started her company with $3,000 and cashed in her 401(k) to make payroll. Jindra Cekan left a high-paying, fulfilling job to go into consulting so she could be home to raise her kids. Is it true that to be an entrepreneur you should not care about making money? Not at all. Paul and Kathy both knew that they had to make money eventually and stuck to their vision with determination to make that happen. Although people most definitely go into business for themselves to make money, it should not be the sole motivator. More often, flexibility, control, desire to make a difference, and career opportunity carry more weight in making the decision to become an entrepreneur than getting rich. Unless you are like Graham Weston, who claims he has been an entrepreneur since the day he was born, there is generally something else driving you. That is why you need to look at what your *real* priorities are.

## Identifying the Glass Balls

Prioritizing is critical. Will this (whatever crisis we are worrying about) really matter in the bigger picture? Will being late to my daughter's doctor appointment change the outcome? Will this late shipment be remembered by the client in one year?

On Christmas Eve 2001, I received a call from my father. His lung cancer was back after nine years in remission. He was upbeat, but I did not share his optimism. I had a bad feeling. Although there was nothing I needed to do immediately, I felt like I needed to see him. Because we had planned an intimate party for 60 on New Year's Eve, I hesitated. My husband helped me put it into perspective: Could I regret going? Sure—it was the holidays, the weather might be bad, the crowds could be ugly, and my stepmother didn't think I needed to come. Then the kicker: Could I regret *not* going? My decision was clear. We canceled the party and I went to spend a few days in Texas. There, I was able to get my picture taken with my dad—the last picture I have of us together.

Over the following six months as the cancer spread to his brain, I spent a great deal of time taking care of him. I was away from home and the business for a total of nine weeks in one- to two-week stints. Even when I was in the office, I was really only half there. My father, who was also my mentor, died on the fourth of July at the age of 58.

Through that time, I was somehow able to play a major role in negotiating a half-million-dollar contract with a new customer. I can even remember standing in the hospital talking to this client while my father was undergoing his chemotherapy treatment. The work was, at times, a welcome distraction. We had our highest revenue ever that year, which I attribute to the strength of my staff and management team. The stall in our marketing effort was nearly lethal, but I would not have done it any differently. Somehow, I was able to juggle it all with a great deal of support from my husband, friends, and family.

The notion of business owners as master jugglers is not new. I believe this extends beyond entrepreneurs to working parents or anyone who has multiple responsibilities and commitments vying for their time. These are the balls we have to keep in the air. My friend Claudia Morrell, who is the director of the Center for Women and Information Technology at the University of Maryland, Baltimore County, has a unique perspective on these balls. She sees some of them as glass and others as rubber. The glass ones, when dropped, are shattered beyond repair. There is no getting them back. These are the priorities that, if lost, cannot be replaced. I also call them the *non-negotiables*. Time with my dad was pure glass. The other balls are rubber—they bounce when dropped. They are recoverable. My business was rubber most of the time, though it was a bit deflated in the end.

The challenge with juggling these balls is identifying the material each is made of. Every person's is different. My ball for attending to a client issue can be glass if the result of not doing it can have irrecoverable long-term ramifications. Likewise, my daughter's championship lacrosse game was glass. She really wanted me to be there, and since I had missed the last two games, I felt like I needed to be there as well. A word of caution: If everything in your life is glass and you are having trouble juggling so many balls, you need to take a closer look. Many more things are rubber than you think.

Being in town for my daughter's birthday was surprisingly rubber. Our client had scheduled meetings that involved colleagues traveling in from out of the country. The only day they could get everyone together was the same day Madison turned two. The meetings were critical to our future contracts. I really needed to be there, but could I miss my daughter's birthday? Thinking about the long-term implications of my decision, I realized she was too young to know when her actual birthday was. We had planned a party for her the weekend after and, to her, *that* would be her birthday. I went to the meetings and let her birthday bounce. It would have been easy to succumb to guilt, but I had to govern how I looked at my decision.

If I had regarded my decision to attend the meeting as sacrificing her birthday, I never would have survived. The word *sacrifice* conjures up negative thoughts and feelings and commonly indicates suffering. No one suffered for what I did. I did not surrender anything for the sake of something else. I made a choice that I had to own. I am by no means the first or the last to make that type of choice.

Pete Linsert found the time to coach his daughters' soccer and basketball teams as he was building a company. He knew it was important to them and to him that he be a real presence in their lives—otherwise, he believes, what's the point of having kids? One year, he was coaching his daughter's basketball team and they made it to the final championship game. The big game was scheduled on the same day that he had an important meeting. He was talking with Salomon Brothers about investing a large sum of money in his company. The principals of the Wall Street financial institution had requested to meet him in person—a meeting it would not have been wise to refuse. Changing the date was not an option, either. Thankfully, he was able to schedule the meeting early so that, even though it ran long, he made it to the game, though he was just slightly late. His team went on win the game, and the company eventually closed on the investment.

Mary Cantando once had the opportunity to take her youngest son, Matt, to the World Series. They were both excited about going, but a big proposal came up and she had to pass on the opportunity. She made a choice. Matt still attended the game, he just went with someone else. As it turned out, Mary did not win the proposal but used this as an opportunity to talk with her son about investing your time wisely without forgoing *all* the fun stuff. She owned her choice but used it as a learning experience for her son.

Viewing our choices as sacrifices often implies that we had no control over them. We were a victim. On the contrary, we see ourselves as powerful when we acknowledge these as choices we made. Additionally, we need to take responsibility for them. In my case, our choice to not look for outside funding may have limited my company's growth. I had to be okay with that and accept the responsibility for our decision. Like Mary, we must accept the consequences of our choices.

One of my clients is a highly educated woman who has been home with her children for a number of years. She was working as part of a team to start a new high-tech company. She had decided that she was very interested in helping to build the company but wanted to work part time so as to continue to be available to her children. She was making a choice. In determining ownership stakes for the company, she started out as an equal partner, but because her partner put more time into the venture, she consequently earned more equity. That was okay. Putting her preference for part-time work on the table and accepting the equity consequence was a huge step for her. She did not make excuses or apologize for what she wanted. By being up front about it, her partner was neither surprised nor resentful. My client did not *sacrifice* her equity in the company. She made a choice and intentionally acknowledged the consequence. How powerful is *that*?!

As we progress through the seasons of our lives and events transform us, our glass balls can turn to rubber and the rubber can become glass. Several years ago, my daily workout was somewhat rubber. I was in good shape, but I was also very active on a daily basis. Now as I approach what may be the median of my life, exercise is becoming more fragile. For those who have health issues, a daily trip to the gym may easily be made of glass.

Furthermore, it is not up to anyone else to judge whether someone's glass ball should be rubber and vice versa. After all, how much do we really know about other people? We see only what they show us of their lives. There is much we do not know about others that could make what we think should be rubber into glass. It is not our place to judge.

Likewise, getting what you want out of life without the guilt demands that you do not worry about how others judge your juggling skills. You cannot worry about whether other people think you are successful; rather, your definition of success is the only one that matters.

## Defining Your Model of Success

One of the most crucial elements of our perception in having it all involves how we define success. The consensus of all the entrepreneurs I have discussed this with is that there is no common measure of true success. Like our perception of pain, success is very personal. Real accomplishment comes from defining what success means for you and your family. Determining the role that your business will play in that model requires that you decide what your ultimate goals in life are. One method that I have used to do that is to write my own obituary.

As morbid as that may sound, scripting your final press release makes you focus on what you want to do with your life. What is the legacy that you want to leave? This is a twist on Steven Covey's second habit (out of the seven), which is "Begin with the end in mind." This is just the ultimate end. The first time I did this was with my mastermind group.

When I developed my obit, my company was not mentioned. My legacy also had nothing to do with information technology or computers. In addition to the loving family section, my vision for my life had two pieces to it. The first one was to prove that you could run a profitable, successful business and still be a good parent. I wanted to demonstrate to others that it could be and was being done. You could be serious about your business and about your family. The second major legacy that I wanted to impart was much vaguer. It entailed using my God-given skills and talents to make the world a better place. While that may sound lofty, I do not believe it is. I may never be personally involved in negotiating a Middle East peace treaty or finding the best renewable energy source, but I believe that every person can make some contribution to the betterment of the world.

This belief was reinforced several years after I wrote my obituary when I read a story in the epilogue of the book *Synchronicity: The Inner Path of Leadership,* by Joseph Jaworski and Betty S. Flowers (San Francisco: Berrett-Koehler Publishers, 1996). The tale is of a discussion between a coal-mouse and a wild dove as they are watching the snow fall on the branch of a tree. The coal-mouse asked about the weight of a snowflake, which the dove agreed was next to nothing. He then related that he had watched and counted as the snowflakes fell on a similar branch. When the 3,741,953rd snowflake fell, the branch broke off. After pondering that for a while, the dove finally concluded, "Perhaps there is only one person's voice lacking for peace to come to the world." Incredible perspective, especially for a bird.

This exercise changed my perspective. I began to see my business as a means to an end, a way to build credibility for whatever lay ahead. The future I visualized was not building ACT into something to pass down to my kids. I wanted to ride the wave, maximize my experience and the financial gain I could get from the company, and then get out when the time was right. At the same time, I wanted to be able to be available for my children so they could grow up to be responsible, productive citizens. I was later able to identify my business as what some may call a *lifestyle* company.

A lifestyle business does not necessarily mean your work is a hobby, part time, or less than serious. As Jeffrey Timmons points out in his book *New Venture Creation* (McGraw Hill, 2006), lifestyle-based businesses can just as easily be a success or a failure. The distinction is more about your priorities. For example, if I had learned that I could be 10 times more profitable if I moved my business to another state, I would not have done it. We have relatives close by, our kids love their schools, and we feel grounded in the community. On the contrary, I would not have hesitated to make the move if my business had not been focused on accommodating my family. The majority of small businesses in this country are lifestyle. Again, that does not mean this type of company does not employ people or count their revenues in the millions. It just means the existence of the business is, in many ways, for the convenience of the owners, which can be a few individuals or even the firm's employees.

The alternative is a business that is focused on economic maximization. In this type of business, the founders are often asked to step down at some point and end up owning a smaller portion of a larger entity. These types of companies are more likely to accept capital investment from people or institutions outside of their friends and family. They are building the company to exploit a technology or an opportunity that they believe has a great deal of economic potential. They make decisions based on maximizing revenues without the lifestyle wants and needs of the owners coming into play.

Neither classification of company is more real, except that lifestyle companies are more prevalent. You can have investors in a business that goes broke or a lifestyle company that sells for millions. The fundamental difference is in how potential investors view it. Outside investors, especially venture capitalists, look to make a tenfold return on their investment in three to five years. To them, this is economic maximization. By that definition, only a small percentage of companies fit this description. All the rest are just, well, businesses. It is these "other" businesses that are driving the largest growth in employment. Besides, what is so bad about building a company to make money and accommodate your lifestyle? Nothing, if you're the one doing it.

It takes a strong person to define his or her own model of success and focus solely on that. For one thing, what if no one else considered their achievements as success? A better question is: Why should that matter? The best part about taking control of our own success is that we are providing a powerful role model not only for our kids but for others as well.

## Providing a Role Model

Children absorb much more about what we do than we realize. I could easily fill another book with the lessons children have learned from their entrepreneurial parents. For example, my daughter learned firsthand business concepts applied to a charity event. I worked with her to create a fund-raiser for the American Cancer Society's Relay for Life. This particular event involved hundreds of people camping on a high school football field overnight while a member of each team walked around the track. At dusk, a touching ceremony was planned honoring survivors and victims of cancer. Having lost my father to cancer a few years earlier, this event held a special place in our hearts. We wanted to do something big. My daughter came up with the idea of selling glow-in-the-dark necklaces. I worked with her to determine a selling price and project our profits. We explored the fact that even though we might collect $300 from the sale of the necklaces, only $200 of that was profit because we had to buy the merchandise. She concluded that if we could get a better price on our inventory or find a company to donate them, we could make more money. I then overheard her explaining to her friends what profit was and why it was important. Isn't this the type of creative, productive thinking we want our kids to embody?

My business experiences have provided many "teachable moments." My kids learned about geography as we mapped out where I was traveling for business. They also learned about time zones. On one of my many trips to Amsterdam, I called home to talk to my kids around their dinnertime. When I told them it was midnight where I was, we got into a discussion about how the earth rotates around the sun. Because they had a tangible example, they were able to internalize the concept. I believe strongly that if you adopt the right attitude, melding business and children can be a positive experience, as Jan also deduced.

Jan's son was only eight when she sold her publishing company. After a hard day of negotiating, she would come home and discuss the process and progress with him. As he reached his mid-teens, she realized that he absorbed a great deal more than she previously thought. He now loves to negotiate and looks for opportunities to talk business with his mom. He still speaks proudly about how his mom ran a company. By not keeping her business and her family totally separate from each other, Jan helped her son to experience a world he might not have otherwise been exposed to at the ripe old age of eight.

Since Linda has always operated out of a home office, her four children have had ample opportunity to observe her efficiency in action. They see her on the phone with clients while dusting the living room or folding laundry and know that multitasking can be an effective tool to getting things done. Her children claim that she makes it all look so easy and are amazed at all she can accomplish. She has used these conversations as an opportunity to talk with her kids about planning and organization. They also see that working for yourself has its own rewards: (1) You are able to spend more time actually working each day on your tasks because you spend less time commuting when you work from a home office; (2) you set your own schedule, and therefore your day may not be as hectic as if someone else were scheduling the day for you; and (3) you are able to be there when your children come home from school. This last point, Linda feels, is absolutely priceless. Her kids knew she would be there to ask about their day, to offer them a snack, and to spend a few minutes of quality time with them before they were off doing their many activities. She believes that it is the "just knowing you're there" that gives them that feeling of security and helps them to grow up to be better parents to their own children when the time comes. She is fortunate to have seen this in action as her daughter parents her own four-year-old son. Living by example, she is convinced, is the best way to raise children and live your life.

Pete believes he has provided a strong model for his children as well. As his daughters saw his efforts over many years, they saw firsthand that growth takes time and learned the importance of endurance. Although he was diligent about leaving his work at the office, he did not hesitate to share his accomplishments and challenges with the family over dinner. In fact, they made a point of sitting down to dinner as a family whenever possible. Through their dinnertime exchanges, Pete's children also learned that delayed gratification is a reality that is worth it, especially for something that is important. In addition, he found he was able to take the patience he learned in building a business into his parenting.

Donna exposes not only her children to business concepts, but she reaches out into the community as well. She conducted a workshop for one of her daughter's groups consisting of several girls ages 10 to 12. The topic of the session was "Be Your Own Boss." The first task she had them complete was to catalog the things that were most important to them. For this age group, shopping and friends were near or at the top of each girl's list. She used these topics to introduce a discussion of money. Where does it come from? *In most cases, Mom and Dad.* How do they get it? *From working.* Do they limit what you spend their money on? *Yes.*

The girls concluded that they wanted to be in control of their money. They realized that the only way to do that is to earn it yourself. Some of the girls had worked for someone else before, but Donna pointed out that they are still at the mercy of the person they worked for. What if your employer decided to close the business down? What if they did not need you anymore? She was not trying to say that they didn't need to work for someone else, because, she pointed out, that is how you learn. Ultimately, however, being your own boss can be an ideal way to have more control of your own money. At the end of the workshop, the girls had completed business plans and were convinced that, someday, they wanted to be their own boss.

While Marissa's sons are still too young to make that kind of association, she believes they will have other immediate connections based on their mom's example. For example, as they get older, they will take it for granted that women can lead. She and her husband both have provided them with a model of partnership in parenting, a base of mutual respect, and the importance of making a contribution. The boys see their parents as equals, while also seeing their mother as extremely capable in her own right. Marissa also takes time to mentor other businesswomen as well as college students. She speaks frequently on work/life balance and is proof that you can have a successful business and still be there for your children.

Margaret's daughter Eleanor learned about the economics of business because she wanted a horse. She was six at the time and, like many young girls, she loved horses and continually pestered her mom to buy one. Margaret's reply to her was that when she is able to sell enough BurpCatchers to make the money they need to move to a house that has room for the horse, she can get one.

From that day on, Eleanor had a keen interest in the number of products going out the door. She had a hands-on opportunity to get involved since her playroom had been converted into the company's warehouse and shipping department. When Margaret returned from her first trade show, Eleanor greeted her at the door with a smile and asked, "How many BurpCatchers did you sell, Mommy?" Margaret grinned at her interest. She replied that they had taken orders for almost 200 products at that one show, which exceeded her expectations. Eleanor's face lit up, she smiled and turned to her younger sister and said, "Bebe, we're going to get a horse!" Although selling 200 was not anywhere near enough, would she have ever been able to learn the valuable lesson about what it takes to get what you want at such a young age?

Kathy has figured out how to get what she wants and models that for her children. She learned how to parent through trial and error but claims she had great role models in her parents. She draws on the same skills at home and in business. She is organized and particular about how things get done in both places. She is a role model not only for her two children but also for her employees. She believes her role as a parent is to be grooming her children for success in whatever it is that they choose to be.

As discussed in Chapter 7 in the section "Training Your Replacement," it was common among entrepreneurs I conferred with to feel as if our job as parents is to train our children to become adults. This likely relates to working parents as well. Many see their children, even as babies, as adults in training, though the expectations are appropriately tempered for their age. Once they are old enough, we teach them to do their own laundry if they want to wear something that is dirty or, in my daughter's case, to sew on a button that has come off. In Jindra's house, her young sons know that they need to help Mom pick up the house and vacuum or they may *never* get to the park. We are teaching them the value of independence.

In my role as parent, I have always felt that I did not hold an exclusive license on positive values and good ideas. Being exposed to other adults whom I knew well and trusted opened my children up to alternative ways of thinking, not just *our* way. Having them around other kids in day care or preschool was good for their socialization and their immune system. Traveling to foreign countries helped them appreciate that there is more than one way to do things, like design a toilet (the one thing they continually noticed!) or get around town (double-decker buses in Paris). By Keenan's and my remaining a constant in their life while also exposing them to a multitude of outside places and ideas, I believe we are raising well-rounded, global citizens.

We are also preparing them for the realities of society by not letting them believe they are the center of the universe. While that may sound harsh, the reality is that they are most decidedly not the axis of existence, and the sooner they realize that, the better off they are. This does not mean that we do not cater to their needs. It is the *wants* that do not necessarily get satisfied or not always in their time frame.

A perfect example is when my daughter wants to play cards. She does not always ask at a convenient time. Sometimes I am able to stop what I am doing and play with her. Other times we make a play date for later. One afternoon she really wanted to play a game, but I was faced with a deadline. I assured her that the next night I would be available for a game of Uno®. The following evening she had forgotten about our date when I came into her room, un-invited, with the deck of cards. The grin on her face told me I had done the right thing. It is not that I was trying to withhold my time or care the night before, but she had to know that Mommy has multiple priorities. While she is tops on that list, she is not the sole name on it. This has gone a great distance in teaching her how to be resilient and flexible. She is still only a kid, so I can't say it has always been an easy or well-received lesson. Since when has parenting been about what is easy?

Paul believes that being an entrepreneur has demonstrated lessons for his kids in the value of taking calculated risks, embracing challenge, and enjoying adventure. He has started to see this influence on his children as his oldest daughter, who was four when he started his company, is in college. She has traveled abroad independently, run her first marathon, become certified as an emergency first responder, and moved halfway across the county to attend college. All of that, he claims, has been accomplished without any pushing from him or his wife. Their daughter discovered her own internal drive as was modeled by her father. Paul was careful, however, to temper their perception of the importance of drive by emphasizing the significance of also making a difference in the world. He wants them to lead balanced lives.

## The "B" Word

Graham maintains that super-driven entrepreneurs are far from balanced people. Often, they are workaholics. I believe, however, that the obsessive workmongers are in the minority. These are just the people and stories that are seen in the press. Perhaps worshiping the people at the pinnacle is not where we should be focused. After all, few of us would trade our lives for theirs if we looked closely enough. How many intensely driven people are still married? Which ones have good relationships with their children or families? Perhaps for them, all work *is* their balance. Who are we to judge? We cannot know for sure if they are truly happy, but in my opinion, lopsided balance cannot last for too long. It eventually catches up to you. We are hopefully in life for the marathon, not the sprint, though there are certainly times we need to run fast.

In starting up a company, there are absolutely times when you have to run as fast as you can. Although the hours involved with being an entrepreneur are often greater than working for someone else, all agreed it was worth it. As one entrepreneur joked: "At least when you are your own boss you have more control over *which* 80 hours you work in a week." Those early days were often hard to balance, but they made it through and eventually found it.

When I think of balance, I envision a teeter-totter or a scale in a horizontal position at perfect equilibrium, each side aligned to make a plumb, straight line. When either of these devices is in balance, there is not much swing or movement. They are almost still. Whose life is like that? I do not know anyone, business owner or not. I have never spoken to an entrepreneur about their company and been given the idea that there was anything stagnant about their lives. I maintain that the traditional ideal of balance is unsustainable on a day-to-day basis, which is why I call it the "B" word."

The word *balance* has unfortunately been overused to the point that discussing it can elicit negative feelings and emotions. Many business owners I discussed it with, especially women, were tired of hearing about it. The men did not understand what the big deal was. Graham has come to believe the word *balance* is used by people to get us to not work so hard. There were some who even feared a common perception that if you were worrying about balance, you were not really serious about your business. While that attitude may exist, I believe it could not be father from the truth. Every ParentPreneur I spoke with claimed to make time with the family a priority whenever possible. The general consensus among them was that there is no one "right" model of what balance is or should be. Like success, it is very personal.

As Sam grew his law practice, he was able to find time to coach his sons' baseball teams. Making it to school events, albeit not to *every* event, was a priority for him, and he worked his business around it whenever possible. There were times, however, when he had to let work take priority over home, but, over time, he was comfortable with the pace at which he was operating.

When we started ACT, I wanted to be able to take time to go into my child's school to help with the Halloween party or field day. If I happened to miss that particular event, I at least wanted to be able to go in for *some* class party; I didn't have to be there for every one.

While Sheila Heinze has adjusted her schedule in order to work from home a few days a week, the best balance for her is to keep her children and her work as separate as possible. She firmly believes that balance is not equal—it is being fully present where you need to be, when you need to be there. She follows the advice of her own mother: "Don't worry about what is going on at home until you open that door." Her need for separation could be due, in part, to the age of her kids—they are both under five years old. She does not bring them into the office except on special occasions when other employees are allowed to bring theirs. She has resorted, however, to putting time with her kids onto her calendar. She found that when she tried to catch what time she could whenever she could, there was no time that worked.

Like many entrepreneurs I conferred with, she cited that none of her life would be possible without an incredible support system, of which her husband is an anchor. They are partners in the business and at home, with both doing whatever needs to be done to make it all work together.

As a single mother, Jindra does not have that option but manages to make it work by building an extended support network. She continues to travel with her business, though only occasionally. When she has ventured out, it is has been over a couple of weeks, and she was able to get the help of family and friends to stay with her children. She has been surprised to find that cell phones work in the remote African villages where she travels. Talking to her sons on her cell phone while living in a hut with natives illustrates to her how far communications have come. She clearly sees how technology contributes to her ability to work and raise a family. To be able to call her sons from a village and describe to them what she is doing has obviously touched their lives. Instead of whining about how much he missed his mother, her oldest son went to school and proudly told his teacher, "My mom is in Africa feeding hungry people."

Part of the impetus for Marissa to start her own company was the flexibility it would provide when she had children. Before she even had children, she queried her employer about the opportunity to telecommute, and it was clear that the chances of that were non-existent. She knew that would be one of the first benefits she would support when she went out on her own. She did not have any kids when she started her business, but they were always in the plans. She also knew that she would choose in-home child care when the time came so she could still be with her children throughout the course of a workday.

Once she had children, working from home with them in the house was a pure joy. Marissa found one of the benefits of working while a nanny cared for her children was periodic oversight. One afternoon, she stumbled across her four-month-old baby left alone on the changing table. The nanny had abandoned him there to retrieve something and was consequently fired on the spot. Had Marissa not been there, the results could have sooner or later been tragic.

Once her children reached school age, she decided to forgo the nanny. Because her husband is also her business partner, they are able to coordinate their schedules so that one of them works from home each day and cares for the children after school. She feels strongly that her sons have benefited not only from the exclusive time and attention they receive from their parents, but also from seeing them accomplishing so much at the same time. Their sharing of the responsibilities in parenting has made it possible for them to attain the heights they have and to continue to reach for higher. Working together, they have found synergy between their family and their business.

Mary Cantando also cites her partnership with her husband as the only way she was able to find balance between home and her businesses. When she and her husband married back in the early 1970s, many of their friends had the mind-set that raising kids was the mother's job, with "help" from the father. They would say things like, "Paul is so great about helping me with the kids" or "Bob really doesn't mind baby-sitting the kids." That kind of language caused Mary to go ballistic. Helping you with his own kids, baby-sitting his own kids—she never understood why other parents maintained this outlook. She and her husband always believed that they were true partners in running the business that was their family, and that parenting was a shared role just like doing the laundry and mowing the lawn.

Entrepreneurship has provided Terry with flexibility few working parents enjoy. She works more hours than she did when she had a "regular" job, but she decides when. If her daughter asks her to stay home with her, Terry has the option to say "yes." She's the boss. She can work while her children nap and after they go to bed. She has found that you can fit in a great deal of work and kid time when you have total flexibility. The downside for her has been that she hasn't had a vacation without her mobile office for seven years. She still feels she has had respite—it has just been piecemeal.

Many entrepreneurs I interviewed considered their ability to balance their lives when they made the decision to venture out on their own, but for many it was not about everyday equity. The common vision that most adopted was to look at balance through a larger lens. They saw the bigger picture and judged whether their life was in balance by viewing it over time rather than from day to day. The secret is in finding your own personal and maintainable balance called a *model of sustainability*.

## A New Model

In their businesses, entrepreneurs have been known to forgo short-term gain for long-term vision. As the CEO of Rackspace Managed Hosting, Graham Weston actually opted out of a $20 million contract with Morgan Stanley because it did not fit the financial criteria they had established for target projects.

Morgan Stanley was looking for a company to host their financial data. In addition to the revenues, the relationship with a prestigious Wall Street bank could help nudge Rackspace into more

Fortune 500 companies as well as position it positively for an initial public offering. The hang-up was that they had implemented a new financial measurement called True Profit. Simply, True Profit requires a company to look at the cost of capital reserved in performing a certain project. It is calculated as their operating profit (after taxes) minus their total annual cost of capital. They will not go into any project where the true profit margin is less than 15 percent. That took the Morgan Stanley deal off the table. While the short-term temptation was there to jump in with such a prestigious client, Graham made the decision to follow their previously decided upon long-term strategy. There have been no regrets. They continued their streak of double-digit growth, which exceeded $200 million in revenues for 2006 (Patricia Gray, "What's Your Magic Number?" *Fortune Small Business*, November 2006).

I, too, have had the opportunity to follow short-term cash and risk my company's long-term vision, though on a much smaller scale than Graham. We were approached by a local company that was interested in contracting a couple of our developers for a project. The engagement was originally expected to take a couple of months, but it was unknown whether it could be completed in that time. There was a good chance it would be extended. The money was good, but the projects would occupy some of our critical development resources, making them unavailable for our customers and needs.

When we created our company's mission and vision statements, we opted to focus on developing skills at a higher level than just contract programming. We even shied away from hiring people without experience to support our claims of providing seasoned resources. We wanted to engage in a consistent type of project where we could leverage the work we had done for other customers. It was about creating value through our methodologies and processes. We wanted to build our intellectual capital so we could work smarter, not harder.

The short-term mentality would have sent me following the waving money, but I had adjusted my perspective. I had to look at the long-term vision. We do this in our businesses, why don't we do it for ourselves as well?

In any one day, it is nearly impossible for our lives to be in perfect balance. One day I had two kids home sick from school and my husband was out of town. That day was all about the kids. A couple days later the very same week, I left my kids at 8:00 A.M. and didn't return home until 11:00 P.M. That day was all about work. It would have been easy for me to feel out of whack or out of balance either of those days. But when we change our expectations and our time frame, we find that it is quite possible to obtain balance *over time.*

Entrepreneurs who report to have it all appear to judge their life balance over a much longer period of time. They recognize that some days may be all about work and others are consumed by kids, sick parents, or their own health. In short, there is a need to focus on other competing responsibilities at some point, and you need to accept that for what it is.

Paul's time frame for judging his balance was 10 years. Mine was more like one to two months. Define your time frame for what works for you—a month, a year, five years. The important point here is that the time frame is expanded. Second, the time horizon needs to be *yours*, not anyone else's. This is where you need to define your *own* model.

The first and most important part of the model is that it truly belongs to you. It does not need to make sense to anyone else; no one else needs to approve it. It is fine to look at others to see how they do it, but take what works for you from their model and throw out the rest. You must stop comparing yourself to anyone else and define the success *you* want to achieve in the time *you* want to achieve it. Rather than striving for "balance" like a teeter-totter or scale, work to develop what I call a model of sustainability for your life.

Sustainability is defined as a balance over time. Looking back, that is what I had been searching for and was able to find through entrepreneurship. There were some days when my life at that point was all about work. I went into the office early and worked late. Other days, when I had a sick child or just felt like spending some quality time with my family, my focus was solely on them. Many days were a combination of the two. I found my own model of sustainability, which made me a better mom and a better entrepreneur. As a bonus, it also helped lift the guilt obtained by focusing on any one day.

The notion that there is a standard measure of *having it all* is indeed a myth. The reality is very personal. You are the only one who can say which balls are glass and which are rubber. The key lies in defining your own idea of what success is, ensuring it is aligned with your priorities, and then realizing the journey is half the fun. If you are concerned about starting your own business because of balance, don't be. Hopefully, the scale and variety of entrepreneurs featured here provides models you can use or combine to develop your own ideal. To do this, it is imperative that you let go of the guilt by looking at the bigger picture and defining your own sustainable model for personal success.

CHAPTER

# The Edge

This book is not intended to encompass everything that is required to make a business or manager successful. Clearly, there is no one definitive resource that can do that, especially given that "success" is in the mind of the beholder. Like children, all businesses are different and require diverse approaches and often divergent paths. What works for one company may not work for another, just like our children.

As I work with a variety of entrepreneurs and businesses, I have observed a myriad of ways to successfully conduct business and virtually no two are exactly alike. There are many different ways to be successful. But as in sharing ideas about raising our children with other parents and seeing what works for us, the same approach should be employed with our businesses.

Similarities abound, however, when you look at some common traits among ParentPreneurs, whether they are working in their own business or within the confines of a larger establishment. The lessons learned and skills obtained, while detailed in this book, can be summarized into five that I believe provide the biggest edge in business. Those are resourcefulness, perseverance, patience, passion, and vision.

## Resourcefulness

I can remember the first thing that I did when the little plus sign appeared on the home pregnancy test (after throwing up again): I ran out and bought a book. In fact, I can recall buying more than one book. I was about to embark on a life-changing adventure and I did not know the first thing about it. I just knew it was something I wanted to do and wanted to digest everything I could about what lay ahead.

As my children have grown up, the learning has continued. After all, I was never trained in child development. When should you start introducing them to the alphabet? What is the best way to talk to children about the birds and the bees? How do you motivate them to do their best in school? I continued to read and talk to other parents about what worked or what did not work for them. I had to be resourceful to find answers or ideas for dealing with constantly evolving issues and challenges.

The same ability to be enterprising as a parent pays off all the time in business. First off, truly entrepreneurial people do not wait for someone to tell them how to do something. They go out and pore over a book or two on the subject and perhaps read about someone else's experiences. They also don't hesitate to talk to others about their observations and ask for help when they need it. Strong entrepreneurs are willing to learn more about themselves, understanding their unique strengths and weaknesses. The good ones hire people to fill the gaps in their information and capabilities and are not afraid to employ people smarter than they are. In short, there is a self-driven desire to learn and to accomplish a specific goal. Resourceful people do not see the trees in the path as obstacles; rather, they focus on the path.

Martek's mop bucket that was used to dry fungus, Terry's purchase of a microwave to replace a specialized lab heater, Graham's lending of his convertible Mercedes to high-achieving employees as an incentive—all of these are creative ways to accomplish a goal. Many also call this "thinking outside the box." It is making use of the resources available to accomplish extraordinary tasks. It is a capability that we build as a parent that helps give ParentPreneurs an edge in business.

## Perseverance

Most parents don't just decide to quit when the going gets tough. We persevere under pressure and wait to fall apart until the situation has stabilized. Mary Cantando had this experience when her youngest son was about three. He fell and she had to take him to the emergency room to get stitches for a cut that was a millimeter from his eye. She was talking to the surgeon, and all of a sudden she passed out. She was on the floor. She had held up as long as needed to get her son taken care of, and then, once she had passed him off, she collapsed.

Similarly, she recalls working day and night on a big proposal. She was at the office for three days without going home. After they submitted the proposal, she went home and fell apart. She was so sick she didn't get out of bed for a week. She had held on for as long as she could, did what she needed to do, and then lost it. This is not an uncommon occurrence in business where the people are committed and passionate about what they do.

Perseverance is a crucial ingredient for leaders in all stages of business. Events and plans rarely work out as intended or hoped, and it can be tempting to quit. Sometimes we can even talk ourselves into abandoning a project or idea before we've gotten started. You have to accept that failure is a by-product of testing your own limits. If you are not failing, you are not taking enough risks or stretching yourself to see how far you can grow. Only by reaching our limits can we identify them. The ability to continue to move forward when the going gets tough is an asset in parenting as well as business.

## Patience

Similar to perseverance is patience. Unfortunately, the only way we get patience is by practicing it. With our children, we sharpen it by holding our tongue or our hand when we're mad so we don't lash out in anger. We also hone our skills when we observe a child making a bad choice and decide to let them learn through failure. Obviously, we would never do this if the consequences would harm them, but bruises gained through doing are lessons that linger.

Pete Linsert acquired extreme levels of patience while working to position his company to turn a profit. While the company was founded in 1985 as a spin-off from Martin Marietta to conduct research on beneficial uses of algae, they did not launch their first commercial product until 1989. The first year they turned a profit was 2003. While this timing may seem extreme, it is not unusual for life-sciences companies to operate in the red (losing money) for 5, 8, or even 10 years. This is delayed gratification to the max. It *always* takes more time and money than you think to reach your milestones. Getting through those periods not only builds patience but also requires great amounts of the next two characteristics.

## Passion

It takes tireless energy to be a parent and a leader. Passion for your kids comes in the way of the bonded love most feel at birth or soon after. I sometimes think it would be insurmountable to make it from day to day without that love, especially when temper tantrums or hormones are rampant.

Many entrepreneurs report that they have never worked harder in their lives. At the same time, they have never had so much fun. There is nothing easy about starting, building, or running a business, especially your own. Without passion, it is almost impossible. People who report to have found their passion have described it as effortless effort. They enjoy what they are doing so much that it hardly seems like work. Many do not have to set an alarm to get up in the morning, while others wake up in the middle of the night with an idea they have to pursue. Like the love a parent feels for his or her child, it is difficult to describe unless you have been there. I guarantee you will know it when you find it. While there are many days that are filled with tasks that are hardly enjoyable, people with the passion focus on the overarching goals or connection with the business or its customers or its impact to keep them moving ahead. They have a long-term vision that continues to fuel their passion.

## Vision

The vision for my children's future started when we first found out I was pregnant. We knew we had to change where we lived so they could have access to good schools or else start looking at private institutions. As they grew, we knew we needed to save money for braces, cars, and college. While we had control over some aspects of their futures, we did not have reign over everything. We had to practice focused flexibility, where we could maintain our focus on the major goals we set for them while also bending to their desires, needs, and capabilities.

It is easy to get mired down in the details of any one day when you are raising kids. When we really pay attention, we are able to see capabilities and traits in our children that they were not yet aware of themselves. We can then help them to build on their strengths and find their special talents. We have access to knowledge of a larger world and experience behind how they might be able to fit into it. We use our vision to guide them along.

It is also helpful for parents to periodically take a step back and see the bigger picture. I have seen too many parents afraid to actually *parent* their children. Many times, parents back down because of guilt—they are not available for their children as much as they think they should be, so they try to make it up to them—or out of fear that their child will not like them. Good parents are able to avoid this trap. They have a larger vision of what their role as a parent is and are willing to accept that while a child may not like a decision you make, it is for their own good in the long run. As parents, we are able to see the bigger picture and help them navigate their place in it.

For entrepreneurs, perceiving opportunities that other people do not see is common. Setting a vision for your company that your employees and customers can buy into is crucial to achieving it. Adhering to the long-term vision for your company keeps you on the right path, and being willing to alter that vision as the world around you changes is imperative as well.

## The Bottom Line

I know for a fact that while business and entrepreneurship are hard, staying home to raise children is equally challenging. It is not my place to say whether one approach to raising children is better than any other. I do believe, however, that the key to being the best parent and the best person you can be lies in your level of fulfillment.

Personally, I would not feel complete without exercising the business side of my brain. Allowing that part of myself to atrophy would only result in my being miserable. Kids perceive more than we know, so hiding my discontent would be impossible. It would *not* make me a better mom. On the contrary, my children would see that I am not fulfilled and grow to believe that that is the way life is supposed to go. I don't want my children to have that kind of future. I want them to know that they can be whatever they want to be. They need to see that the right family model is to support each other in our choices rather than conforming to some preconceived notion and being miserable. I want to model what it is that I want for them: to be a complete person who is not afraid to follow her dreams and be fulfilled. I believe strongly that whenever you are living a fulfilled life, you have an edge in everything you do.

# Index